Y0-BKY-427

STAFFING
EUROPE

STAFFING
EUROPE

An Indispensable Guide to
Hiring and Being Hired in
the New Europe

Max Messmer
Chairman and CEO
Robert Half International Inc.

ACROPOLIS BOOKS LTD.
HERNDON, VA.

© Copyright 1991 Acropolis Books Ltd. All Rights Reserved.
Except for the inclusion of brief quotations in a review, no part of this book may be reproduced or utilized in any form or by any means, electronic or mechanical, including photo copying, recording or by any information storage and retrieval system, without permission in writing from the publisher.

ACROPOLIS BOOKS LTD.
13950 Park Center Rd.
Herndon, VA 22071

Attention: Schools and Corporations
ACROPOLIS books are available at quantity discounts with bulk purchase for educational, business, or sales promotional use. For information, please write to: SPECIAL SALES DEPARTMENT, ACROPOLIS BOOKS LTD., 13950 Park Center Rd., Herdon, VA 22071.

Are there Acropolis books you want but cannot find in your local stores?
You can get any Acropolis book title in print. Simply send title and retail price. Be sure to add postage and handling: $2.25 for orders up to $15.00; $3.00 for orders from $15.01 to $30.00; $3.75 for orders from $30.01 to $100.00; $4.50 for orders over $100.00. District of Columbia residents add applicable sales tax. Enclose check or money order only, no cash please, to:

ACROPOLIS BOOKS LTD.
13950 Park Center Rd.
Herndon, VA 22071

```
         Library of Congress Cataloging-in-Publication Data

Messmer, Harold, 1946-
    Staffing Europe : an indispensable guide to hiring and being hired
  in the new Europe / Harold "Max" Messmer, Jr.
       p.     cm.
    Includes index.
    ISBN 0-87491-994-0 : $24.95
    1. Americans--Employment--Europe.  2. Corporations, American-
  -Europe--Personnel management.  3. Manpower planning.  4. Europe
  1922.  5. Labor market--Europe.   I. Title.
  HF5549.5.E45M47   1992
  658.3'11'096--dc20                                          92-8702
                                                                 CIP
```

Contents

INTRODUCTION	The New Europe	1
Section I	**The European Business Arena**	
CHAPTER ONE	A Look at the European Arena—Then and Now	9
CHAPTER TWO	One Europe? A Matter of Perspective	25
CHAPTER THREE	An Overview of Each of the EC Member States	35
Section II	**Staffing the Euro-Company**	
CHAPTER FOUR	Locating Candidates	67
CHAPTER FIVE	The Hiring Process	91
CHAPTER SIX	Making the Job Offer	111
CHAPTER SEVEN	Pay and Benefits	123
Section III	**Elements of the Workforce**	
CHAPTER EIGHT	Achieving an Effective Workforce Mix	139
CHAPTER NINE	Temporaries, Part-Timers and Para-Professionals	151
CHAPTER TEN	Women	161
Section IV	**Fitting In**	
CHAPTER ELEVEN	Keeping European Staff Motivated	169
CHAPTER TWELVE	The Family Fit	179
CHAPTER THIRTEEN	Retrofit: Protecting Your Investment	195
Epilogue	**The Other Europes**	
CHAPTER FOURTEEN	Non-EC Europe	205
CHAPTER FIFTEEN	Afterword	217

APPENDICES

Important EC Headquarters — 221
Investment Information Offices — 222
Chambers of Commerce and Trade
Associations of EC Member States — 224
Overseas American-Sponsored
Elementary and Secondary Schools — 229

INDEX 235

Prelude

Staffing Europe is a book that had to be written, and no one is better qualified to have done it than my friend and colleague, Max Messmer.

In 1986, a public corporation of which Max was president, acquired the company I had founded in 1948, Robert Half International. He immediately put into effect a long-range program of expanding the company, particularly in Europe. In addition to being a brilliant CEO, Max has a keen understanding of the myriad of differences between the workplace in Europe and the United States. It is this understanding, coupled with the input of the many fine people with whom he works, that will benefit every reader of this book—employer and job seeker alike.

Max recognized that many top-flight U.S. business executives, as good as they might be in hiring domestically, were not sufficiently prepared to effectively staff expanding or start-up European operations. He also recognized that job candidates interested in working in the "New Europe" were, for the most part, uninformed about the right way to find and land desirable positions abroad.

Staffing Europe fills the gap on both sides of the desk.

Congratulations, Max, on a splendid book.

Robert Half
Founder
Robert Half International Inc.

Acknowledgments

Staffing Europe is the result of not only my own experience, but the experiences of numerous other people who graciously contributed their thinking and advice. These include many clients of Robert Half International, who have dealt with our European managers; those managers themselves; and hundreds of job candidates, whose success in finding employment in the "New Europe" prove there is a right way to go about it.

Thank you John Hackl, my publisher, who saw the need for a book like *Staffing Europe,* Donald Bain, Tony Tedeschi and Lynn Taylor for your input and encouragement.

And, certainly, my gratitude to Robert Half International's founder, Robert Half, whose many books have provided invaluable help to both employers and job seekers over the years, and whose friendship and continuing counsel have meant a great deal to me.

*For my wife, Marcia,
and my sons, Michael and Matthew,
who have brought me so much happiness.*

*And for my mother,
who taught me years ago
that the right people make all the difference.*

Introduction

DECEMBER 31, 1992—THE NEW EUROPE

On this date, the economic heartland of Europe is, at least conceptually, to be transformed into a confederation of open borders and expected to create a single market with a commonality of purpose. That goal: a "New" Europe that is the match for, if not superior to the established trading blocks in North America, or along the Pacific Rim. In essence, this new Europe seeks to bring about the socio-economic achievement that centuries of strife, and countless battles for dominance could not.

But what does this New Europe look like to the outside observer? Is it a fortress, as pessimists insist, or an opportunity, as optimists suggest?

One thing is certain, and beyond debate. Europe—all of it—is a place where recent changes have been swift and dazzling. Eastern Bloc nations have shed the yoke of Communism and seek to enter the fold of political freedom, and the resulting free-market prosperity. The two Germanies are now one. The Soviet Union is gone, replaced by a loose confederacy of republics that may or may not pass the test of time.

Keeping up with and anticipating future changes is a daunting challenge for every business.

For those optimistic U.S. companies that see opportunity, there is no question that the potential is great. An economically unified Europe holds the promise of a vast market where U.S. industry can sell its goods and offer its myriad services. Simultaneously, it is home to a pool of skilled labor for the production of those goods, and for the delivery of those services.

The economies of the 12 nations that make up the New European Community (EC) generate, by conservative estimates, a combined five *trillion* dollars per year, and that figure does not take into account the still ill-defined opportunities in Eastern Europe and the newly defined Soviet Union. The best perspective on the size of this market is to compare it to a U.S. economy of five trillion dollars in 1991, or a Japanese economy of three trillion.

As visionary companies prepare to enter this market, a vast array of strategies must be formulated; hard decisions must be made. But, as with all business plans (whether they be conceptual or functional), they are only as good as the people who formulate and implement them—the men and woman charged with turning paper programs into positive action. While the critical function of hiring is a considerable challenge for any business expansion—anywhere—it is especially problematic when it involves a foreign country or, in this case, a diverse and nationalistic group of nations seeking to function as a unified economic entity. As those who have tried to staff foreign operations based purely upon U.S. precepts have discovered, when you are on the other team's field you must play by its rules or game plans disintegrate.

Andreas Van Agt, head-of-delegation for the Commission of the European Community, used his own sports metaphor in the summer of 1990 when addressing the Royal Institute of International Affairs in London. He said, "Sometimes the United States behaves like John McEnroe at Wimbledon, scolding the umpire and the linesman, instead of just acknowledging that other players have risen to eminence."

American executives who attempt to apply the John McEnroe approach to doing business in Europe will undoubtedly find rough sledding.

If Europe '92 and beyond is the call to action for corporations seeking to be serious players on this enhanced international playing field, assembling a top staff (uniquely qualified to meet its many demands) will be one of the most critical and difficult assignments facing U.S. management. If I were to design a course called "European Expansion 101," the core lecture would have to be "People," or to be more specific, "Human Resources." And I would begin that lecture by pointing out that effectively staffing overseas operations will be intensely competitive for many reasons, including sociological situations beyond the control of human resource professionals.

Not only must companies vying for market position in the new Europe seek to find and retain the best people, they will have to accomplish it in a world in which the number of qualified employees is small to begin with, and shrinking with each passing year. Irrespective of population increases in segments of the Third World, numerous studies show that a declining birthrate in the industrialized world, combined with a lowering retirement age among senior staffers, is creating a situation in which the supply of skilled personnel is considerably less than the demand for these same people.

Staffing European operations will not be simply a matter of finding warm bodies to fill jobs clearly defined within an environment that U.S. companies intimately understand. These positions will demand a whole new set of job skills and experiences, combined with an ability to apply these skills, and to utilize these experiences in a setting that is foreign in more than simply a geographic sense. Creating the best marriage of employer with employee will be no easy task, and much will depend upon the ability to do just that.

But figures and surveys alone about population shifts do not directly address all of the specific demands that will be made upon executives asked to manage penetration by U.S. companies into the European market. If you take into account the ingrained U.S. attitude that the world ends abruptly at our borders—then add to it differences in culture and a different European business psyche—the problems of staffing for European expansion become painfully apparent.

While U.S. businesses have the economic resources, the technological excellence and the latent potential to compete effectively in the New Europe, they will have to devote a great deal of attention to finding the right people to pull these attributes together in order to make their overseas formulas work. At the same time, they will have to learn how to do business in each of the individual countries in which they establish operations. That alone will have a significant effect on how they hire. To the uninformed, Europe may look homogeneous from the outside, but the person doing business abroad will still have to deal with individual idiosyncrasies—Greek executives who will not meet with a U.S.

representative without a proper introduction from an acceptable organization; or Danish executives who have elevated punctuality to a level of sanctity, and who call off a meeting with a new marketing director of a U.S. company because she has been delayed by crosstown traffic.

"Getting a handle" on all this is what *Staffing Europe* is about. In subsequent chapters, the opportunities, challenges, and solutions to the human resources needs of U.S. companies committed to succeeding in the environment of the new European Community are addressed.

At the same time, people looking to find career success in the economic unification of Europe will discover many valuable, practical tips for turning international aspirations into career reality.

While the process of staffing an operation in Europe will be complex, a dedicated and effective human resources program will be well worth the effort. The 1990s will lead many businesses away from their national fiefdoms and into a global market posture for the 21st Century. A strong entry in the European market will be critical for those companies committed to globalization. The professionals who staff these European entries will not only be critical to success in Europe, they will become among the most important resources of companies addressing the ever-expanding opportunities that lie ahead in every business sphere.

It is my intention that *Staffing Europe* be an invaluable handbook that helps get the process started properly, as well as a reference manual for those companies committed to maximizing the effectiveness of their human resources on an ongoing basis. The book is not intended to be a treatise on the laws of any EC country or jurisdiction.

Staffing Europe mainly focuses on Western Europe and the 12-member nations of the European Community. Nevertheless, the recent massive changes in Eastern Europe make it an intriguing and promising region for expansion, despite its challenges. The former Eastern Bloc is the subject of Chapter Fourteen.

In Robert Half International's 44 years of finding the right career opportunities for skilled professionals, while working with companies across the globe to help them find, hire, and retain the best possible talent, matching candidate to job has been the linchpin of our success. For any man or woman looking to build a career overseas, particularly in the unified Europe of post-'92, knowing a company's personnel needs is the first step to landing a job with that company. Readers of this book who seek such opportunities will learn about how to prepare themselves to offer what expansion-minded U.S. companies will surely—and sorely—need.

Introduction

Before any company can tackle the specifics of staffing in Europe, the decision makers must have an understanding of the playing field upon which their company will be operating, including the reasons why the New Europe came about.

Robert Half International has, for many years, conducted ongoing surveys of the workplace that have been widely published. Until recently, these surveys have focused upon the U.S. workplace, with the exception of the United Kingdom where we have done business for more than 25 years. But as this company, like so many others, prepares itself for significant expansion into the broader EC, we've turned our survey attention to that evolving amalgamation of countries, and the results are reported throughout the book.

In the next group of chapters, we take a look at the European arena, how the European Community evolved, how it works, and whether it is becoming a single economic entity in fact as well as in theory—or whether its individual states are still a geographic quilt of socio-cultural differences.

Harold Max Messmer, Jr.—Menlo Park, California, 1992

Section I
The European Business Arena

One
A Look at the European Arena— Then and Now

> 31 December 1992, is not simply a deadline. It is the gateway to Europe's political future. The objective of creating an area unhampered by internal frontiers therefore affects every one of us and will affect future generations, which is why we need everyone's support, although we are aware of the difficulties the current program may entail for some. We are nevertheless convinced that our future role in the world economy is at stake.
>
> Martin Bangemann
> Vice President
> Commission of European Communities
> "Europe without Frontiers: Completing the Internal Market," February 1989

For any company seeking to penetrate the European marketplace, and committed to fielding the most productive team to compete in the New Europe, it is imperative to understand the dynamics that have led to this remarkable experiment in unity. U.S. men and women who aspire to adding European experience to their resumes will also benefit substantially from understanding the genesis of this imposing new unified marketplace.

While the shooting war in Europe ended officially in 1945, the truce was anything but comfortable. Ominous signs were manifest almost immediately, then dramatically underscored with the breakdown of the Moscow Conference in April 1947. The conference had been called to resolve the situation of a divided Germany; instead, it resulted in a further polarization of Eastern and Western Europe.

The consolidation in the late 1940s of Soviet satellite states, the Berlin blockade, and the formation of the North Atlantic Treaty Organization—and its counterpart, the Warsaw Pact—institutionalized, in rapid succession, the division of Europe. The successful explosion of a Soviet nuclear weapon in 1949 heightened the level of perceived fear, and pushed the political face-off to center stage, relegating economic issues to a position of lesser importance and increasing the potential for long-term economic problems.

An early and ominous example of these problems developed in the coal and steel production regions on the borders of France and Germany. Demand for steel was slackening, and producers were showing early signs of forming a restrictive cartel. Fragile post-war economies would suffer from restrictions on steel production, coupled with unrealistic pricing levels.

Robert Schuman, the French foreign minister, was given the assignment of defusing the situation. With the assistance of a learned colleague, Jean Monnet, he hammered out a compromise. In the process, they set in motion a much grander design—the reintegration of Germany into the basic fabric of post-war Europe. This compromise also laid the early foundation for Pan-European cooperative efforts.

At a press conference on May 9, 1950, Schuman declared:

> It is no longer time for vain words, but for a bold, constructive act. France has acted, and the consequences of her action may be immense. We hope they will. She has acted essentially in the cause of peace. For peace to have a real chance, there must first be a Europe. Almost five years to the day since Germany's unconditional surrender, France is taking the first decisive step to rebuild Europe and is inviting Germany to play its part. This will transform the situation in Europe. This will open the door to other joint activities inconceivable hitherto. Europe will emerge from all this; a Europe that is firmly united and solidly built; a Europe where living standards will rise as a result of the pooling of production and the expansion of markets . . . .

Schuman's proclamation more than 40 years ago may have been premature as a Pan-European prediction, and perhaps overly optimistic for that early point in time, but his words were nonetheless prophetic.

On June 20, 1950, at an international conference in Paris convened to solve the coal and steel problem, France invited overall European representation. Belgium, Italy, the Netherlands and Luxembourg sent representatives to join their French and German counterparts. The result was a treaty establishing the European Coal and Steel Community (ECSC), with headquarters in Luxembourg, and Schuman's colleague, Jean Monnet, as president. The seeds of modern European economic cooperation had been sown.

Meanwhile, in the post-war era of the early 1950s, the United States, secure in its position on the other side of the Atlantic, dominated the world economy. Per capita income in the United States was multiples higher than that of the nations of Europe or the Pacific Rim, each of these areas devastated by war and in need of monumental rebuilding efforts to restore even the most basic elements of infrastructure. The United States, on the other hand, had no balance-of-payments problems; was responsible for almost 40 percent of the world's industrial output; and possessed more than half of its monetary gold. The United States also provided most of the world's Nobel laureates, and held an undisputed and seemingly impenetrable lead in new technological developments. The United States even managed to take command in industries that had traditionally been the industrial domain of Europe, such areas as pharmaceuticals and chemicals.

From the U.S. perspective, nations devastated by the war seemed destined to play only a supporting role for the foreseeable future, especially countries in Europe where the Iron Curtain's east-west division compounded post-war confrontation and created ongoing tension.

Those whose vision would relegate the nations of Europe and the Pacific Rim to second-class positions as industrial powers were, however, shortsighted. From the unclouded perspective of hindsight, we now can look back on four decades of rebuilding, reestablishing traditional areas of strength, and repositioning business and markets, all of which resulted in perhaps the greatest economic renaissance in world history.

At the onset of the 1990s, the great leveling process that anchored this renaissance of the European Community and the Pacific Rim—at the expense of U.S. market share—was firmly established. Productivity levels, particularly in Asia, exceeded those of the United States during this intervening 40-year period, and brought the living standards of the Japanese and Western Europe to, or near, parity with the United States.

To a sizable extent, the economic renaissance of Europe was made possible by a growing understanding that cooperative programs among nations (even long-time adversaries such as the French and Germans) were necessary if European neighbors were effectively to utilize their resources. Joint efforts like the ECSC were early indications that the long-standing enmities of the war had already fallen victim to new and pragmatic economic and political realities.

Then, as the '80s turned the corner into the '90s, the failure of the Communist experiment resulted in the collapse of post-war alignments in Eastern Europe and, most strikingly, the dissolution of the Soviet

Union itself into a loose confederation of states now called the Commonwealth of Independent States. There was the very real sense that after a half century or more of economic sacrifice—including shortages of even basic necessities—that the nations of Eastern Europe were anxious to partake of the good life they had seen in the West.

One of many dramatic examples of this ecumenical attitude was the collapse of the Berlin Wall and resulting steps toward reunification of West and East Germany, whose economies had been divided by the political barriers of the Cold War. That economic integration was foremost in the minds of the leaders of both East and West Germany. It was testified to in the almost immediate adoption of West Germany's powerful deutsche mark as the currency for both Germanies—even before political reunification had become a reality. The business sectors of the long-divided nation began to meld just as quickly.

"The words 'management,' 'marketing' and 'consultant' were not in the East German dictionary during four decades of Communism," the *New York Times* reported shortly after the fall of the Wall. "Now, from lexicographic oblivion . . . have emerged two of East Germany's first private management and marketing consultants. Their rise comes as many companies are turning to consultants for help in evaluating the potential of the unified German market, as difficult as it may be, in finding joint-venture partners. And, a number of West German and U.S. consulting groups are rushing to build networks of contacts and a base of information on East Germany."

The dizzying pace that followed the collapse of Communism was obviously not for the faint-of-heart, or the slow-to-move. If consultants were rushing in, could the avalanche of business opportunists be far behind? A great deal clearly had to occur, however, in the prior half-century to make this bloodless political and economic revolution possible.

Between the end of the "hot war," and the thaw in the Cold War during the 45 years that followed, there were a series of meetings that served to reshape the face of Western Europe. The perception in Western Europe of a need for economic integration as a source of strength was pervasive, irrespective of the depth of national differences. These meetings resulted in the Treaty of Rome, signed on March 25, 1957, by Belgium, France, Italy, Luxembourg, the Netherlands and West Germany. This treaty established the European Economic Community (EEC), which was legislated into existence on January 1, 1958. During a 12-year period mandated by the treaty, these original six countries were to ease customs restrictions and scale back tariffs and quotas, while simultaneously establishing an external tariff for non-members.

In response to the formation of the EEC, seven other countries established a competing group—the European Free Trade Association (EFTA)—consisting of Austria, Denmark, Norway, Portugal, Sweden, Switzerland and the United Kingdom. But, it soon became clear that the EEC would be the more powerful of the two organizations, and several members of EFTA sought membership in the EEC during the 1960s and 1970s. By the end of the 1980s, the EEC had accepted some converts, and had expanded to 12 members, adding Denmark, Greece, Ireland, Portugal, Spain and the United Kingdom. The name of the confederation was shortened to the European Community, or EC.

While the name may have been simplified, the EC's composition, administration and decision-making elements have grown predictably complex. It has become a multi-chambered organization, headquartered in Brussels, and employing more than 20,000 people in administrative, executive, legislative and judicial functions. Although the heads of the individual governments of member states provide overall policy directives and establish long-term objectives for their particular delegations, the principal advisory and decision-making bodies of the EC are: the Commission, the Council of Ministers, the European Parliament, the Court of Justice, and the Economic and Social Committee. (There are, predictably, hundreds of sub-committees and other units.)

A brief description of these major governing bodies is necessary if the function of the EC is to be truly understood.

• • •

The **Commission** consists of commissioners appointed by the 12 member governments, and is the initiator of EC policies. For the most part, it has the exclusive right to propose EC legislation, and is the powerful body that drafts rules and regulations which ultimately govern the operations of the EC. The Commission is also the executive arm of the EC government, implementing—or at least overseeing—adherence to the policies.

There are 17 commissioners—two each from France, Germany, Italy, Spain and the United Kingdom; one each from Belgium, Denmark, Greece, Ireland, Luxembourg, the Netherlands and Portugal.

The commissioners each serve four-year renewable terms. A president and vice president are chosen from among their numbers to serve two-year renewable terms. Regulations, directives, decisions and recommendations are drafted by the Commission for action by the Council of Ministers.

While the commissioners are appointed by their respective nations, the Treaty of Rome dictates that they be impartial in their actions, and not be beholden to their respective governments.

On the other hand, the **Council of Ministers,** is the body that directly represents the interests of member states. It is made up of government ministers from each country, with the number of votes allocated each member weighted in favor of the larger nations.

The Council is the principal decision-making body of the EC, and rules upon the adoption of regulations and directives after taking into consideration the recommendations of the Commission, as well as of the European Parliament.

The **European Parliament** examines and reports on proposals made by the Commission. While the Parliament's recommendations are non-binding, it exerts powerful influence in other important areas. The Parliament has budgetary powers over the operation of the EC apparatus, and is empowered to dismiss commissioners.

The 518 members of the Parliament are chosen by direct election in the member states, and serve five-year terms. In effect, the Parliament's comments on proposals presented by the Commission before the Council of Ministers represent the only direct expression of the will of the people of the various member states.

The **Court of Justice** is the judicial arbiter of EC conflicts. The Court settles treaty disputes, and is the ultimate interpreter of disagreements over regulations, directives and decisions. Each of the Court's 13 judges serves for six years, and there must be at least one judge from each member state.

The **Economic and Social Committee** serves in a purely advisory capacity. The Council chooses its members from lists submitted by member states, and the number per state is, once again, according to size. Members serve four years. One of the Committee's responsibilities is to provide feedback on programs under consideration by the Commission, and by the Council.

There is also the **Court of Auditors,** which examines the soundness of EC financial management on a regular basis; and three small units—the **Publications Office,** the **Centre for the Development of Vocational**

Training, and the **Foundation for the Improvement of Living and Working Conditions**—each attached to the Commission.

Although not part of the formal structure of the EC, the **European Council,** which is made up of the heads of state of the 12 member nations, meets twice each year with the president of the Commission to discuss overall policy and direction for the EC. Obviously, positions strongly held by the heads of state will work their way into the decisions of the Community.

Also created by the Treaty of Rome was the **European Investment Bank** (EIB), "with the task of contributing, through its financing, to the balanced development of the Community." It is an independent entity, within the EC, that raises its funds on the capital markets, and that lends on a non-profit basis to finance priority investments. EIB's loans are not confined to the Community, however. It also has made loans to countries in Europe outside the EC, as well as to nations in Africa, the Caribbean and the Pacific.

The concept of unification carries with it a tacit belief that simplicity will follow. It's obvious, however, from even this cursory look at the structure of the EC that simplicity will hardly be the eventual outcome. Already, the bureaucratic structure is large and complex, and undoubtedly will grow more so in the years ahead.

• • •

With the organizational structure of Europe's multi-nation economic concept firmly established during a period of more than 20 years—and with the early experiences of the EEC to draw upon—the bold step to move the member states into a single-market entity was finally taken in the mid-1980s. A white paper—"On Completing The Internal Market"—issued by the Commission in 1985, outlined the single-market concept, and provided a basic blueprint under which it would take effect at the end of 1992, i.e., the elimination of physical, technical and fiscal barriers.

The Single European Act (SEA), adopted by all 12 member states in 1987, officially established a European market larger than the United States and Japan combined. With a population of more than 320 million condensed in an area less than a quarter the size of the United States, the countries of the EC export more than either the United States or

Japan (even excluding trade among member states), and import about the same percentage of the world's products as the United States. Where it lags behind both the United States and Japan is in per capita gross domestic product (GDP), and that is an imbalance the SEA seeks to rectify.

Also proposed were hundreds of legislative directives, whose enactments were necessary to make the 1992 transition a reality. By the end of 1992, it is expected that approximately two-thirds of these directives will have been enacted, with the other one-third phasing in during the remainder of the decade. Key directives include those regulating such areas as product standards, import quotas, local content, rules of origin, corporate law and mergers and acquisitions.

From the perspective of U.S. companies, the question, then, is: with this monolithic apparatus in place, what is the general effect on a company seeking to do business in Europe post-1992, and what new breed of executive will be required to make it work?

Beyond the need for a basic understanding of how the EC works, it should be clear to any prospective U.S. company seeking success in a unified Europe that member states of the EC are, to some extent, reinventing their own version of the wheel. Many pro-unification efforts have occurred over 30 years to create the framework for the unity of purpose that their heralded 1992 transformation to a new Europe seeks to establish. In the process, member states have implemented programs and policies that work for them, and that are designed to make them an even greater force in the global marketplace.

The management of foreign businesses seeking to expand into Europe must have an appreciation of the EC's complexity, along with a clear understanding that it was created for the benefit of its members—a force to compete against the world's other powerful economic zones.

In fact, after the collapse of the Uruguay round of international trade talks in late 1990, the *New York Times* editorial put the blame squarely on the shoulders of the EC and its special interests. It read in part:

> All this was undermined by the European Community. To protect its 10 million farmers, it keeps food prices high by shutting out foreign imports. The high prices, in turn, generate huge surpluses that it dumps on world markets at subsidized prices. That amounts to economic warfare against farmers from the U.S., Canada and the Third World.

There is, in effect, a high degree of chauvinism in the EC's creation. An outsider seeking entry into this venue is precisely that—an outsider.

While this does not necessarily presage a we vs. they attitude, it does dictate that heavy-handedness on the part of foreign corporations will not be appreciated, perhaps not even tolerated.

Diplomacy will be.

I should emphasize here that the overall objective of this economic unification is to generate business, and to foster economic development for all. We cannot, however, lose sight of the fact that there is now a history of 30-plus years, and an intricate organizational structure in place to weight any economic balance in favor of the EC member states.

It is true that one large, integrated market, without physical barriers and with better access to end-users, will make intra-EC marketing and distribution easier and less expensive, even for foreign companies operating in Europe. It is also true that standardization will be the general order in the New Europe, which will provide benefits to foreign businesses.

Specifically, standardization of excise and value-added taxes will ease some of the more troublesome problems of price competition that have caused prices to vary—sometimes dramatically—in different member states. Furthermore, the free flow of goods without the impediment of physical barriers—i.e., customs posts and transportation restrictions that previously favored national carriers—will reduce the costs of moving goods within the EC by as much as 50 percent. Elimination of this kind of red tape will save as much as seven percent of the EC's gross domestic product.

But, if the time does arrive when a U.S. company decides to fight city hall—EC style—the enlightened Euro-executive will understand that he or she is up against a multilayered bureaucracy in which decisions to adopt new directives, or to modify or repeal old ones, could take years.

All of this takes into account the EC as it basically exists today. The final decade of this century will undoubtedly see numerous changes: the expansion of the list of member states and adoption of a European currency being the most probable phenomena. There is already, however, a basic philosophical split as to how the EC should approach the future. Nations seeking to maintain a degree of exclusivity have been labeled "deepeners"; those favoring expansion are called, "broadeners."

The deepeners, whose titular head is France, favor consolidating the present membership and bonding even further via a Euro-currency and Pan-European political integration. Broadeners, led by the United Kingdom, lean toward expansion to include the Swiss, Scandinavians and some Eastern European states.

Compromise may result in the adoption of elements from each camp, with the printing of currency most likely mirroring the deepeners' position, and elements of expansion growing from the broadeners. Ties with EFTA (now composed of Austria, Finland, Iceland, Norway, Sweden and Switzerland) are already in place and likely to grow stronger.

To understand the ramifications of these changes, and to deal with them on a day-to-day basis (not to mention to compete effectively in a market where competitors from member nations are already well established), will require careful recruiting, training and allocation of human resources. For the U.S. company, good business sense dictates combining the best of local talent (who understand the local marketplace, rules and business protocol), with U.S. professionals (who understand the company's products, services and modus operandi).

Arriving at the most productive mix is a challenge in its own right, further complicated by outside forces, sometimes pulling in opposite directions.

For example, while European countries have restrictive employment codes for aliens (not unlike the U.S.'s "green card" regulations), Western Europe has been experiencing a dramatic decline in birth rate, which will make it increasingly necessary to go outside the borders of the EC for talent.

Although 2.1 children per mother are necessary to maintain a constant population, the average for the EC is less than 1.6 (with Italy, Spain and Germany at less than 1.4).

Meanwhile, the EC workforce is shrinking from the opposite direction. Of its 324 million, about one-third are already over age 50, and their number is increasing at a rate greater than that of the rest of the population.

The result is an ever-increasing spiral of more people leaving the workforce, while fewer enter it. Add to this estimates of as many as two million *new* jobs created by the single market, and the shortage of labor becomes even more extreme.

At the same time, the aging workforce is driving up average salaries, and the growing popularity of early retirement is putting a further squeeze on skilled labor. (Soon, the number of retirees in the EC may be greater than its number of workers.)

Part of the shortfall in human resources will be made up by reinstating the unemployed. Vacancies will also provide more opportunities for women to enter the labor pool. But existing human resources will not be enough. Supply vs. demand will raise the cost of enticing young, talented professionals into U.S. companies seeking to take advantage of business opportunities in the EC.

The situation dictates that European business operations will have to look elsewhere for skilled help. That spells opportunity for foreigners.

Problems of poverty and local conflict in North Africa, Southern Asia and the Middle East (as well as population rates as much as three times greater than Western Europe) will increase pressures on migration from these areas. But deep cultural, religious and other sociological differences between citizens of these areas, and the societies of Western Europe, will mitigate against mass European immigration. Furthermore, these emigrants from impoverished areas lack required skills—in the required numbers—to effectively staff Europe.

In France, for example, an organization called S O S Racism, has grown from a campus club in 1984, to a membership of 17,000, with 350 chapters nationwide, largely handling complaints of bias against second-generation French citizens of African and Middle Eastern descent. Eight percent of the French population—or 4.5 million people—are immigrants from those areas, but the customs and traditions of their original homelands are alien to the long-held traditions of the indigenous French.

Conversely, the affinities of culture, and areas of overlap in business that exist between Europe and the United States, will provide opportunities for U.S. companies and for their highly skilled men and women.

U.S. companies which will have the greatest advantage in post-1992 Europe are those that have had the benefit of operating there for years, and that have established networks of offices continent-wide. In many respects, these U.S. companies might have advantages even over some of their European competitors, many of which have major operations in their native country, but a lesser presence outside their own borders.

U.S. firms that have seen the effects of the EC's single-market concept coming since the mid-1980s (or even before), and have consolidated their positions on a Pan-European scale, will be in the best position to capitalize on the opening of borders. Many are in solid positions. Companies such as IBM, DuPont, Hewlett-Packard, Citicorp, and Ford have long histories in Europe, and have brought their European executives to the States for tours of duty while sending U.S. managers to Europe. They have executives who are multilingual throughout their global networks, and at all levels.

For others, the potential to succeed is also there—provided, of course, that their expanded U.S.-European staffs are up to the task. There will be some obvious economies of scale.

For example, the so-called elimination of national borders will facilitate the consolidation of manufacturing operations and distribution centers, with a consequent reduction in duplicated efforts.

Similar consolidations on the part of European customers will permit U.S. suppliers to target their marketing efforts at key decision makers in fewer locations.

Where U.S. companies are faced with decisions of consolidation, conventional wisdom will dictate a close look at the geography. The cost of doing business in Germany is high; it is considerably lower in Spain. Both, however, are part of the EC. Goods from Spain, therefore, have the same access to the rest of the EC as do those manufactured in Germany.

The possibilities for expansion within the EC are similarly limitless.

A Dutch accounting firm will be able to set up practice in Copenhagen. An Italian shoe company may open a factory in London. A Portuguese seafood cannery might well open a distribution center in Dublin. The flow of goods will be greatly improved. Dozens of separate customs forms will be replaced by a single document. Business people who enter one of the EC's member states can travel to the other 11 without having to confront another immigration or customs checkpoint. The overland movement of products will speed up substantially with the elimination of these border checkpoints. Goods should move as easily between Madrid and Edinburgh as they do between Chicago and New York City.

Citizens of EC member states can now travel with their burgundy-colored European passports, and can buy "Europlates" for their cars.

The critical point here is that as borders fall, and as corporations gain expanded access to the multinational or global arena, it is the *company* as an entity that gains in importance, while the importance of the country, or political entity, declines. New cross-border companies will operate on a global scale, with the effect that developments in one corner of a company's operations will impact upon other corners of the operation.

The benefits of new research and development, for example, will flow across borders. Products and people will move more freely from state to state. Financing will come from widely separated geographical sectors. Mergers and acquisitions will further blur the role of national regulatory agencies.

A *Newsweek* magazine analysis concluded, "global product managers are asserting power over country and regional managers."

U.S. companies with global operations already in place have obviously developed their own cadre of global product managers. But these U.S. firms represent only a small percentage of companies that will be competing in post-'92 Europe. Where will the new breed of global product manager come from? Are there a sufficient number of U.S. men and women already preparing themselves for the daunting challenge of managing not only their company's European operations, but for dealing with the even broader perspective of integrating those operations into the whole? Executives capable of filling this crucial role are, to paraphrase an old saying, made, not born. Good ones will be a long time in the making. Companies with aspirations in the New Europe, but who have not recognized the need for a long and careful nurturing of such individuals, will find themselves stymied for an unnecessarily long period of time. There is, of course, the potential of hiring away seasoned, experienced global managers from other companies, but that well is not deep. The time to begin developing Euro-managers is now.

The once-dominant system whereby product managers reported to top management at headquarters via separate channels has become old fashioned. It is "too bureaucratic, too slow and too expensive in today's market," a member of the Corning Glass board of directors told *Newsweek*. "It's getting to the point where there is no *American* corporation," Harvard Business School professor Robert B. Reich added.

The magazine cited the example of a new electronic elevator system developed by six United Technologies research centers in five countries for UT's Otis subsidiary. A group in Connecticut managed systems integration, one in Japan developed motor drives, France was responsible for the door systems, Germany for electronics and Spain for small-gear components. According to Otis, this global cooperation sped up development from four years to two, at a savings of more than $10 million.

The EC rules of origin have tested Japanese reluctance to transfer technologies and appoint non-Japanese to top management posts. But in order to be considered legitimate EC corporations, such moves must take place, and the Japanese, not a people to pass up a business opportunity, are complying.

Beyond actual hands-on assistance, U.S. companies are turning to foreign business executives for help via advisory councils. More than 300 U.S.-based companies consider such councils critical enough to highlight them in their annual reports, while perhaps four times that many utilize them as well.

Staffing the new borderless corporation should benefit from such new EC regulations as those permitting the freer movement of locals. While differences in educational approach and professional qualifications are still in effect among member nations, the EC has been working to minimize, and to eventually eliminate these differences by establishing community-wide qualification standards, beginning with certain specified professions.

The greatest progress has been made in the critical healthcare professions—doctors, nurses, dentists, midwives. These professionals now enjoy the right to establish their own practices throughout the EC. Progress has also been made in areas such as agriculture, forestry, mining, power, gas, oil and water. While standardization is proceeding more slowly in other areas, the progress made in these fields is encouraging, and hopefully prophetic.

The globalization of business and its effect on the blue-collar segment of the workforce, however, have caused concern in organized labor. In the first half of 1990, the 700,000 members of the Communications Workers of America joined with the 40,000 members of the Communications and Electrical Workers of Canada to confront "the globalization of business, which is one of the most serious problems the labor movement faces." Presidents of the two unions told the *Washington Post* their concern was that the "fast approaching domination by stateless corporations" would exploit cheap labor wherever they could find it.

The Brussels-based International Federation of Chemical, Energy and General Workers' Unions has been expanding its reach in attempts to organize chemical, pharmaceutical and rubber-producing firms throughout the world.

This growing movement toward global oversight by organized labor was an early warning shot that while making the most of available personnel resources around the globe will be to a corporation's advantage, exploitation of workers, and its deleterious effects on the livelihood of skilled labor, would not be tolerated.

Larger U.S. companies, with long-standing relationships in Europe, are already taking advantage of improvements that affect their operations. There are many of them. In 1990 our company surveyed hundreds of executives among the nation's largest 1,000 companies. Slightly over 50 percent reported that their companies currently operated in Europe. Of those whose companies were not, as yet, operating in Europe, 54 percent felt that they would be expanding there within the next five years. Thirty-eight percent saw Eastern Europe as a potential setting for overseas expansion during the same five year period.

Smaller U.S. companies, including those without highly developed networks, can learn a great deal from the experiences of these larger companies. And, in fact, other surveys have shown that as many as one-third of U.S. small to mid-sized firms, with sales from $10 million to $300 million, have already set up operations in the EC, each facing an ongoing need to enhance and supplement staff with the caliber of people to meet intense competitive challenges.

Of course, the extent to which U.S. companies, large and small, enter, or expand in post-'92 will depend upon numerous factors outside their immediate control. The recession towards the end of 1990, and which continued into 1992, is a prime example. The effects of such a recession, coupled with the impact of currency exchange rates, caused many U.S. firms to re-think, or to curtail the extent of their commitment to European expansion. As the dollar continued to sink in relation to European currencies, it became more expensive to open offices abroad. On the other hand, once opened and operating, these offices stood to benefit from a sinking dollar, and to become more profitable. In the final analysis, such world economic events dictate that companies be more deliberate in their planning, and more serious in their purpose, lest they become discouraged by start-up expenses and early losses of operation. But for those with well-conceived plans and a certain amount of endurance, richer rewards could certainly be anticipated.

The potential for European expansion by U.S. firms represents an opportunity that must be carefully examined even by those companies with what initially may appear to be only minimal interest in foreign markets. The EC represents an opportunity that cannot be ignored, but only those committed to intelligent planning, including diligent manpower considerations, will prosper. Managers with tunnel vision, who see only domestic or nearby markets, may ignore a chance to sell their products to the EC's sophisticated consumers.

A good example of entering, and prospering in the European market, is Medical Concepts, Inc., founded near Santa Barbara, California, in 1984. The company found an expanding market for its product in Europe just two years later.

Medical Concepts manufactures mini-video cameras for viewing endoscopic procedures, such as orthroscopic knee surgery performed on athletes. The cameras are also an important piece of equipment in a new procedure to remove gall bladders endoscopically.

In 1986, Medical Concepts conducted research revealing that some U.S. manufacturers of endoscopic equipment that utilized their cameras were selling a considerable number of their products in Europe. Medical Concepts decided to explore the potentials of marketing their products directly to Europe, and ultimately developed a network of distributors in Europe. As the usage of their cameras increased—particularly in the United Kingdom, France, Italy and Germany—a service center operation was needed to shorten the distance for repairs and modifications. The company contracted with a firm just outside of Amsterdam.

"The market was primed for our product," says Angeli Mancuso, product manager. "As consumers became more aware of endoscopic medical procedures, they demanded them from their doctors who, in turn, demanded the equipment from their hospitals.

Within three years of the establishment of the Dutch service center, sales outstripped its capacity, and the company had to start planning for the establishment of its own sales and service operation, staffed with a combination of local employees and augmented by U.S. staff. As the European operation grew in tandem with Medical Concepts' domestic sales, staffing Europe took on new and important meaning. "Our success in Europe basically just happened," says Mancuso. "We hadn't had the time, or the luxury, to plan how to fill our human resources needs overseas. Now that Europe is an established reality for us, and the future looks even brighter, we're putting a lot more thought into the type of employees we need to manage our growth there."

• • •

Now that we've had a chance to examine, however briefly, the single-market concept and the movement of the European public and private sector in that direction since the close of World War II, can we assume that the lofty objectives of the EC will be met? Is the EC really creating a European homogeneity, or will centuries of factionalism, heterogeneity and outright conflict mean that the EC is little more than an exercise in bureaucracy?

In broad strokes, what will the structure of a unified core of 12 nations in the heart of Europe require in terms of creating a team there qualified to effectively manage and prosper?

These are some of the questions we'll explore in ensuing chapters.

Two
One Europe? A Matter of Perspective

Can a continent whose various sovereignties have filled history books with centuries of conflict, and whose cartographers have revised its maps countless times, finally find unity in an economic-inspired confederacy? While the recent history of the EC encourages a positive response, opinion is divided.

Officials at the EC are obviously upbeat. "(T)he process of completion of the single market is now irreversible . . ." a recent progress report declared.

There is third-party endorsement, as well:

"Before the end of the century there will be a single currency in Europe," the chairman of Holland's giant N.V. Philips manufacturing conglomerate told a business school class in Switzerland. "Much of Eastern Europe will be in the EC and 20 years from now there will be a Europe of 700 million people able to be equal partners with the United States, Japan and the rest of the world."

Agreements struck by EC member nations in Maastricht, the Netherlands, in the latter part of 1991 lend credence to this optimism.

Still, others remain less sure:

Business Week has foreseen ongoing rivalries, such as Britain's "fear of a loss of sovereignty," or France's "mortal terror of German power," as slowing the process of integration, if not derailing it, at least in a de facto sense. The magazine sees other serious problems that must be overcome: " . . . trying to bring in the basketcase economies of Eastern Europe as the EC struggles to absorb such poorer members as Portugal and Greece may be more than the system can bear."

Josef Joffe, U.S. editor of Munich's *Suddeutsche Zeitung,* is downright pessimistic. He wrote in the June 1990 issue of *Commentary:*

> . . . the EC as we know it will not survive the passing of the Cold War . . . Suitably reformed, Hungary, Poland, Czechoslovakia and Romania have at least as much of a claim to entry as had Portugal and Greece. Why keep out Switzerland, Sweden and Austria once the EC is no longer the economic core of a Western defense organization? One thing is certain. More members equal more heterogeneity, which, in turn, will postpone political union indefinitely. The EC [will be reduced] to a Europe-wide free-trade zone.

Even such a strong supporter of the EC as president of the European Commission, Jacques Delors, views the reality of a truly unified Europe as perhaps being beyond the capability of the individual states to achieve. He told the European Parliament in late 1990, "There are those who want an economic and monetary union so beautiful, so perfect, that it will never get started, it will never be born."

Mr. Delors based his view on the seemingly impossible task of creating a single currency within the EC, which took centerstage at that time. Unification efforts on other fronts have proceeded more smoothly. But, many American companies, and their men and women charged with finding success in a unified Europe, must be prepared to function in this promising, yet turbulent business atmosphere.

As indicated in Chapter One, barriers, both physical and economic, have and will continue to come down between member states of the EC. But long-standing individual histories that have differentiated Romans and Goths, Saxons and Gauls, have spawned and nurtured socio-cultural differences in the way Europeans from different geographic regions conduct their daily lives. The midday siesta is as foreign to the daily routine of a London banker as a Copenhagen product manager's obsessive punctuality would be to the marketing manager of a Neapolitan shoe manufacturer who has made a unilateral decision to delay meeting with his advertising reps.

Similarly, the member states of the EC approach the 1992 unification date in various states of readiness. While many feel—and fear—that Germany is on the verge of dominating the community (it represents about a third of the EC's Gross Domestic Product), others appear to be in considerably weaker positions.

Italy, for example, has had much higher budget deficits than France or Germany, markedly higher inflation rates in recent years, less liberal internal markets, and a long-term inability to bring state-owned industries into a more efficiently run private sector. Furthermore, while Italy's diversified business base provides a degree of insurance against downturns in specific segments of the economy, growth in its traditional products—shoes, wine, furniture and textiles—has been sluggish across the board in recent years.

"Unless Italy changes its ways," an analyst in *Business Week* concluded, "many fear it could wind up a second-string player in the post-1992 European game." Perhaps an unduly harsh assessment. Under the magnifying glass, other EC members could suffer similarly critical analyses.

Italy's problems should not result in the assumption that the country lacks clout within the EC. It was while Italy held the rotating presidency of the EC, and held the line on the establishment of a European currency—aligning 11 member states against the United Kingdom—that Margaret Thatcher's intransigency on the subject began to erode her support among her Conservative Party colleagues. This eventually led to her resignation in the autumn of 1990.

The point remains, however, that there are definite disparities among member states as they enter the single-market zone. Furthermore, there are even more dramatic differences in the attitudes of those Europeans who have lived in the Eastern Bloc during the post-war years.

Consider that with the reunification of Germany, many of East Germany's 170,000-strong armed forces found the job security of a career in the military a faded memory. The unified German military has been able to absorb less than half of its East German counterparts; the rest were forced to seek work in the private sector.

For the U.S. company planning expansion into Europe, the advantages of the borderless EC will be moderated by socio-cultural differences among member states. In fact, in many instances, U.S. nationals are far more likely to view Europe as a single entity than their European counterparts. Old-line business executives in Europe have, for years, grown up in a system that views with mistrust a single European entity.

It may take years to reverse that thinking, if it can be done at all. It is the hope among the forward-thinkers in Europe that these nationalistic business people will be replaced by the emerging class of junior executives who will live and prosper under their heightened sense of unity.

How, then, are current differences likely to affect staffing decisions by corporate management? What can management do about them?

To gain a proper perspective from which to approach staffing Europe, managers of U.S.-based corporations must understand that while they may gain entrance to the EC via an office in Dublin, which in turn throws open a vista of 11 additional national markets, their base is nonetheless in Ireland—and they must acclimate to the Irish business mentality.

On the other hand, the Pan-European perspective of the EC sometimes comes into conflict with local laws, creating for the American business person on-coming traffic where he or she had thought they'd seen a one-way sign. For example, the May 1990 issue of *Target 92*, a newsletter produced by the EC Commission, reported a judgement of the Court of Justice in favor of a Belgian supermarket that was distributing leaflets across the border in Luxembourg, which violated some of the latter's advertising regulations.

"The EC Court of Justice takes the view that Europeans have the right to buy where they like within the 12-nation European Community, and to be kept fully informed of bargains on offer," the article noted.

Advertising, of course, is the conduct of business through the impersonal conduit of print and broadcast media. On the person-to-person level, a whole new set of considerations come into play.

While it is difficult to generalize about the "psyche" of the European business person, suffice it to say that even the most basic business approaches, methodologies and motivational factors may be markedly different from what the U.S. manager is accustomed to.

Specifically, with a business structure in place long before the founding of the U.S. republic, Europeans are often more set in their ways. Some are inherently suspicious of the terms of a business arrangement, and more likely to make decisions based upon their evaluation of the trustworthiness of the person making the offer.

U.S. nationals may find some of their European counterparts less amenable to risk-taking, at least as risk is perceived by many U.S. managers. Americans working closely with European counterparts may find—in midstream—that they are standing in hip-deep water, in unfamiliar surroundings, minus the services of their local guide who has disappeared behind the treeline.

Perhaps a basic philosophy for conducting business would start with:

"Assume nothing,"

followed by:

"Proceed with diplomacy,"

and hopefully arrive at:

"Gradual change."

Navigating these waters will require the assistance of local experts in such fields as law, financial services, real estate, accounting, etc. Local rules and regulations may intercede while other plans are being made.

For example, while your company makes a unilateral corporate decision to forgo an audit of U.K. offices one fiscal year, you then discover that U.K. law requires an audit every year, and that you will have to comply, irrespective of the effects on corporate convenience.

Obviously, interpersonal relationships play a critical role in the day-to-day conduct of all business. In many segments of the European industrial community, such relationships will be critical to the ultimate success or failure of U.S. firms doing business there.

In deference to the need to understand such relationships, Roy Bostock, the CEO of the D'Arcy Masius Benton & Bowles advertising agency moved to Europe for two months as the agency's European business began to overtake its U.S. revenues a few years back.

"Europe has become so important to us that it is imperative that I get to know our business over there," he told the *New York Times*. "The best way to understand what's really going on is to just plop myself down in the thick of it."

This type of action was not unusual in the advertising industry. Ad giants such as J. Walter Thompson and Grey Advertising have set up European boards of executives to manage clients' Pan-European business.

Understanding differences in local, national or regional sociology goes well beyond knowing how to advertise to the marketplace. The most successful marketers will understand how people are likely to react to the product or service being offered.

When Citicorp, one of the largest banking companies in the United States and the only U.S. bank among the world's top 20 in terms of assets, decided to emphasize its highly successful credit card business in overseas markets, the bank came to understand that different cultures approach debt from different backgrounds. Germans, for example, are uncomfortable with debt. *Schulden,* the German word for debt, also means guilt. To overcome this indigenous aversion, Citicorp had to coin a new term for its credit card services: *rackzahl-wahl* or "credit that empowers."

Differences in the meaning of words between languages is something that every successful Euro-exec will have to understand. Language skills are critically important to any U.S. national looking to succeed in the European Community. I talk more about this in subsequent chapters, and a list of language training resources appears at the end of the book.

Before we even get to the specific issues and challenges of staffing Europe, it would be helpful to examine, briefly, how a U.S. firm is likely to enter the European market and what that will mean in the overall picture of human resources.

From a general perspective, there are three principal ways American companies enter the European arena:

- merger with, or acquisition of, an existing operation;
- an international joint venture with a European business or foreign-based company with operations in Europe;
- starting an operation from scratch.

One of our surveys of U.S. companies asked executives to project how they feel most U.S. firms will expand in Europe. Sixty-eight percent viewed joint ventures as holding the most promise. Twenty-four percent saw acquisitions as the method of choice. Approximately seven percent felt that the start-up of new operations would prevail. Let's briefly examine each of these from the perspective of their impact on staffing.

Merger or Acquisition—The attraction of 1992, as well as the fear of being left out, has spurred near frantic activities in international mergers and acquisitions. *Translink's European Deal Review,* a publication that monitors M&As, has recently reported such activity at more than 350 major deals per quarter, valued at between $15 and $20 billion in each quarter. While the United States has been a major force in this, European companies' activities increased markedly, too, and the Japanese went on a near feeding frenzy, with a particular appetite for smaller German companies.

By acquiring or merging with a European company, the U.S. firm assumes a staff already in place. If the company is to be allowed, for the most part, to operate as it has been, there is little to consider in terms of staffing. But to assume any acquiring U.S. firm will maintain a complete hands off policy is unrealistic.

There will be staffing challenges in an M&A environment beyond those of employees that come with the purchase of the European company, including oversight responsibilities in such key areas as operations, finance and marketing. Effectively overseeing the European subsidiary will be a difficult task unless key U.S. executives in those areas have the requisite understanding of how the Europeans operate.

International Joint Ventures—IJVs involve a separate organizational unit, owned by two or more "parent" companies, with at least one of the parents being outside the IJV's country of operations—in our case, a U.S. company joining with a European company to create a separate venture in Europe.

From a staffing perspective, the managers at the European entity will have to deal with such human resources concerns as split loyalties and the concurrent potential for friction, a diverse workforce, long-distance communication and a sense of isolation. The staff members of an IJV, unlike those at a regional operation for a purely U.S. firm, will not have the sense of security that goes with being an employee of a parent corporation.

Recruiting for this type of operation is difficult and delicate, and it is not surprising that there is often high turnover, along with an accelerated failure rate for IJVs in general. However, if staffed and operated efficiently, an IJV can be an effective way to enter the European marketplace.

General Electric's joint venture with Snecma, a French aerospace company, is a prime example. Wanting a crack at the jet engine contracts for the Airbus (itself the product of a multinational European cooperative business venture: Airbus Industry), GE launched a joint venture with Snecma. The IJV permitted both companies to share the risk of $800 million in development costs, which each, individually, was reluctant to undertake.

General Electric's joint venture won the engine contract for the Airbus 320. The result was a high-performance, low-pollution engine that was so impressive, the venture has sold them for use on the American-made Boeing 737s as well.

Not that there weren't ongoing cultural problems. The French side had an affinity for bringing in outside experts, often from the military, who insisted upon detailed briefings that took a great deal of time. At the same time, the French were uncomfortable with the U.S. national's more intuitive approach to problem solving.

Start-up of a European operation—The pros and cons are almost innumerable in starting and staffing a new operation in Europe. Challenges range from the costly labor intensive preliminaries (feasibility studies, legal research and preparations, the securing of charters, licenses, etc.) to the construction or acquisition of property, penetrating the market and, finally, making a profit.

Unquestionably, this approach is, more than anything, an exercise in the importance of staffing. Human resources are *the* critical element.

• • •

The question of whether the competition will be there is already being answered. KPMG Peat Marwick, in one of its surveys, found recently that despite the debate over the reality—or even the prospects—of a single market, one-third of U.S. executives perceive such a market already exists, and six of 10 U.S. companies have taken action, or plan to take action, in response to the new Europe.

Meanwhile, as they are looking at the business vistas in front of them, U.S. business people will also have to keep checking over their shoulders. No one expects the Japanese to be anything less than fierce competitors. They have even become adept at challenging the Europeans on their home turf.

For instance, Mitsubishi Electric Corporation was the center of controversy when it received more than $8 million in subsidies from the EC for a semiconductor manufacturing plant it was building in Germany. Competing European companies were outraged. But it turned out Mitsubishi was the beneficiary of incentives provided for locating manufacturing facilities in depressed areas. The plant was designed to employ 450 people in a region that had been hurt by losses of jobs in the coal industry.

Entry into the New Europe, consolidation of operations already in place there, the strengthening and expansion of a presence—all of these important business thrusts will require careful consideration. Business plans that detail short-term actions are necessary to plot immediate moves. Longer-term analyses must be prepared in order to forecast where a company will want to be positioned, after the initial rush to stake out appropriate sectors of the European business arena subsides.

U.S. executives should already be examining directives and regulations issued to date by the Council of Ministers to determine which apply to them, and how they will be affected. In fact, if possible, they should try to keep abreast of proposals *before* they become directives, or even before a consensus is reached. Once the bandwagon begins to roll, it is difficult to reroute it.

The U.S. banking industry has, to a large extent, committed itself to doing this. It has taken a cautious approach to Europe based upon its analysis of EC directives and laws that might affect growth, positive and negative. As the decade of the '90s arrived, many large U.S. banks began pulling back on their European expansion, and focusing more on domestic operations. This was in response to a decision by the EC's Ministry of Finance to allow European banks and securities firms freely enter each other's domain, a move that will give these European firms a strong competitive edge over U.S. banking companies. Depression-era laws such as the Glass-Steagall and McFadden acts prohibit U.S. banks and securities firms from crossing over. But American banks are convinced that these archaic laws will fall by mid-decade. This contemplation, coupled with having to compete in Europe with banks that have enjoyed years of experience under the EC deregulation, have caused many U.S. banks to contract in Europe, rather than to expand. The danger in this short-term strategy is that European banks are aggressively expanding in this country. With their head start in combining banking and securities trading, these banks may benefit the most from changes in our laws.

Whether this scenario holds true or not is conjecture. The salient point is that U.S. companies, in any industrial or service sector, must keep a sharp and continuing eye on what the EC and its member countries elect to do that might impact upon operations there.

Companies should be asking such key questions as:

- What will be needed to modify products to meet new regulations?
- How will logistics be affected?
- What will this do to the pipeline from vendors?
- What will it do for customers?
- How will marketing efforts be affected?
- Will the changes affect customers needs?

- Will international competition grow more intense?
- How can a U.S. company combat increased international competition?
- Who are the men and women with the appropriate education, experience, and sensitivity to the myriad cultural and socio-economic differences of the EC's member states to effectively perform such crucial tasks?
- How will recruiters know them?
- Where will they be found?

In the next chapters, we look at the individual EC member states in order to better understand the challenges of staffing an operation within specific countries. A similar, but necessarily less detailed view of non-EC states, as well as nations of the former Eastern Bloc, appears later in the book.

Three
An Overview of Each of the EC Member States

Each member state of the EC enjoys unique and precious national characteristics. There have been dozens, perhaps hundreds of books written about each one and its people—books that provide interesting and helpful insight. This chapter is not intended to add to that rich collection of analytic work. I do feel, however, that by briefly highlighting a few selected views, commonly held in each EC nation, readers will gain at least a sense of the cultural differences they and their employees will face. Each person who has ever visited a foreign land will have something to add, based upon their personal experiences. I recommend that anyone looking to relocate to the EC read as many books as possible about countries in which they'd like to work, and to benefit from the personal experiences of others who have been there.

Geographic proximity does not ensure common customs. For instance, while Spain and Portugal occupy the Iberian Peninsula together, Spaniards tend to be more demonstrative in public; friendly embrace during a greeting, is acceptable, if not common. The Portuguese, on the other hand, are more reserved, and such physical contact is often unwelcomed.

At a business lunch in Brussels, a U.S. business woman would find it virtually impossible to pick up the check for a male colleague or client, even if she has initiated the invitation—*unless* she has given the maître d' her credit card in advance, and has insisted to her guest that her company is paying for lunch.

If a U.S. national is invited home to dinner by a European business colleague, a gift is appropriate. But while a bottle of wine might be the perfect gift in the United States, it is not appropriate in many areas of Europe where hosts pride themselves on their wine cellars. Of course, a bottle of U.S. wine, accompanied by the suggestion, "I thought you might like to sample one of the fine wines from my country," is acceptable.

The potential is great for missteps in business situations, or at business-related social functions in a foreign country. The only long-term preventive medicine is to study the rules, practices, customs, protocols, and mannerisms of the host country, and then spend considerable time there putting what's been learned into practice. And, of course, to ask for guidance from European conterparts.

For those interested in a detailed introductory package that answers initial questions about doing business in each of the individual countries, all of the EC member states maintain foreign investment advisory offices in either New York, or Washington, D.C. Some have additional offices in other major cities across the United States. A list is found in the Appendices at the back of the book.

BELGIUM

General Business Overview

There are two distinct cultures in Belgium, the Dutch-speaking Flemish population, and the French-speaking Walloons (plus a small, German-speaking population). The twain does meet occasionally; the EC is headquartered in predominantly French-speaking Brussels, but is smack within the Flemish north. The language split is fairly sacrosanct, with one or the other spoken in specific geographic regions. This works in favor of English-speaking foreigners, since English is a kind of bridge language, frequently used in communications between the Dutch- and French-speaking populations.

EC headquarters plays a dominant role in the city of Brussels, with its architecturally modern—some would say radical—buildings.

Aside from its position as the seat of power for the EC, Belgium's north-central location also makes it a transportation hub relative to the rest of the Community. Brussels International Airport is a major passenger and freight center, the port of Antwerp is the third most-active seaport in the world, and Belgium's railway network is one of the most dense on earth (with three miles of track for every two square miles of territory).

In the international trade arena, Belgian business takes considerable pride in its highly skilled, multilingual workforce. It also has a long history as a global trader. Almost two-thirds of Belgium's GDP comes from exports.

To encourage foreign investment, Belgium offers incentives such as interest rate subsidies, exemption from certain taxes and cash grants. The most liberal incentives are granted on the basis of a company's potential for positive strategic impact on Belgian trade, and for the potential to create new employment opportunities.

Further incentives are offered for research and development, employment and training of locals, and the creation of Belgian-produced products for export to non-EC countries.

Operations in Belgium, as in most countries of Europe, may be set up as subsidiaries, as branches of U.S.-based companies, as joint ventures with Belgian firms, or as the result of mergers or acquisitions. Laws and regulations, of course, govern how each of these operations are established and how they conduct business. However, the Belgian Ministry of Economic Affairs has stated:

> [Belgian law] guarantees the advantage of the freedom to set up a company and transfer capital to all foreign companies and to any foreign investor who wants to settle in Belgium in order to start a commercial or industrial operation. . . . Foreign capital may be brought into Belgium without restriction. Income and operating profits may be repatriated by them without limit.

The Belgian treatment of foreign firms has obviously had a positive effect on multinational corporations. More than 14,000 foreign firms have established operations in the country, including such giants as Caterpillar, Kraft, Mobil, Monsanto, and Japan's N.V. Asahi Chemical.

And what of the workforce in Belgium? It comprises 4.2 million workers who are required to complete 12 years of schooling, much of it dedicated to the acquisition of employable skills. It is predominantly male—59 percent to 41 percent. Twenty-three percent of the working women hold part-time jobs, as opposed to just two percent of working men. Overall cost of labor in Belgium has traditionally been about eight percent lower than in the United States.

Foreign firms recruit employees by direct methods, such as advertising and conducting their own interviews. They may also take advantage of the government's Regional Employment Services, which recruits by advertising job vacancies on TV and radio, or they may hire private recruitment firms.

Robert Half International has long been impressed with the business climate of Belgium and with its local workforce. Since 1988 we have opened two offices in Brussels and one in Antwerp, to take advantage of these attributes, and to better position ourselves to grow with the EC in the years ahead.

Customs and Protocols

As the seat of the EC, Belgium in general, and Brussels in particular, are distinctly international. They are also expensive. Americans doing business there should be conscious of this, and sensitive to its impact upon locals. For example, when being treated in a restaurant be conscious of menu prices in order not to saddle the host with a big check. A safe procedure is to ask about national favorites or specialties, and to suggest that the host or hostess do the ordering.

Belgians tend to be formal, especially in business and business-related situations. When in doubt about what to wear, overdress. Unless you are well-acquainted with a business colleague, use last names and titles. Initial meetings are invariably to get acquainted. Trust between business associates in Belgium is important, and often takes many meetings to develop. Forceful, "U.S.-style" pressure is inappropriate, and usually proves counterproductive.

American human resource professionals may find certain hiring practices in Belgium to be unusual, perhaps even bizarre. Managers at our Robert Half offices in Brussels report the rather frequent use of psychometric tests and graphology (handwriting analysis) in the recruiting and evaluation of candidates. Some Belgian clients will not consider hiring a candidate without the graphologist's report on what his or her handwriting indicates about that job seeker's character.

As in most countries, making an effort in Belgium to learn even a few phrases in the local French or Dutch—greetings, menu items, common expressions—will be interpreted as a demonstration of goodwill, even if they result in the occasional humorous mistake.

Familiarizing yourself with local tastes is important, too, and may prevent faux pas. For example, ordering "scotch" in a Belgian bar will usually get you a glass of the local brand of beer.

DENMARK

General Business Overview

The entrepreneurial spirit reigns supreme in Denmark. The Danes are business-like people, and the country is much more than the fairy tale kingdom with which many foreigners become acquainted as children. A high percentage of Danes, who begin their careers with large corporations, often strike out on their own when they have amassed the knowledge, experience and capital to do so. They then build these ventures into successful companies.

Whatever Denmark's particular formula is, it works. Denmark has the highest per capita GDP in the EC.

The labor force in Denmark splits 54 percent to 46 percent in favor of males. More than one-third of the working population is employed in service businesses, and about one-fifth in manufacturing.

More than 2,000 foreign companies are located in Denmark. While European-based firms predominate, American and Japanese corporations also have strong representation, including IBM, Motorola, Milliken Textiles, Exxon, Hitachi and Matsushita.

Like other EC countries, Denmark prides itself on a workforce that is multilingual, highly educated, flexible and mobile.

The international airport at Copenhagen provides efficient passenger and cargo connections to and from the rest of the world, while Copenhagen's seaport facility provides key access to the Baltic region (so much so that Sony Corporation has installed a high-tech distribution center there for servicing markets in Denmark and the rest of Scandinavia).

In terms of providing an investment climate for international firms, Denmark boasts one of the most favorable corporate tax structures in the industrialized world. According to the Investment Office of the Royal Danish Consulate, corporate income taxes in Denmark are among the lowest in the world, expressed as a percentage of total taxes (4.5 percent vs. 8.1 percent in the United States and 22.9 percent in Japan), or as a percentage of gross domestic product (2.3 percent vs. 2.4 percent and 6.9 percent respectively).

As for recruiting employees for new operations in Denmark, the Danish Employment Department operates some 150 local job centers, utilizing computer data bases to match candidates with employer job specifications. The service is free-of-charge. Various business development units in local communities also assist foreign companies in locating employees, again without cost to the employer.

The most prevalent methods of locating and recruiting employees, especially skilled workers and managers, however, is via direct advertising and informal networking. Established companies also keep updated waiting lists to help fill vacancies, especially for those in blue-collar categories.

Denmark is actively involved with positioning itself as a major player on the ever-expanding free market gameboard of Europe. According to Uffe Ellemann-Jensen, Danish foreign minister, and a former editor of one of the country's leading business papers:

> Denmark is a staunch NATO ally, an active EC member state, but also a Scandinavian country and a neighbor to the Baltic countries of Eastern Europe. You can hardly find another country more involved, more respected by all sides or better located to service all these markets. . . . Any realistic assessment will demonstrate that Denmark is a competitive and advanced industrial society, and a favorable location with many advantages. . . . [particularly with] knowledge-intensive companies where quality, skills and performance are essential.

Customs and Protocols

Punctuality is important—in business and social settings. This does not necessarily mean formality, however. For example, if you are invited to dinner at a colleague's home, casual clothes (even neat, clean jeans) most likely will be acceptable, but ask first just to be safe. On the other hand, withhold comments on other guests' clothing. In many countries in Europe, personal comments about clothes, hair styles and jewelry are not considered to be in good taste.

Another attitude Danes share with most of Europe involves eating. If food is on your plate, there is an assumption that it will be eaten. If you are sure you do not—or will not—like something, take small portions, or insist politely, that you are already full.

Many U.S. citizens consider themselves burdened by excessive taxation, but don't complain about that to a Dane. Denmark, along with other Scandinavian countries, is among the world's highest taxed. In return, of course, its citizens receive a number of social welfare programs that are not available in the United States. The Danish personal income tax structure is a popular topic of conversation, and there are as many opposed to the system as there are those who enthusiastically support its benefits, which include full health care and a comfortable retirement.

Denmark, like many other European countries (and certainly Japan) enjoys certain aspects of U.S. culture that have found their way there. Leading the list is American jazz, which has enjoyed immense popularity throughout Europe but especially in Denmark and France. A number of U.S. jazz musicians have moved to Copenhagen and other European capitals over the past half-century, and there are statues in many European cities and towns saluting the greats among their midst. Nightclubs featuring this form of music abound throughout Europe. Any U.S. national hired to work in Denmark, as well as in these other European nations, would benefit from learning something about jazz which is an indigenous U.S. art form.

FRANCE

General Business Overview

The outsider's perception of France as chauvinistic is perhaps the most prevalent stereotype affixed to any nation in Europe. While the fairness of the label can certainly be debated, suffice it to say the French will come at business discussions from a decidedly Gallic perspective. If at least one member of your team does not have an excellent command of French, including all the appropriate business terminology, you will be at a very real disadvantage.

On the other hand, France is also deeply involved in the ecumenical attitudes of the New Europe. The Council of Europe is headquartered in Strasbourg. Established in 1949 to foster greater cooperation among the nations of Europe, the Council's aims are to work for the greater unity of European nations, and to improve living conditions, uphold the principles of parliamentary democracy, and advance the causes of human rights. Twenty-three nations belong, including the 12 member states of the EC and the six member states of EFTA, plus Cyprus, Liechtenstein, Malta, San Marino and Turkey.

While the American perspective focuses upon how U.S. companies can crack and staff the European marketplace, we should not lose sight of the fact that European businesses, some of them among the largest in the world, are also on the prowl for acquisitions in other countries—the United States in particular. The French have been particularly aggressive during recent years, buying controlling interests in U.S. vehicle manufacturers and drug companies, among others. The French objective appears to be the same as that of many U.S. companies—i.e., penetration of specific markets in the post-1992 EC. In this case, however, the shoe is securely on the foot of a European master.

This is not to say that the French are not actively seeking foreign investment in their own country. The French government's industrial development agency, Délégation l'Aménagement du Territoire et de l'Action Régionale (DATAR), in a publication aimed directly at North American companies, declared:

> Increased emphasis made by the government to encourage foreign investment has resulted in major changes, including significant new tax advantages for the establishment of regional headquarters in France, and particularly in Paris. In addition to the benefits that France offers in the [EC]—a centrally located country with excellent transportation, the availability of highly qualified professional help and a well-known quality of life—these new developments make France the best choice for a European headquarters.

Anyone even peripherally familiar with Europe knows that the French can make a strong case for locating a business in their country. Paris has two modern, efficient airports with nonstop service to more than a dozen North American cities via international carriers of France, the United States and Canada. While Paris itself is off the coast, the port at Le Havre is nearby, and the port of Marseilles is connected via highway and modern rail lines, including the high-speed TGV (Train a Grande Vitesse) which travels at speeds approaching 170 miles per hour.

In the larger cities of France, a wide array of support services—legal, financial, accounting, administrative and personnel—are available, staffed with a growing number of locals who are bilingual. (Today, in an acceptance of world business realities, three-quarters of the school children in France are studying English as a second language). There are also incentives for those companies who train locals in new career disciplines.

Training incentives are not the only ones offered to prospective employers. For example, cash grants of up to 25 percent are available via DATAR to finance a physical plant if at least 20 new jobs are created. There are also incentives for R&D programs, as well as tax exemptions and tax credits for various facilities or programs that are deemed helpful to the local economy.

Recruitment in France is conducted in complete freedom, provided that "legal requirements and fair practice are observed." A specific right of priority to employment is granted people in certain categories, i.e., women returning from maternity leave, disabled people, those returning from military service, workers unemployed because of redundancy in their previous positions and young people.

The principal advertising outlets are the country's three main daily newspapers, *Le Monde, L'Express* and *Le Figaro*.

The National Employment Agency can provide candidates from its registry of unemployed personnel, by job category. The National Management and Professional Staff Employment Agency maintains a registry of personnel in various management categories.

Large American national and international recruitment firms are active in Paris and are ready resources to help fill key positions.

Customs and Protocols

There is, of course, that air of refinement in France, particularly in the large cities. Dress tends to be more formal than for similar social situations in the United States. Personal conversation about family, or style of clothing is not appropriate. People are also likely to be judged by how they comport themselves, i.e., negative impressions result from loud voices, demonstrative gestures and slouches.

At a business lunch or dinner, foreign guests are expected to sample the local wine, especially in such renowned wine regions as Burgundy, Bordeaux and Rhone. While some French citizens may drink wine as a substitute for water, in France—as in many of the wine-favoring regions of Europe—to overindulge is in bad taste, and creates a strong negative impression.

As with the other Romance regions of Europe, many small and provincial businesses shut down between noon and 2 P.M., so the business day must be planned accordingly. Large and international companies, however, are beginning to forego this custom. Also, August finds many French businesses closed for vacation.

GERMANY

General Business Overview

Many of the stereotypes applied to Germany over the years, particularly those evolving as a result of World War II, do not accurately position the German business person of today. To consider Germans as cold and calculating is to do a great disservice to what this country—devastated by two world wars—has accomplished since the mid-'40s.

Politically partitioned for more than 40 years, West Germany nonetheless managed to forge one of the strongest economies on earth, and was therefore one of the few countries in a position to absorb, as it did in 1990, a region as economically depressed as its eastern sister. To achieve what they have, Germans have had to be creative, innovative, willing to take risks and possess the requisite expertise to make those risks work for them.

While Germany does not have the EC's richest economy (based on GDP), it has managed to achieve its per capita riches with a much larger population base than the smaller leaders of the EC financial register. It is considered by many the country most likely to emerge as the leader of the continental business community.

Given the high regard in which German business is held, it is not surprising that the country appears extremely confident of its abilities to perform with the best in any free-market economy of international proportions. Restraint of competition is prohibited by law in Germany, although the government will allow cooperative arrangements for small or mid-sized firms if it deems such arrangements likely to foster competition with larger companies. The government also offers incentives in the form of tax concessions to smaller firms to overcome "unfair disadvantages" in trying to compete with large corporations.

The Federal Office of Foreign Trade Information declares that recent German business history has been built upon a free-market economy that encourages competition from many sources:

> [I]t is seen as particularly important for competition that markets should be open to outside suppliers. Every government in the history of the Federal Republic of Germany has pursued an open-door trade policy in the realization that the international division of labor is one of the keys to world affluence.

A mainstay of German business is its highly skilled labor force. One of the most effective elements in achieving this highly developed human resource is vocational training. As a result of the Vocational Training Act passed in 1969, German businesses may participate in a dual system of training, which brings young trainees into their plants and offices for on-the-job instruction three-and-a-half to four days a week, coupled with vocational schooling one to one-and-a-half days. This system, of course, provides participating companies with an excellent source of well-trained employees, who have spent a good deal of their time learning how the company conducts its business.

Customs and Protocols

While "cold" is not an appropriate description of the citizens of Germany, "deliberate" might be. It will generally take Germans a little longer to respond to your efforts to become better acquainted, but that is a part of the national character.

They will respond with similar slowness to business proposals, feeling that quality is more important than speed or quantity. If challenged on this, Germans are likely to point to their successes in business and their reputation for quality. The atmosphere in a business meeting is apt to reflect this sense of seriousness, and attempts at levity can fall flat.

Also, local contacts are important. An introduction will go a long way toward gaining you access to a client or other prospective business associate.

Incidentally, in Germany as in other areas of Europe, a letter addressed to a specific individual is likely to remain unopened if that person is away. If you need a quick response, address your letter to the department you seek to query.

GREECE

General Business Overview

Greece has one of the lowest per capita GDP in the EC, but many international businesses are impressed with the country's low labor costs and attractive government incentives for locating a business there.

The other principal attraction of Greece is its location at the commercial crossroads between Western Europe and its democratizing Eastern

Bloc cousins, as well as its geographic access to the Middle East and North Africa.

A country of 10 million, 40 percent of Greece's population lives and works around the capital of Athens and the country's principal port city of Piraiévs. The result is a concentrated labor pool, and a concentrated market population. The second principal business center is Thessaloniki in the northern part of the country.

Greece ascended to full membership in the EC in 1981, after an associate membership dating back to 1962. While seeking to exploit the advantages of access to markets offered by full membership in the EC, the Greeks have also instituted local programs designed to make the country more attractive to foreign investment, including tax incentives, grants, subsidies, reduced duties, and repatriation of foreign capital and profits.

The types of businesses that qualify include everything from energy to manufacturing, high-tech to agriculture, tourism to shipbuilding. Investment categories include construction of new facilities, rehab of existing facilities, purchase of equipment, R&D and relocation expenses, among others. Grants ranging from 10 percent to 100 percent of an investment also have a geographic component, which skews toward those regions where business development is most needed.

While their membership in the EC is extremely important to the Greeks, they are likely to bring their national predilections into the international arena, the most emphatic of which is a great sense of national pride.

Customs and Protocols

In many respects, Greece is as informal as other European countries are formal. In most cases, first names will be appropriate, and personal topics of conversation are not only acceptable, but probably will be initiated by a Greek host or hostess.

This informality extends to many aspects of Greek life, business and social. Danish punctuality would result in hypertension in Greece. If you are on time for a business meeting (not to mention early), you may be the only one there. And if you are on time for a dinner engagement, you *will* be the only one there.

Greeks tend to be demonstrative and spontaneous. Nightlife is an integral part of the social fabric, and many Greeks will insist foreign guests keep sampling the local wine or liqueur; tomorrow's business appointments are tomorrow's concerns. Also, plan to eat hefty meals; it is a sign of respect for the host or hostess.

On the other hand, in day-to-day business dealings, the Greeks tend to place an emphasis on trust, i.e., the who-you-know syndrome predominates. There is a wariness, if not downright suspicion, of authority. Consequently, they will want to get to know you better if there is to be a solid, ongoing business relationship. This also means lengthy sessions to work out business details; the Greeks will not be rushed into a decision, nor be pressured to meet predetermined deadlines.

IRELAND

General Business Overview

The image many Americans have of Ireland is a land of lush green meadows and small farmers taking produce by horse-drawn wagons to village markets. The Irish Industrial Development Authority (IDA), however, has another story to tell.

Positioning Ireland as the "skills center of Europe for the electronics industry," IDA points to U.S. Department of Commerce figures that show U.S. manufacturing investment in Ireland is realizing a 23 percent return—almost four times the EC average.

While other EC member states are experiencing declining populations, with a parallel decline in the number of high school and college graduates, Ireland is the exception. The IDA points out:

> Almost one-third of the Irish population is in full-time education. Continuous and enlightened State investment is producing more well-educated, English-speaking and computer-literate students than can be absorbed.... 50 percent of the Irish population is under 28 years of age; half of all high school graduates enter third-level education; and 55 percent of college students are pursuing business, technological and computer disciplines. The availability of these skilled people is making Ireland the software center of Europe.

The message is proving to be an effective one. Major U.S. corporations have set up operations in Ireland, including Apple, IBM, Microsoft, GE, and Digital Equipment, to name just a few. Not to be left out, Japanese technological giants, such as Fujitsu and Nippon Electric Company, are also represented there.

Our eight Robert Half International offices in the United Kingdom have found, over the years, that the Irish talent pool provides highly qualified and imminently salable candidates for companies in the United Kingdom, the rest of Europe, and even in the United States where immigration quotas from Ireland were increased in the late 1980s.

A small island economy makes Ireland more dependent upon import-export trade than other countries of Western Europe (more than twice as dependent as the United Kingdom as a percentage of GDP—and more than four times U.S. levels). To help counter this situation, Ireland offers some attractive incentives for foreign companies considering establishing operations there.

For example, tax incentives guarantee no more than a 10 percent tax on corporate profits through the year 2010. There are capital grants toward the cost of physical plants (based on the potential for employment created), grants of up to 50 percent of costs to establish R&D programs, and grants of up to 100 percent for worker training. Attractive appreciation allowances include a 50 percent write-off on certain capital expenditures during the first year of operation.

Infrastructure improvements in communications and internal transportation, as well as three international airports—at Dublin, Shannon and Cork—make for efficient access to suppliers and markets, both intra-country and with the rest of the EC.

While the business language of Ireland is English, the Irish are extremely proud of their heritage and of their native Gaelic tongue. They may lapse into Gaelic among themselves, including during business discussions, as other nationals sometimes do with their native tongues.

A word of caution: The sensitivity to the Northern Ireland situation is very real, and should never be discussed without an acute awareness of its significance. The best approach is to avoid the topic all together.

Customs and Protocols

Protocol is not sacrosanct in Ireland. Faux pas is less likely here. Unfriendliness, or a lack of compassion, are more apt to cast a foreigner in a negative light.

Pubs provide a focus for much of Ireland's social life. If you cannot, or do not wish to drink, beg off for reasons of health, or sip very slowly. Incidentally, there are time-honored protocols for behavior in Irish pubs. For example, unescorted ladies repair to the lounge, not the bar. Also, women are expected to order half-pints of ale or stout, while a man ordering less than a full pint will attract stares, perhaps even a comment on occasion.

The Irish tend not to keep to tight schedules; experience will dictate a safe multiplier to determine how much leeway you can allow for a business appointment, or when invited to a social function.

ITALY

General Business Overview

Cultural attractions, particularly art and architecture, have brought visitors to Italy for centuries. In fact, UNESCO estimates that about one-half of the world's art and architectural wealth resides in Italy. This Italian flair for design has stood the country in good stead in such areas as fashion, industrial design and automobile manufacturing. But today, Italy is expanding or actively reinforcing its traditional business affiliations with emphasis on such diverse areas as aircraft manufacturing, energy production and financial services.

To understand something of where Italy is heading involves a look at where it has been, and an understanding of its geographic divisions.

Italy has two distinct personalities, with Rome as the dividing point. The north is industrial, and contains most of the important centers of business; the south is predominantly agrarian, and is home to smaller businesses. While Italians are extremely conscious of their own internal geographic factionalism, they are nationalistic where outsiders are concerned.

The positive performance of the Italian economy during the 1980s stimulated dramatic increases in direct foreign investment. By the end of the decade, there was more than 10 times the dollar amount at the beginning of the decade, with a healthy 50–50 split between the manufacturing and service sectors of the economy.

U.S. companies control about a third of the foreign-owned companies in Italy, while Germany, France, Switzerland and the United Kingdom account for more than 10 percent each. Of the U.S. companies, Exxon, IBM and Mobil are the big three, while Kraft, Dow, and 3M also have significant operations. AT&T and Honeywell also have a presence in Italy, which along with IBM, makes the United States the dominant foreign player in the Italian information technology field.

While the number of locals employed by such companies has leveled off—even decreased in some sectors—the Italian government attributes this to increases in productivity as employees become more highly trained, and more familiar with the specific operations of their new employers.

As with the other countries of the EC, Italy offers incentives to foreign companies considering the location of businesses there. Many of the incentives are geographic in nature, focusing on the lesser-developed areas of North Central and Southern Italy. Business categories are also a determinant, with the electronics, telecommunications, computer and chemical sectors among those eligible. Subsidized financing and non-refundable loans of up to 50 percent of certain specified expenses are available for firms that meet the criteria. Paramount among them are creating facilities for new technologies, research and development operations, distribution operations, facilities that aid in pollution prevention, and those that purchase local raw or semi-finished materials.

A subject for concern in Italy involves the potential negative impact of the country's membership in the EC upon economic redevelopment in the Mezzogiorno Region in the South. EC pressure to reduce large national deficits may substantially reduce the billions of dollars in government funds that have been funneled into the region during the last decade. Pressure from poorer countries, or from the poorer regions of richer countries, however, will likely result in a substantial increase in funds available to these areas via the EC's European Regional Development Fund.

Another major shift involves business ownership. There is a strong and growing movement toward the privatization of Italy's giant government-owned holding corporations, with a parallel and substantial opposition to the movement. The three largest government-owned companies, EFIM, ENI and IRI, include such subsidiaries as Alitalia, the national airline; Agusta and Aeritalia, aircraft manufacturers; RAI, the national TV network; AGIP and SNAM, energy corporations; and three large commercial banks.

"Supporters of less state involvement underline two main reasons for wanting the boundaries of Italy's wide public sector to be rolled back," it was pointed out in a special advertising section to the *Wall Street Journal*. "First, state ownership is often equated with low efficiency. Second, Italy's public sector accounts would obtain a much-needed boost from the sale of assets."

The change-over will not be easy. In a country where five political parties share government control, lobbyists and pressure groups hold a good deal of power, much of which derives from their ability to provide jobs to party loyalists. A loss of control of large segments of the commercial sector will mean a loss of these political patronage jobs.

Customs and Protocols

"We are convinced that improvement of the quality of life in an advanced society is achieved by cultural development," wrote Gianni Zandano, president of Turin's Instituto Bancario San Paolo, in the *Wall Street Journal*. Mr. Zandano's bank has been supporting social and cultural programs since its founding in 1563.

The Italians have been synonymous with culture since the days of the Roman Empire, with a significant booster shot during the Renaissance. This flair extends to everyday life as well. Italians are very fashion conscious, for example. Clothing styles here will lead by months, or even years, the introduction of the same fashions in the United States. Even jeans are apt to be cleaned and pressed, and considered part of a larger fashion statement.

A national pastime is to be seen during the popular two-hour evening walk—*la passeggiata*. Many first and second generation Italian-Americans continue this custom in the ethnic neighborhoods of larger U.S. cities, where neighbors know all their neighbors via the evening stroll. It is a time when Italians network, mostly in a social context but also for business discussions, although never in a formal manner.

Eating and drinking are important rituals in Italy. Sample the wine, but don't overindulge; drunkenness is a sign of weakness (there is no minimum drinking age in Italy).

While you may politely decline the initial offer of seconds during a meal, the host or hostess will probably insist, and you will be expected to fill your plate again.

Italians believe that people are at their worst during the time when digestion is taking place, a time when moods are somber and humor is scarce. That's one of the reasons they favor after-dinner drinks they call *amari*, also known as digestives. There are more than 300 varieties of amari. They're made of herbs and roots, are often bitter in taste, and are alcoholic (40 to 90 proof).

This Italian belief about the troubling effects of digestion could help explain why the business lunch and dinner have never been institutionalized in Italy the way they have been in other countries. Italians prefer to digest their food in friendlier surroundings.

Foreign business people have to adapt to the midday closure of businesses and, as with France, August is a slow time for business in Italy, with many companies closing for the entire month.

LUXEMBOURG

General Business Overview

"Because of its historical and geographic position between much larger neighbors—who invaded and occupied it often—Luxembourg has developed a keen sense of national identity and self-preservation that allows it to approach closer European union without fearing an erosion of national character," says the EC magazine, called *Europe*.

Mightier than its tiny size might indicate, Luxembourg has one of the highest GDP's in the EC. Although it is only 1,000 square miles in total area, it benefits from its central location between Belgium, France and Germany. Its population of 365,000 is largely multilingual—French, German, and the local dialect called Luxembourgish are spoken by most of the population.

Luxembourg City, the capital, is one of the top three cities in the EC, with the European Parliament, Court of Justice, European Investment Bank and Court of Auditors headquartered there.

Luxembourg is also one of the financial centers of the continent, with more than 180 banks, and some 50 insurance companies. That amounts to one of the highest concentrations of banks per square mile, and per inhabitant, of any place in the world. The country's liberal banking laws have established it as a tax haven, which may suffer somewhat under new EC-wide banking regulations. Ever conscious of any potential for erosion in their prime business base, however, Luxembourgers are diversifying into other businesses.

With a manufacturing base once largely dependent upon the steel industry, Luxembourg has diversified its heavy industry to include plastics, rubber products, mechanical and electric equipment, chemicals and textiles. The country is also after high-tech business, and has been actively pursuing the world's major computer firms.

Dependent upon international trade to both feed its industries with raw and semi-finished materials and to buy the products it makes, Luxembourg's future potential appears closely tied to the EC.

The country's favorable tax structure extends to foreign investors, as well, and includes incentives for companies that contribute to the expansion and/or structural improvement of the economy.

Other attractive non-tax incentives include interest rate rebates for fixed assets and equipment, training or retraining for employees, studies and research work related to new product development, and investments that protect the environment.

The resident workforce of 150,000 is supplemented by French, German and Belgian workers who commute to Luxembourg each day. This workforce is highly skilled, especially in the country's traditional businesses. It is also highly motivated, boasting the lowest absentee rate of EC member states.

Customs and Protocols

Despite centuries of invading armies, and current waves of French, German and Belgian workers, Luxembourgers are sensitive about their national identity, and are quick to correct foreigners who mistake them for any nationality other than their own.

The local language, Luxembourgish (called Letzeburgesch by the natives), is a German dialect, so entwined with local phrases and idioms that even the Germans have trouble understanding it. It has become a written language only within the last decade. English has recently become favored, especially in commercial and financial sectors.

Since there are no major universities in Luxembourg, professionals journey outside the country to continue their education.

In terms of customs and traditions, Luxembourgers are most like their Belgian neighbors, i.e., they tend to be formal rather than casual, use last names and titles where appropriate, and consider first meetings primarily as a session to get acquainted. Trust between business associates is always a key factor.

THE NETHERLANDS

General Business Overview

Historically a trading nation, the Netherlands has developed its long-standing affinity for international commerce into an effective, modern-day business acumen. Giant international corporations such as Shell Oil and N.V. Philips anchor a solid Dutch business sector. Long considered to be frugal, as well as extremely tough negotiators, the Dutch are to be taken seriously in any business transaction.

Perhaps the most important source of the Netherlands' success in international business over the years has been the country's emphasis on education. The Ministry of Education and Science has the highest budget of any government ministry, with about 17 percent of the national budget spent each year on education. The population also boasts the highest mastery of foreign languages in Europe, which is quite an accomplishment when you consider that Belgium, Luxembourg and Switzerland have more than one official national language.

Transportation is the backbone of Dutch business. More than a quarter of seaborne EC traffic passes through ports in the Netherlands, particularly Rotterdam, the largest and busiest port in the world. Rotterdam, which already handles almost 300 million metric tons of cargo each year, has earmarked a half-billion dollars for port improvements by the end of 1992 in order to handle anticipated increases in traffic.

Schiphol, the international airport near Amsterdam, is one of the most active in Europe—fifth in terms of passenger traffic, fourth in freight. It has also been consistently rated the best in Europe by the *Business Traveller* reader survey. KLM, the national airline, is a truly globe-spanning carrier with wide-ranging passenger and cargo services. Airport authorities project a doubling of passenger traffic by the year 2000, and dramatic increases in freight tonnage, particularly after 1992. Almost $2 billion in expansion and improvement of services and infrastructure are planned by the turn of the century.

With a modern network of roads, and an extensive waterways system of rivers, estuaries and canals, intra-country transportation is efficient and quick. The far-reaching road and river networks also link the Netherlands to its neighbors in the EC.

The Netherlands takes particular pride in the performance of foreign investors who choose to locate operations there. At the close of the 1980s, Prime Minister Ruud Lubbers gave this assessment:

> An increasingly important contributor to our ever-growing exports is the output manufactured or assembled by many of the 1,500 American companies with Dutch operations.... In the Netherlands, the average rate of return made by U.S. corporations in the 1984–1988 period was 26.14 percent, some 25 percent higher than the EC average.

More than a third of U.S. companies that have located in the Netherlands since 1980 are in the modern, high-technology sectors of biotechnology, medical and diagnostic systems, information technology and specialty chemicals.

Aside from workforce and infrastructure attractions of locating a business in the Netherlands, financial incentives include one of the largest venture capital pools in Europe. There are also tax incentives for companies locating particular types of businesses in the country, and in designated locations.

Other incentives include wage subsidies for training designed to improve the working environment, and to stimulate employment in job skills that are difficult to fill.

The Netherlands' Foreign Investment Agency offices in New York, the San Francisco Bay Area, and Los Angeles will provide endorsements from the many U.S. companies that have been attracted by the favorable business environment of the Netherlands.

Customs and Protocols

The present-day Dutch, like their forebears, travel a great deal. Make business appointments well in advance and reconfirm them. Planning, in fact, is important to most aspects of Dutch business conduct. The Dutch like to know what is coming; they don't react well to surprises—even last-minute luncheon invitations.

This is not to say the Dutch are not receptive to entertainment; they pride themselves on being masters of the art. Attention to detail is always important. In fact, in retail shops, a sales person will wait on one customer at a time, from entrance to exit.

In restaurants, sample the food, the wine and the world-famous Dutch beer. It will be expected, and you are not likely to be disappointed.

PORTUGAL

General Business Overview

Portugal ranks among the poorest of the EC member states. The population is still struggling to rebuild an infrastructure allowed to decay during an autocratic regime that was removed in the mid-1970s.

Despite the democratization that has occurred, a small percentage of the population still controls a disproportionate amount of the wealth.

Much of the country's manufacturing base and infrastructure need rehabilitating or complete rebuilding. Transportation facilities and roads still require a great deal of work.

The country is making slow, but steady economic progress, however, with its unemployment rate on the decline, and an economic growth rate higher than the average for EC member states.

TAP, the national airline, connects the capital city of Lisbon with the rest of Europe and North America. And sea traffic has been an important part of the country's commerce since the great Portuguese navigators of the Age of Exploration crossed the uncharted Atlantic, and helped open the Western Hemisphere 500 years ago.

While the manufacturing sector of the economy is growing as a proportion of overall GDP, agriculture is still the principal business in spite of generally poor topographical and climatic conditions. Agricultural products dominate the country's exports. Portugal ranks first in the EC with the highest specialization rate in the sector of textiles, footwear and clothing. Other principal exports include cork, paper and additional forestry products.

Since Portugal's entry into the EC, foreign investors have begun to "discover" the country, and the attraction of its inexpensive labor pool. Incentives are available to investors, as well as opportunities that may develop as a result of the EC's European Regional Development Fund, which will be putting money into the country's less-developed regions. According to the publication, *Panorama of EC Industry:*

> In response to the gradual liberalization of the finance sector, inward investment . . . increased 24 times. Thus, the structure of total inward investment to Portugal shows much the same pattern as in other EC countries, with a heavy concentration on services. Due to further privatization, foreign investment (including Spanish) in the financial sector is likely to intensify . . . . with the lowest labor costs in Europe and a growing liberalization of the equity market, industrial investment is also likely to increase sharply in the run-up to 1992.

There will be business opportunities, especially for companies in high-tech industries, which are seriously lacking in Portugal. Service industries are also on the rise, employing more than 40 percent of the workforce, and now accounting for more than half of the GDP.

Tourism is a principal source of capital inflow; Portugal is third among EC member states (behind Spain and Greece) in terms of capital generated by tourism as a percentage of balance of payments.

And, it is important for any foreign company to remember that entry into Portugal will provide entry into the rest of the EC.

A common misconception is that Portugal is virtually indistinguishable from its Spanish neighbor on the Iberian Peninsula. To the uninitiated, the languages may sound similar, but they are really quite different. Portugal has long-standing relationships with other countries that are stronger than its links to Spain. The United Kingdom in particular has been a steady market for the country's exports.

Customs and Protocols

The Portuguese love their food and wine. They are world famous for their port and rose wines, and for their local dishes, especially seafoods.

Business schedules tend to be relaxed, but protocols are observed and titles honored. Dress tends to be formal, and reactions reserved.

Unlike most of the other EC member states, English is not widely spoken in Portugal, so expect to work through an interpreter for both oral and written communications.

SPAIN

General Business Overview

"We had been excluded from Europe for 200 years and there was a national yearning to join Europe and be part of the world again," Pedro Solbes Mira, Spain's secretary of state for the EC, wrote in *Time* magazine. "Much of our existence has been shaped by isolationism and protectionism. That had to change. Our only possibility to be a global player was through Europe."

Spain has suffered much turmoil over the past 50 years. The Civil War, which began in the 1930s, resulted in the dictatorship of Generalissimo Francisco Franco, which forestalled the democratization of Spain until the late 1970s. Years of political division left deep-seated factionalism. The attitudes and cultural differences between Catalonia, Andalusia and the Basque region, for example, are as strong as the differences between many foreign countries. An acute consciousness of these regional differences is critical to doing business in Spain, and that of course, involves doing homework.

A country proud of its national heritage, Spain is often perceived as arrogant. Like most stereotypes, however, this perception often does not stand the test of a specific business relationship.

Playing catch-up with the other nations of Western Europe has not been easy for Spain. Periods of positive economic growth have been sandwiched between longer periods of negative movement, while the country has battled longer-term problems, such as inflation and unemployment.

There are encouraging signs, however. The country's negative balance of payments situation began to improve in the mid-1980s, while the government and private sectors grew optimistic about increasing interest on the part of international partners in utilizing Spain's pool of low-cost labor.

Membership in the EC on January 1, 1986, was seen as the most positive development toward Spain's long-term pursuit of economic parity with its European neighbors. The association began to bear fruit immediately. From 1986 through 1989, the Spanish economy was one of the fastest-growing in the EC and one of the fastest growing in Europe. International businesses had begun to arrive, and their interest in the country was growing. In the early 1990s, four Japanese banks and the Sony Corporation had set up operations there.

Spain has also become the principal beneficiary of the economic assistance meted out by the EC's European Regional Development Fund, created to assist underdeveloped regions, particularly in the poorer member states of the Community. Almost a third of the fund's allocations have gone to Spain. For example, the Austrias region has received millions of dollars for a new industrial park, a bridge, a series of new roads and other improvements.

The fall of the Franco regime ushered in a new sense of freedom, followed by a free and often combative press. The country's young are better educated, more women are entering the workplace and the birth rate has been falling.

Although the government declares no preferential incentives for foreign investors in excess of those received by domestic business, those fiscal incentives that are granted can be a real benefit to a company locating a facility in Spain. This, when coupled with the low labor costs and the access to EC markets that Spain provides, makes for an attractive combination.

An Overview of Each of the EC Member States

Incentives that are granted take the form of tax deductions, subsidies, and low-cost loans, most linked to the number of jobs created by a new enterprise. There are also geographic sectors that qualify for special consideration. These are called Economic Promotion Zones, areas that are considered to "have suffered severely the effects of industrial readjustment."

Incentives are also offered for certain industries that have provided traditional employment (such as tourism, fishing and agriculture), or industries that the country seeks to attract (such as high-tech business, textiles, automobiles and industrial support services).

Various agencies and commissions also offer financial support for research and development, as well as technologies that decrease the country's dependence upon imports (and that increase its exports).

The transportation systems throughout Spain, while not as sophisticated as some of its wealthier neighbors, are generally good. Iberia, the national airline, has an excellent domestic route system, as well as connections to major cities throughout Europe, and transatlantic routes to North America. Roads connecting principal cities are adequate, but tend to back up, since auto travel is the favored form of domestic travel. Rail service is also adequate, but sometimes slow.

The Ministry of Public Works has made the improvement of roads a major priority during the next decade. "We simply could not be part of Europe without a comparable network," Javier Saenz Cosculluela, former minister of public works, said. "We are tripling the amount of Spanish auto routes by the end of 1991 ... and are planning to add another 4,000 kilometers between 1992 and 2000." He said renovation of 27 of the country's major seaports is another priority.

Customs and Protocols

While Spaniards tend to be demonstrative and sometimes openly emotional, they have a long tradition of deference to title and age, and it is important for foreigners to act accordingly.

Spain is trying to alter its national character somewhat. "A new Spanish character, one that contradicts all the past images, is just being defined," wrote Ernesto Ekaizer, director of *Cinco Dias*, a Spanish financial daily. "At the moment we are almost infantile in our enthusiasm and vitality and have trouble defining ourselves."

One tradition that will take some initial getting used to by U.S. executives is the Spanish custom of assuming both the father's and mother's last names. On the other hand, while the double name is used in written communication, it is not used verbally. (Incidentally, unless your written Spanish is impeccable, correspond in English rather than risk a letter that is less than appropriately formal.)

Conversations, even business discussions, tend to be open forums, with interruptions expected and not considered rude.

As in Greece, personal contacts will go a long way toward arranging a business introduction.

UNITED KINGDOM

General Business Overview

The United States has closer ties to the United Kingdom than to any other EC nation. They are bound by common heritage, language and, most recently, common approaches to the shifting international political scene.

From a business perspective, the two countries have been close trading partners. Some 3,000 U.S. companies have operations of varying size and scope in the United Kingdom, including all but a few of the *Fortune* 100. The reasons for locating in the United Kingdom go beyond the obvious bonds of heritage, culture and language, however.

"Pall Corporation considers Britain to be the perfect location for manufacturing in the EC," said Maurice G. Hardy, president of the Long Island-based manufacturer of filters, one of the largest such companies in the world. "No matter what kind of analysis we have run over the last 29 years, we've never been able to make a better case than Britain."

In 1977 the Invest in Britain Bureau (IBB) was created as part of the government's Department of Trade and Industry. IBB provides information on all important aspects of locating a business in the United Kingdom: advice on dealing with the various bureaucracies; how to locate essential services, and how to gain assistance with grants, loans and site selection.

The decision to create the IBB to offer such assistance has proved to be an effective one for the U.K. economy. During the first decade of IBB's existence, overseas direct investment in the United Kingdom has increased by more than 50 billion pounds (at the current exchange rate, approximately $100 billion). Of all U.S. direct investment in EC member states since 1950, more than a third has been in the United Kingdom. The Germans and Japanese are also major investors there.

One of the principal attractions for U.S. companies is the labor force. Surveys indicate that workers in the United Kingdom are very receptive to innovation, particularly when it involves new technologies. This enthusiasm to retrain and upgrade has translated into greater job-related efficiencies. The decade of the 1980s saw a productivity improvement of almost 60 percent, one of the most impressive in the industrialized world. And, the cost of labor is significantly less expensive than the world's other industrialized powers—40 percent below Germany's, 20 percent below Japan's, and 18 percent below the United States'.

There are, however, some marked differences between the way business is conducted in the United Kingdom and in the United States. British business has traditionally been extremely hierarchical, based on social positioning and family ties. While the business structure has been liberalized, and an entrepreneurial attitude has taken root and flourished, foreigners should be conscious of the significance of traditional connections. In the conduct of their business, the British tend to be very formal. Decorum, including punctuality, and a respect for appropriate formalities and protocols, is always considered important.

Financial incentives to locate a business in the United Kingdom include a maximum corporate tax rate of 35 percent (and the government is on record as wanting to reduce it even further). There are also allowances of up to 100 percent for R&D (during the year in which the expenditures occur), and up to 100 percent allowances for construction costs, particularly in designated Enterprise Zones.

Grants are available to those companies locating businesses in Assisted Areas, those areas of the United Kingdom that are most in need of industrial development; Northern Ireland heads the list with tax-free grants of up to 50 percent of project costs. Financial assistance is also available for the training of young people, the unemployed who wish to re-enter the work force, and the "longer term, but well-motived unemployed."

The potential of the British market is an attraction in itself. The population of more than 56 million spends almost 300 billion pounds per year on goods and services. From an industrial perspective, the United Kingdom is a major buyer of goods, including more integrated circuits than any other country in Europe.

Access to markets in the United Kingdom, and to other international markets from the United Kingdom, is enhanced by one of the most effective transportation systems in the world. British Airways ranks among the world's busiest international airlines, while there are state-of-the-industry airport facilities at Heathrow and Gatwick, two of the busiest airports in the world—with more than 7,000 international flights each week, and more than 5,000 domestic ones.

The ports at Southampton, London, Dover, Felixstowe, Harwich, Hull and Liverpool handle more than a half-billion tons of freight each year. Domestic rail and highway access is modern and efficient; no point in Britain is more than 75 miles from the sea.

Links to the continent will be greatly enhanced with the completion of the Channel Tunnel, scheduled for the summer of 1993.

Information on locating a business in the United Kingdom is available from IBB offices across North America.

Customs and Protocols

The staff members at our Robert Half International offices in the United Kingdom like to remind us that their homeland, and the United States, are often described as two countries divided by a common language.

The assumption that a U.S. national will fit into the British business world and its customs and protocols without skipping a beat is naive in the extreme. Even menu items are not a given; Yorkshire pudding, for example, is a puff pastry that Americans would not likely consider a pudding.

The long-held image of life in the United Kingdom as sedate and sophisticated, a land of private clubs and Rolls Royces, Shakesperian theatre and regal formalities has, over the past 30 years, expanded to include an alter ego of heavy-metal music, outrageous fads and outlandish fashions. Somewhere in between lies the real England.

Formality and a respect for protocol are still, and perhaps always will be, important in the United Kingdom. To jump your position in line is to risk a serious rebuke. A certain casualness, however, has become more apparent in recent years—in dress, carriage and even business conversation. The shift to first names, for example, comes much sooner in a relationship than it once did.

The midday break is foreign to the British, who will utilize lunches to conduct business. Younger managers have taken to the business breakfast as a means of extending the workday, while their older, more traditional counterparts, may offer an invitation to business dinners.

• • •

With a basic foundation now of how the EC was formed, how it operates and what, in general terms, can be expected in each of the member states, let's move on to "Staffing the Euro-Company."

SECTION II
STAFFING THE EURO-COMPANY

Four
Locating Candidates

For business people taking the pulse of the world economic body, the vital signs for Europe give every indication that it is there that business will be the healthiest during the last decade of the 20th Century. That prognosis takes into consideration the deep and prolonged recession in the United States that extended its effects to other nations of the world.

Business Week's first annual "International Hot Growth Company Survey" of the decade, taken in early 1990, found: "The brightest stars are in the European constellation . . . virtually no venture capital is going to Japan. The great Hong Kong market is floundering. But billions are pouring into Europe to help start-ups not only in technology but also in marketing, hotels and consumer goods."

That opinion was not limited to smaller companies.

"The advertising volume in Europe is so much greater," the chairman of Grey Advertising told the *New York Times*, "it is conceivable that whoever is running Grey a few years from now will be working in Europe."

A survey we conducted on the importance of overseas management experience produced the following: When asked whether experience in managing European operations had become a more important asset for future success in top management at major U.S. companies, 81.5 percent replied they thought it had. Thirteen percent did not feel that way, a small percentage did not venture an opinion.

That level of excitement about the continent's growth potential, and parallel opportunities for enhanced management training, will engender a similarly intense feeling of competition, not only among companies, but for a new breed of executive capable of succeeding in this hot environment.

Bigger companies are consolidating, *Business Week* found, and "the little guys could get steamrollered unless they find cozy niches. So they are sharpening strategies, rejuvenating management and merging."

The struggle to merely survive in this type of environment, let alone prosper, will not be successful with absentee management (witness the Grey prediction that even the highest level of management will be based in Europe by the mid-1990s).

The human resources trade publication, *HR Magazine*, estimated "that as many as five million new jobs throughout Europe ... will transform the continent into a unified major world economic power." The magazine declared that for U.S. companies to establish effective offices in Europe, there was "an urgent need for administrators who understand European politics, labor and tax law legislation, and personnel."

To staff an effective operation in Europe, a company must proceed with an effective plan. Transferring existing personnel resources to hastily established European offices, or recruiting without a carefully considered system of staffing, is likely to prove counter-productive.

For example, Medical Concepts, Inc., the California manufacturer of cameras for endoscopic equipment, saw its business in Europe, based upon what was functionally a U.S. marketing plan, mushroom only three years after the company had been founded. Europe was developing so rapidly that the company had to quickly contract with a distributor of similar equipment in the Netherlands in order to service its burgeoning list of customers.

When the company outgrew its Dutch partner, it was faced with the pressing need to put into place its own operation—its own people. Most of what it had done in the early stages was accomplished on-the-fly to meet unanticipated demand. Setting up its own operation, including critical staffing considerations, demanded careful, anticipatory planning.

U.S.-based Continental Bank, on the other hand, has been operating in Europe for 30 years. During that period it has had plenty of time to get ready for 1992, to the point where the official debut of the single market concept will have little impact.

"We have integrated into local markets and tied them back into our own business base in the states," explains William M. Goodyear, the bank's managing director based in London. "We have local professionals imbedded in key markets and are able to provide clients back in the United States with insights and access into information in banking they otherwise would not have from a U.S. bank."

Fundamental to that strategy is including locals and third-country nationals as key elements of an employee mix.

"The kind of people we look for have good language skills and are globalist in their business outlook," Goodyear explains. "I call them fluent and flexible. They are the kind of people who can move from assignment to assignment, and are extremely valuable."

Determining Human Resource Needs

Let's begin with the assumption that an agreed-upon business plan, detailing the operational, marketing and financial objectives for doing business in the European marketplace has been formulated. Such a plan will constitute one of the principal elements upon which to build an effective human resources program.

Any personnel management staff faced with this daunting challenge must necessarily begin by translating the business plan into a human resources plan; to achieve business objectives, staffing needs must be determined, and a parallel plan created to meet them.

Some of the critical questions to be addressed in determining human resources needs are:

At what level will a European operation be established?

- Will it begin with a tiny satellite operation and grow the business from there?
- Will it open with a full-blown subsidiary operation that takes on the competition with a concerted frontal attack?
- Or, will it buy into an existing operation?

What are the company's principal levels of interface with the European business sector?

- Who will be the suppliers? European? U.S.-based? A combination of both? Will there be third-country suppliers?
- Where are the markets? Are they in the U.S. company's European country of operation? Or, spaced throughout the EC? Back in the United States? Elsewhere?
- Where does the company interface with the in-country infrastructure?
- How much contact will be necessary with government authorities and agencies?
- What are the ongoing administrative needs, including legal and accounting?

In answering these questions, and others that are specific to a particular business, those charged with staffing EC operations must be continually sensitive to the environment within which their employees will operate. The rules and regulations governing employment within specific EC countries, as well as with those EC human resources directives that apply across the single-market community, must be researched and thoroughly understood, and a sensitivity to the nuances of doing business in the EC developed. Ideally, senior human resources executives will spend productive time with members of the appropriate governmental and private sectors during the process of formulating a sound hiring plan.

(As a source of such information, a list of trade and commerce associations for individual countries is provided in the Appendices at the back of the book.)

Determining Job Descriptions

A key element in any comprehensive European staffing program is the writing of carefully shaped—and realistic—job descriptions.

The creation of job descriptions is too often considered a routine, cursory task in U.S. companies. To view it that way when staffing operations in the EC is to court potential difficulties. These job descriptions should be as detailed as possible because a mistake in an overseas placement creates a far more difficult situation than does a domestic one.

In writing job descriptions, the European environment in which new employees will work looms large. While there might be a tendency to fall back upon U.S. experience in defining certain job categories, the need to examine all staffing descriptions within the context of Europe and the EC cannot be ignored.

For example, while it may be acceptable for a chief financial officer of a U.S. corporation not to be a certified public accountant, that qualification is virtually a given in the United Kingdom. On the other hand, while it is most unusual for a person in senior management in this country not to have a college degree—in many cases advanced degrees—hands-on experience is weighted more heavily in Europe.

Staffing Europe cannot be approached based wholly upon U.S. concepts. For instance, there may be pressure to consolidate job functions, particularly in smaller, start-up operations. But the feasibility of such consolidations succeeding in the culture and laws of any single EC nation cannot be forecast based upon the U.S. experience with such management decisions.

In this country, consolidating sales and marketing functions may make sense, but if you are manufacturing in Spain, Portugal or Greece—and selling in Germany, France or the United Kingdom utilizing a sales force made up of appropriate third-country nationals—you may find yourself having to deal with expanded marketing and sales functions, with resulting divergent chains of command.

Here again is a reason for paying particular attention to the writing of job descriptions. A problem faced by all personnel placement professionals (and a problem for personnel service companies such as our own) is filling positions whose job descriptions are inaccurate or, at best, ill-conceived. Some job descriptions demand so much of a candidate, are so unrealistic, that the employer ultimately ends up with someone who quickly becomes discouraged with the workload and begins looking elsewhere.

Another problem created by unrealistic job descriptions is in the salary structure for any given position. Some employers demand extensive education, experience and knowledge, yet offer a salary commensurate with candidates possessing far fewer qualifications. This is another invitation to rapid job turnover.

In line with this, it is important for everyone involved in the hiring process not to overstate the potentials of a job. Ironically, companies are as prone to this failing as are candidates. We assume that candidates sell themselves through their resumes, letters, references, and interviews—and that companies are sold by them. The truth is that when a company wants very much to fill a vacancy, especially when the candidate pool is shallow, there is the tendency to "sell" the best candidates on coming to work there, and thus ending the arduous hiring process.

Unrealistic promotion and salary expectations, however, soon lead an employee to disenchantment, and a search for another job. When such individuals have been sent overseas at considerable company expense, losing them through less-than-honest promises only compounds the cost. Short-term goals might have been met. Longer-term problems are the inevitable result.

It is only after the business objectives of a company have been accurately determined that the focus can shift to human resources needs. A lack of coordination between various elements of a company—administration, marketing, sales, accounting, legal—is sometimes gotten away with by companies that deal in small, domestic spheres. A similar lack of coordination in staffing overseas is an invitation to chaos and, potentially, overall failure.

Candidate Criteria

If a relatively accurate job description has been formulated, is that sufficient reason to go out and begin seeking candidates to fill the job?

In the case of overseas staffing, it isn't. Not only must the job description be accurate, a careful analysis of the priorities within it should be undertaken. Again, specificity is crucial. What's needed is to develop a job description, including subtle priorities, that are not based upon generalizations, but that take into consideration the unique demands of having to function in a European country, or any other foreign nation for that matter.

Every employer, no matter what the industry or profession—and no matter where the job is to be performed—looks for certain employee attributes. Initiative, creativity, a sense of teamwork, dedication, hard work and other such similar strengths are what every employer hopes to find when hiring someone for a key position. As far as staffing Europe is concerned, add language skills, sensitivity, diplomacy and other less tangible, not easily measured traits, which will become requisites for success in a foreign environment.

Some critical questions should be answered before proceeding to the first step in identifying and hiring employees to fill overseas assignments.

For example, what kind of educational background is required? Will background requirements be different for staffing Europe? How will you know? Our experience in Europe has caused us to ask many such questions, and the answers have not always been what we anticipated.

When we place accountants and financial officers in the United Kingdom, or other EC countries, we know that a college degree is less important than it is in the United States. Accountancy in Great Britain places greater emphasis on technical training and experience than on academic degrees. That is not to say that recruiting a U.S. national to fill an important accounting or financial position in the EC should neglect to seek those candidates with the best possible education. It does mean, however, that such academic credentials might not carry the same weight in the European Community that they do here. Experience will count more than education.

What about education in general when seeking candidates to fill overseas positions?

If human resource professionals depend upon the criteria generally used in the United States, they might overlook some splendid candidates whose attributes and abilities are less easily measured than what they are accustomed to. A degree that might prove especially useful in Denmark does not necessarily have the same impact (or, indeed, have provided the same training) as it would in Greece, or in Germany. To write a job description for a cost analyst or MIS manager is not enough. General qualifications with which we are used to dealing may leave a gap when filling positions in the EC.

As noted in earlier chapters, within the EC itself is a movement to standardize educational programs, evaluations and degree designations. But, outside of a few areas where limited progress has been made, a uniform system of rating and evaluation is years away. Therefore, a general list of qualifications must be analyzed and expanded, based upon the country to which a candidate will bring his or her background and experience.

Once that is accomplished, the intangible qualities of candidates must be redefined by U.S. managers. A U.S. national with a high degree of technical skills, and who might fit in and prove to be a valuable member of a company's staff in the United States, could also prove to be less effective when asked to employ those skills in a foreign land.

A technically trained and experienced person must also have a highly developed sense of diplomacy in order to function effectively away from home base, and in a foreign business culture. That may be asking a lot, which is why the competition for such people is, and will become, even more intensely competitive. How many men and women can there be currently who have developed the skills necessary to succeed in this complex technological age, but who are also comfortable with the less tangible demands of diplomacy, and who possess sensitivity to the way people live and work in foreign environments?

Along with diplomacy and sensitivity, flexibility must also be considered when choosing a candidate for an overseas post with a U.S. company. In the United States, men and women who have been taught highly technical skills have, in effect, also been taught not to be flexible. Technical skills demand adherence to a proscribed set of parameters, leaving little room for flexibility even though career counselors consistently implore such people to develop "people" skills such as written and verbal communication, and sensitivity to human needs.

The supply of people who have mastered technical fields, but who also possess a keenly honed sense of diplomacy, sensitivity and flexibility is short. This raises the natural question of whether a U.S. company seeking to expand into the EC should depend upon finding such individuals, or take the longer-term position of having to *create* them.

Because flexibility is one of the key factors in determining the potential success of U.S. executives overseas, some companies are focusing upon finding less-experienced men and women, and then training them in the requisite skills and attitudes of successful overseas management.

Language skill is a particularly good example of this. Are we expecting too much of our human resources professionals to ask them to go out and find a highly skilled accountant, with a splendid education, years of solid professional experience, finely developed ambassadorial sensitivities and skills, *and* a working knowledge of Italian, German or Luxembourgish? There are such people, of course, but when hundreds of U.S. companies are out there looking for them, supply simply does not meet demand.

In-house language training (or contracting for these services) may well become a routine business practice in the near future. Will it be expensive? Of course. But it also will be vital to any company with a sense of long-range purpose and commitment to the EC.

Opening an office in Hamburg, London or Madrid, is not analogous to opening a new branch in Kentucky or California. Companies that take this somewhat parochial position have found their experiences in Europe tough sledding. Those who commit themselves to expending the time, energy and cost of answering the hard questions about staffing stand a greater chance of finding the right people and, by extension, finding ultimate success in the New Europe.

Assuming we know what we need and want in overseas positions, we're faced with the next hurdle—finding, evaluating and ultimately hiring the right people to fill them.

There are three basic ways of doing this, although the unique demands of staffing Europe might find U.S. companies adding other, more unconventional methods of recruiting.

The three time-honored means of finding good candidates are advertising, recruiting from within and direct recruiting from outside sources (with special emphasis on networking). We'll begin with a look at advertising.

Advertising

Advertising for candidates is a relatively cost-effective means of reaching a wide audience, providing it is undertaken with an intelligent understanding of what is to be accomplished. The negative, of course, is that advertising invariably generates hundreds of resumes, all of which must be screened. And that means maintaining a larger human resources staff than might be necessary. Of the responses received to an ad, most will not merit more than a cursory look, particularly if the target audience has not been sufficiently identified.

Although advertising for candidates throws open the field to a vast pool of unknowns, its primary markets can be analyzed and chosen in the same way as the advertising of a company's products or services. Careful planning, and working with a realistic job description, are the keys to selecting media that will reach the most potentially rich field of candidates.

Some media that have proved to be effective recruiting vehicles over the years are:

- The *New York Times—Daily and Sunday Classified Section*—The top talent in the New York, New Jersey and Connecticut metropolitan areas browse these sections regularly, even if they are seemingly secure and happy in their present employment. Ambitious professionals use these sections to monitor their market value. The prospect of gaining European experience, especially at a time when Europe is poised to be a hot topic in the business community, could serve to entice otherwise contented executives to respond to ads offering these kinds of opportunities.

The News of the Week in Review, and Sunday Business Sections—These two sections, also of the *New York Times*, are where senior executive candidates routinely search for job opportunities. Since the *Times* is now a wide-reaching national publication, professionals in myriad specialties, middle-level management candidates and senior executives from across the country keep their eyes on these ads . . . "just in case."

This is especially true in this era of mergers, takeovers and acquisitions. The concept of lifetime employment—the "gold watch" syndrome—no longer exists, on either side. U.S. companies, faced with increasing global competition and growing domestic economic pressures, meet swings in their competitive postures by adjusting staff levels. U.S. workers *expect* to change jobs a number of times during their careers. As a result, turning to the "Help Wanted" ads is no longer done only when a job is needed, or a change desired. It is—and should be—a regular part of career-building.

- *Wall Street Journal*—"The Mart" is the daily exchange of available positions and situations. The *Journal*'s reach is national, indeed international, and it is read by a highly educated, motivated, career-conscious audience.

  There are other national publications such as *USA Today*, but they do not run much employment advertising and advertising in them is not generally cost-effective.

- *Regional and Local Newspapers*—The *Los Angeles Times* has become one of the largest circulating dailies in the United States, and is an effective vehicle for reaching the important California market, particularly the Los Angeles and Orange County regions. The *Chicago Tribune* has long been entrenched as the midwest's most widely read newspaper. The *Washington Post, Boston Globe, Denver Post, San Francisco Chronicle* and other newspapers are well-read, and have proved effective at reaching audiences in locales from which promising Euro-execs might be culled.

  Advertising in these publications should not be indiscriminate, however. In the Los Angeles area, there is a high concentration of scientific and engineering professionals working in the defense industry. In Boston, specialists in the area's famous high-tech and computer technology sectors can be targeted. Hartford and Omaha have a high concentration of insurance executives. In Washington, the audience you wish to reach may include executives with foreign service experience. Knowing in advance the precise demands of a job to be filled goes a long way in making these determinations.

- *Periodicals*—Magazines and trade journals do not offer the immediacy of daily newspapers and broadcast media, but they are among the most-effective methods of advertising to narrowly selected audiences.
  - *Business Publications*—Weeklies such as *Barron's, Business Week, Industry Week* and *Crain's New York Business* reach business-oriented audiences. Monthlies such as *Money, Inc., Fortune* and the *Harvard Business Review* reach similar audiences. These publications can be prohibitively expensive, however, and should only be used on a targeted basis when seeking the highest level of Euro-executive.
  - *Career-Specific Publications*—Publications directed at specific industries, such as *Advertising Age, American Banker, Chemical Engineering, The New York Law Journal, Purchasing World, Personnel Journal, Management Accounting* and hundreds of others allow a direct advertising approach to specific job categories.

    There is a similar selection of parallel publications published throughout Europe, and the number grows. As U.S. companies increasingly turn to finding good candidates from the European talent pool—as they undoubtedly will—these magazines and newspapers will be important recruiting tools in the overall process of staffing.
  - *University Publications*—For college and university audiences, there are numerous school newspapers and magazines, predictably cost-effective vehicles for reaching those about to graduate. This audience is, of course, virgin territory for recruiting entry-level management candidates who are often more pre-disposed to relocate than those ensconced in jobs and careers. Companies whose management decides to stress hiring people in order to mold them into the sort of Euro-executives they seek should undoubtedly make good use of college and university publications.

- *Intellectual Publications*—Publications such as *Harper's, The Atlantic Monthly, The Smithsonian* and *Scientific American* can prove a creative buy. Their readers are highly intelligent, have a greater disposition to thorough reading, as opposed to skimming articles and text ads, and tend to view life, personal and professional, on a more global basis.

European Media—Aside from professional journals published in Europe, there are European counterparts to all U.S. print and broadcast media, including nationwide and local TV and radio operations in each of the EC countries, and prominent print media including France's big three, *Le Monde, L'Express* and *Le Figaro* newspapers; the Netherlands' *De Telegraaf;* and Spain's *El Pais.*

While, in general, concepts and media plans may be similar in approach and execution, don't count on it. Assistance should be solicited from advertising experts in each country. Naive, idiomatically incorrect, and crudely constructed ads in inappropriate media, will be a waste of time and money, especially given the level of employee being sought.

Many assumptions we make in terms of U.S. advertising may not apply to Europe. For example, age discrimination is not against the law in many countries of Europe.

Also, there are nuances of approach. German ads tend to be aggressive in their message and selling techniques. French ads are more like bulletin boards in their approach. In the United Kingdom, it takes a lot more advertising to generate good candidate inquiries because there are a large number of competing recruiting firms there, including specialized firms like Robert Half. Frequent advertising is necessary to meet this continual competitive challenge. If you calculate advertising as a percent of revenue, the formula used in the U.S. probably won't apply in Europe.

Working for a U.S. firm is, very often, attractive to Europeans. Many U.S. products and services have been in Europe for decades, have become household words, and have highly regarded reputations for quality. While U.S. companies suffer from what many Europeans perceive as a hire-fire syndrome, this is often outweighed by the feeling that in working for a U.S. company, you are working for a proven winner.

Despite recent slippage by some U.S. companies—and European disdain for an aggressive business style—the majority of U.S. companies are still highly regarded.

Recruiting (Internally)

To staff a European operation, the obvious place to begin is at home. Within your own company will be staff members who would like to go overseas, and who have the credentials to merit careful consideration. The advantages to a company are obvious:

- Their capabilities, strengths and weaknesses are already known to management, a luxury not enjoyed with new hires;
- Company veterans are familiar with the product or services, and methods of operation;
- It is one of the cornerstones of an effective personnel policy to offer opportunities first to those already on staff.

Given the familiarity with internal candidates, the operative issue is whether their abilities mesh with those that have been identified as necessary for productive overseas assignments. Since the abilities of these candidates are known, a company has the luxury of concentrating on the less-obvious attributes necessary for overseas success—"the fit."

Naturally, by making it known to existing domestic employees that overseas positions are open to them, and then having to reject them, can result in morale problems. Here is where the fit can be useful.

By pre-determining the *type* of person management wants in Europe, it takes the onus off having to reject a valued employee in favor of someone from outside. The rejection, therefore, is positioned as not based upon the individual's skills and knowledge—or lack thereof—but upon the fit overseas, which is determined by many factors, including the specific requirements of the host country. This approach enables management to stress that the employee's continued role in the domestic operation of the company is of great value and much appreciated.

To further maximize the potential of finding the best candidates internally (and to minimize the sensitive situation of having to reject valued employees), careful attention should be paid to the pre-selection process.

Pre-screen for potential internal candidates by discussing overseas objectives with their department heads. This obviously must be done diplomatically, since the perception of favoring certain candidates without giving others a fair chance for the position should be avoided under any circumstances.

Of course, if you have a particular department that could be a source of multiple overseas candidates, its manager might well balk at the notion of having some of his or her best people taken away. Whether couching the conversation on the basis of the company's "greater good" will appease that concern is conjecture.

Job-posting is the tried-and-true method of apprising employees of available positions because it is the fairest method. However, certain rules should be considered when posting overseas positions.

First, if jobs are posted, don't let the program fall into the bogus suggestion-box syndrome. Companies that establish suggestion boxes for show in the misguided notion that it will boost employee morale—and then routinely ignore suggestions, good and bad—not only don't elevate morale, they eventually lower it. The same holds true for job postings that are not legitimate. If jobs are to be posted, make sure those jobs are fairly available to all qualified company employees.

Before posting overseas jobs, procedures should be in place as to how, once applications are received, the internal screening process will be conducted. Confidentiality will more than likely be a key issue with employees, who may not want their managers to know they are applying for another position.

There may be different criteria for overseas positions. For example, foreigners in your present employ, who are resident aliens in the United States, may have greater difficulties relocating to an EC position. Also, an employee's family situation could militate against relocation.

In the long run, these internally recruited staff members can become one of your most valuable assets. Once you have your European operation firmly established, there probably will be an ongoing exchange of middle-level managers on each side of the Atlantic, creating the best possible team of U.S.-Euro executives who are multilingual, have cross-cultural experiences and who, by extension, have probably developed a healthy sense of corporate loyalty.

Recruiting (Externally)

While advertising will probably constitute the core external recruiting approach for staffing an EC operation, to neglect other avenues is to limit the potential of finding the best person.

Because the subject of Europe post-'92 will probably be of inherent interest to virtually everyone in business—whether they are seeking opportunities there or not—the press, particularly trade magazines, are increasingly open to article suggestions on this subject. By mounting a public relations campaign through which the editors of magazines are queried about having top people in your company write articles for them, you have the opportunity to expand upon what the company has to offer without the appearance of self-serving advertising. In addition, articles, as opposed to advertising, carry with them an implied third-party endorsement by the publication. They have a high credibility factor.

Naturally, such articles cannot be blatantly commercial, but that requirement actually works in a company's favor. A well-written article on how an executive from the company sees opportunities in Europe after the 1992 unification can be an infinitely more effective "sell" than even the best-crafted ad. U.S. nationals toying with the idea of looking for opportunities in Europe will, after reading such pieces, identify the company as a leader in European expansion. The possible result: inquiries into the potentials of joining the company by qualified people in the company's field who might not have considered seeking a new job.

Recruiting on college campuses is another area to which increased attention should be paid. The extent to which this is pursued, however, depends upon the philosophy within the company as to the amount of training it is willing to commit.

If your company has determined that the best approach to developing Euro-executives is to take relatively raw talent, and then shape it into the company's desired image, the college campus is a solid vehicle for identifying such people. And, as I mentioned before, young people who have not developed family and community ties are more likely to respond quickly and favorably to the opportunity of working abroad.

One company committed to college recruiting is Pall Corporation, the manufacturer of filters mentioned in Chapter Three.

"We are very interested in young, bright people whom we can mold into our particular corporate culture," says Donald G. Nicholls, group vice president, sales and marketing for Europe, the Middle East and Africa. "The competition for the best talent, however, is intense."

To outflank this competition, particularly the larger companies with more readily identifiable names, Pall plays to its principal strength: a long history as a growth company in a high-tech business, where something exciting is always happening. And, the company gives recruiting the priority it deserves.

"We consider the recruitment process one of the most important functions of senior management," Nicholls explains. "We don't delegate that responsibility to juniors. Junior managers are involved, but there is always a strong senior management role, as well."

Where Pall does recruit in the experienced job market, the company is more interested in skills than experience with a competitive product.

"The type of experience we don't need is with another filter company," Nicholls says. "We'd much rather take a good scientist or engineer and train him or her in our methods of filtration than take people who think they know what filtration is all about and have to retrain them out of their bad habits." And he emphasizes, good jobs are never easy to fill, even during periods of high unemployment.

Such a dim view of the competition is not always the case. And that's where networking can play a key role.

Networking

Networking has always been a staple approach for men and women looking to change jobs. It has also been used effectively by certain companies to identify top talent working for competitors, determining whether they are interested in seeking new opportunities, and pursuing them after making such a determination.

In the case of staffing Europe, a beefed-up system of networking can pay dividends. If employees currently with the company have been made aware of European opportunities, and have been given a fair chance to compete for them, those who have not pursued such opportunities should be actively encouraged to spread the word to others outside the company who have the requisite background and skills. The importance of your company's expansion into Europe should be stressed whenever possible, and current employees should be asked—and perhaps even rewarded—for coming up with good people through their professional and personal networks.

Of course, the concept of networking for the best possible candidates to fill jobs is at the heart of what every professional recruiting organization does. That is their primary function, and those firms that have proven themselves over a long period of time are generally able to find the right people quickly, usually at a cost considerably lower than if the company did its own hiring.

Larger recruiting firms with international networks are not only in touch with prime candidates for overseas assignment, they have devoted considerable resources to understanding the special needs of each EC country. By extension, they are in the position not only to find people, but to effectively screen them, and to work closely with human resources departments in shaping job descriptions that most accurately reflect the realities of the job, and of working in the EC.

As with utilizing any outside service, care must be taken in choosing the right one. Research should be undertaken on both sides of the Atlantic to assure that the firm, or firms that represent you are operating in your best interests.

The tendency of some firms to employ the same methodologies worldwide will not be the way to recruit for positions in the EC. For example, we gained a major U.S. investment bank as a client after it had a bad experience in Europe. The bank had hired a team from a highly regarded New York personnel services firm to recruit staff for a London operation. The recruitment firm sent its team to the United Kingdom and exercised iron-fisted control over every aspect of the procedure, right down to hiring clerical help.

The *modus operandi* was U.S.-oriented. It did not play well in Europe. Candidates were put off by the forceful approach, combined with an unimpressive lack of knowledge of local rules and customs. The bank finally decided that local representation would be more effective and less costly—an unbeatable combination.

A final point on recruiting from the employer's perspective: Try not to be locked into preconceived notions, no matter how historically correct they have proven to be. The head of one of our United Kingdom offices provides an interesting example of the downside of this.

He was contacted by a U.S. insurance company seeking to recruit a candidate for the position of controller at the company's office in Copenhagen. The company wanted a Dane, and directed our recruiters to use a search approach, i.e., direct recruitment via known contacts. Our manager suggested advertising, despite the seemingly narrow specs for the job. After much cajoling, the company agreed, however reluctantly.

The candidate they finally hired worked for a company in the same building, one floor above the insurance company's Copenhagen office. The insurance executive who retained us was initially angry for having to come to England to hire a Dane, who ended up working one floor above his own Danish office. Our manager pointed out to him that a search approach would not have identified such a candidate. The winning candidate had no previous insurance experience, and was more junior than the profile originally presented. Advertising was the *only* way to locate that particular individual.

• • •

Having dealt with recruitment from the perspective of the employer, I now would like to provide the prospective candidate with a checklist to prepare him or her for finding a position in the new Europe, and in the process help generate a symbiotic relationship that will work best for both sides of the equation.

Advice for the Candidate

Any candidate who has read the preceding chapters should have some idea of the methodology many corporations will utilize in seeking to hire a team for European operations. In order to be recognized as a potential member of such a team, the successful candidate will need to know where to look, and how to position himself or herself to best advantage.

The ideal way to do that is to understand where and how the employer will be looking for candidates, and to respond accordingly. The following suggestions summarize the approach that should be taken by candidates seeking European positions.

Be prepared. Employers seeking to staff their European operations will be looking for certain abilities, types of training and levels of experience. It goes without saying that any candidate, for any job, should possess the requisite education and skills called for in the basic job description. But, where staffing Europe is concerned—and as I've pointed out in previous chapters—there are a number of other, less tangible assets a candidate should be prepared to offer.

The most obvious is language proficiency, even though English is widely spoken throughout Europe. If you are still in school, proficiency in one or more of the predominant European languages will be a tremendous asset, because it allows you not only to communicate with Europeans in their own language, but it demonstrates a degree of respect that will stand you in good stead with your contemporaries.

If you are no longer in school, you can take non-matriculated courses, study at one of the many professional language schools or take advantage of such organizations as the French or Spanish institutes in larger U.S. cities.

Gain the necessary schooling. Study the type of training and qualifications employers are seeking for their European staff: computer literacy, business schooling, skills in international business, etc. Business education does not end upon graduation from college. If Europe *is* in your future, devote the time and energy to analyze your strengths and weaknesses, and pursue the education necessary to fill the gaps.

Young people in Europe are acutely aware of enhanced educational needs, and are aggressively preparing themselves before going out into the job market. A recent study for the EC by The European Foundation for the Improvement of Living and Working Conditions found that:

> Young people are staying longer in the educational system. There is a strong element of "qualification explosion" and "creeping credentialism" wherever high qualifications are required in order to compete effectively in the labour market. Jobs which previously required school leaving certificates now require college or university degrees or diplomas.

Enhance professional experience. U.S. companies will undoubtedly place increased emphasis on professional qualifications when choosing Euro-execs. It behooves any person eyeing the new Europe as a career move to identify those professional skills that will be in particular demand and, if his or her current skills aren't on that growing list, to acquire them.

Presently, EC countries are predictably seeking to attract high-tech industries, particularly information services and communications technologies. In addition, international banking, finance, and many other management skills necessary to help countries from the Eastern Bloc make the painful transition to a free market society are disciplines that offer excellent opportunities.

Polish your "people" skills. Diplomacy, tolerance, flexibility and an ability to appreciate the other person's way of doing things will be valuable skills. If you are a rigid, head-strong, inflexible person, who has a reputation for intransigence and ruffling feathers, your potential for success in an overseas environment is limited.

By extension, every U.S. company assigning people to European operations—and I cannot stress this too much—must screen carefully to avoid sending such people as their representatives. This means adopting new methods of evaluating resumes, analyzing personality traits during interviews and perhaps even injecting into the hiring process new forms of psychological testing. The human resource professionals of the future will, of course, play a critical role in shaping such new and innovative approaches. The astute candidate will know this and adjust accordingly.

Know where to search. You should be studying the pages of the appropriate trade journals in your career field, as well as the leading business publications for the kinds of opportunities you seek in Europe. In the "Advertising" section of the chapter, I gave many examples of where I feel the most effective ads should be placed. Obviously, they are the places you should be looking.

Pay careful attention to what the ads are asking for, and don't waste your time, or the time of a prospective employer, if you are not a good fit. If your credentials and skills do match up, and you have a serious commitment to working overseas, you will find your response to such an opening will be welcome. But, as with pursuing any job, do your homework first. Research the company. Research the country in which the successful candidate will be posted. Finding—and landing—the right overseas job will take a concerted effort beyond the usual demands of domestic job hunting.

Stay up to date on your own company's overseas plans. Check job postings, company memos, employee publications and the business pages of local newspapers. Sometimes, to a company's chagrin, the press uncovers stories about it before the company is prepared to announce them. European expansion plans could be such a story.

If your company is planning to establish operations in Europe, you have an insider's advantage. But don't assume that you won't have to "sell" yourself with the same vigor and skill as an outsider. With so much at stake in staffing Europe, your company is not likely to select a present staff member of inferior ability over a better qualified outsider. It has always been my belief that every employee should approach each working day as a potential job interview. This means always dressing properly, attaining visibility within the company on every possible level, understanding more about the company's goals and operations beyond immediate responsibilities, and maintaining good relations with every level of colleague.

Employees with designs on working in Europe, but working for a company that has not announced plans to locate—or to expand there—shouldn't wait for such an announcement to be made. Begin preparing now, and make it known that you are taking language courses and pursuing other learning opportunities. You may not be able to put your new skill to use in your present company, but when you're ready to pursue other overseas positions, you'll certainly be better prepared.

Your advantage over outside candidates will naturally be your understanding of company products, services and methods of doing business. But understand, however, that there might well be requirements concerning the hiring of locals in the EC country of operation that are beyond the control of your company's management. You may not be hired for a position, even though you know you are a strong candidate.

Practicing diplomacy should start on your present domestic job. If you are a prime candidate for assignment to fill a position in Europe, your current boss will be reluctant to lose you. Diplomacy on your part might be the key to winning approval.

Bear in mind that even overseas positions, which appear to be the same or similar to jobs in the United States, and to which you consider yourself uniquely qualified, may be quite different because of local requirements and long-standing methods of operations. Locals trained and experienced in the means of doing business in their particular locale could be considered more valuable than U.S. nationals being sent to assume such jobs, especially in the short run.

If your company is seeking to become a legitimate global corporation, it will be looking to identify and train bright stars who gain the international experience to lead it into its multinational future. These executives will likely come from both sides of the Atlantic.

Know the job market. If you are interested in overseas employment with a company other than your present one, you will have to become a student of the market. That involves more than scanning help wanted ads. Be alert to articles announcing the start-up of U.S. operations overseas, acquisitions by U.S. companies, and joint ventures between U.S. companies and European partners. This information will serve two critical functions. It will provide you with valuable leads on where to look, and it will make you a knowledgeable person concerning important news in your field, a plus when being interviewed for an overseas job. At the same time, begin reading about countries to which you might be assigned. Gain a sense of the history of those countries, and steep yourself in the local customs and culture. Not only will this be necessary for success when working in them, it establishes you with prospective employers as a thoughtful, keenly interested candidate.

Along with independent efforts to identify positions in the EC that are available to U.S. candidates, the use of professional recruitment firms that have offices or affiliations in the countries in which you are interested, is an effective approach. The best of these organizations are skilled at evaluating candidate abilities and principal sell points. It is their role to apprise candidates of their strengths and weaknesses—especially as they apply to the potentials of landing a good job in the EC—and to suggest how to strengthen a candidate's appeal. And, of course, they know where the jobs are and how best to go after them.

Network. Networking via professional organizations is an excellent way to come up with good job leads, domestic and international. Involvement in professional organizations should be an ongoing commitment throughout everyone's career, not just when something is wanted from these affiliations. I suggested in the first section of this chapter that companies seeking to get out the word that they are expanding overseas operations, and are looking for good people to staff them, write articles on the subject for trade publications. This advice is equally appropriate for men and women who wish to be recognized as possible prime candidates. Visibility is an important ingredient for overall career success, and using the written word, as well as speaking to groups within an industry, goes a long way to obtaining this continuous visibility. If you are at all shaky in these areas of communication, by all means take whatever steps are necessary to correct these deficiencies.

Consider the long way around. A longer-term approach is to seek employment in the United States with corporations which have long-standing operations in Europe, then work your way to a European assignment from the inside. While taking this approach doesn't include any guarantees, you may find that you've joined a company that meets your career objectives, whether overseas transfer occurs or not. If it does eventually lead to a European assignment, taking this patient route to achieving that goal will be a pleasant and welcome bonus.

But don't limit your thinking to only U.S. multinationals. Annual foreign investment in the United States is estimated to be in excess of $200 billion, and such investment has increased each year despite U.S. recessions, and through periods of both inflation and deflation. As was pointed out in a 1991 article in *Graduating Engineer,* "The blue chips of today might be companies with names like British Petroleum, Mannesmann AG, Mitsubishi or CIBA-Geigy."

Finding jobs with foreign companies doing business in the United States, and using them to eventually find transfer opportunities to Europe, can be an effective approach. But, keep in mind that at present, and in the foreseeable future, foreign-owned companies doing business in the United States prefer to reserve upper management jobs for executives from their home nations, much as U.S. companies tend to do.

Locating Candidates

• • •

Having formulated overall business objectives and job descriptions and then having started the search process, a U.S. company now prepares for hiring.

Five
The Hiring Process

> Finding and training the best cross-border managers will be crucial to reaping the benefits of 1992 . . . The future belongs to companies that not only find the whiz kids but also hang on to them. The winners will be companies that stop paying lip service to 1992 and prove they believe in it—creating exciting, cross-border jobs that tomorrow's Euro-managers thrive on.
>
> "The Hunt for the Global Manager"
> *Fortune*—May 1990

The magazine went on to cite some of the problems of over-demand and under-supply that have pushed some salaries to "a very un-European $500,000 a year."

Whom to hire for a European operation, and how to find that person involves attention to good basic hiring practices. At the same time, sharp focus on those unique aspects of effectively staffing Europe must be maintained. Concurrently, there is the added pressure of knowing that the value of legitimate Euro-executives is continually escalating, and that those with the "right stuff" will be the subject of intense competition for their services. Time, therefore, becomes an additional factor.

Hiring for Europe follows, for the most part, many standard procedures that human resources professionals have used for years when hiring domestically. These procedures will always play a major role in staffing any company, anywhere, and for any job. But, because the sort of person who will succeed in the EC should possess additional traits and attributes, the evaluation process, at every stage, must take this into consideration.

The nuts and bolts of hiring begins, of course, after the human resources department, or recruiting firm, has sifted through stacks of resumes—or curricula vitae—and has identified candidates who best match the hiring criteria. Once that has been accomplished, the elimination process begins. For domestic hiring, this involves four basic steps; but we've found in our recruiting efforts for U.S. companies staffing Europe that a fifth step is needed.

Here are those five steps. The first is specific to the requirements of Europe 1992; the next four should be part of any well-established hiring program:

- Research and thoroughly understand the specific requirements imposed by various nations on staff members working in the target European country.
- Evaluate resumes and curricula vitae with careful attention to what they say, and what they don't.
- Determine the candidate's real level of proficiency in those specific skills that will be required of European staffers.
- Conduct an effective interview.
- Give appropriate emphasis to reference checking.

The ultimate objective is to reach a meeting of the minds between employer and candidate that results in a job offer and acceptance.

Hiring Considerations for Europe

By this point, all those involved in the hiring process should be aware of company staffing needs (based upon the business plan discussed in earlier chapters), as well as EC employment requirements. In addition, the European country to which employees will be assigned will undoubtedly have its own labor laws for those areas in which the EC has not reached a consensus, and has not issued Community-wide directives. Failure to become intimately familiar with these factors could render European staffing efforts an exercise in futility.

For example, while there is freedom of movement for citizens of member states across the entire expanse of the EC, foreign nationals—in our case, U.S. citizens—are not EC citizens, and do not enjoy the same freedom to move to new jobs in other member countries.

Furthermore, since foreign nationals are subject to the employment laws of the particular country in which they are working, if they seek to move to another member state, they must qualify under, and abide by, the employment rules of that country.

There are also differences in credentialing. To an outsider, the wide range of different educational and professional qualification requirements in specific countries can be confusing. Aside from those professions whose qualifications have been standardized by the EC, each country has its own hierarchy, and develops specifications for professional training accordingly. How much professional training is called for can vary depending upon the level of schooling a person has completed.

Training to qualify as a certified public accountant in the Netherlands can take three to 10 years; how far a candidate has gone with secondary school and university training helps determine this.

Another example came to light when one of our offices in the United Kingdom proposed two British candidates for the same accounting position. The client's headquarters in the United States summarily eliminated one candidate in favor of the other because the human resources manager recognized the letter designation of that candidate's credential, but not the designation after the other candidate's name. We pointed out to the client that the rejected candidate's credential was a level *higher* than the candidate who'd been chosen. Despite that information, the decision to hire the less qualified candidate was not reversed.

While as many as three out of four managers at U.S. firms have college degrees, the ratio for Continental Europe is only about two of three, even lower in some countries such as the United Kingdom where its prime minister, John Major, does not possess a college degree.

In the United States, an MBA may be an important credential in and of itself in a business candidate's educational background. In Europe, the school from which a student receives a degree may carry considerably more weight.

An additional wrinkle in staffing Europe results from rules in many countries that dictate that locals be employed first to fill positions, even with foreign-owned firms. To overcome these restrictions, it must be shown that the foreign employee designated for the position has a "defined specialty," which cannot be duplicated locally.

One effective method of meeting this defined specialty requirement, which has worked for some U.S. firms with which we've been involved, is to show that the employee's knowledge of the company's unique product, service or *modus operandi,* cannot be duplicated locally. Diplomacy, however, dictates that this argument will only work if a fair percentage of locals are hired and trained to work in areas perhaps otherwise reserved for U.S. nationals. An attempt at fairness is always appreciated by European host countries.

Along with being a sound diplomatic move, hiring locals helps a U.S.-based corporation gain that degree of mobility only afforded citizens of EC states. In any event, hiring locals should in many cases be an important element of an employee mix because of the particular areas of expertise they offer, and the contributions they can make. (Achieving this mix is the subject of Chapter Eight.)

While citizens of EC member states are free to cross borders, they are restricted in what they can do outside their home countries. Although it is a stated objective of the EC to achieve as close to total occupational freedom across national borders as possible, the process is proceeding step-by-step, in many cases profession-by-profession.

For each profession, laborious negotiations are under way to define exact qualifications, and to specify training requirements, often in minute detail. For example, directives to allow architects to practice throughout the EC took 17 years to be enacted; for pharmacists, it took 16 years. It may take many more years before there is extensive freedom of movement in the skills that are most important to U.S. companies.

Citizens of an EC member state are guaranteed a right of residence for five years in other member states, with a possible extension of an additional five years. Therefore, once a U.S. firm has hired a foreign national, it has the benefit of his or her contribution for a minimum of five years, and possibly 10. On the other hand, local laws may make it difficult to terminate such hires once they've become part of the organization.

Absentee management back in the States must be sensitive to the local situation and act accordingly. For example, if a U.S. company is experiencing a systemwide slump, but the operation in Europe is doing well, local management will naturally be resentful of layoffs there, or even a hiring freeze.

It all boils down to placing a tremendous additional burden upon human resources professionals. It has been hard enough for them in this economic climate to find people who can keep a company running smoothly despite significant staff reductions. Now, for companies looking to expand into the New Europe, they must also become experts on the many additional employment regulations there, and keep up with new laws and changes to existing ones that seem to be written every day.

Despite this, the job must get done, and that means applying professional staffing skills to the step-by-step, time-consuming and often frustrating process of evaluating candidates who have applied for overseas jobs. In most cases, the initial contact is via a candidate's resume.

Evaluating Resumes and CVs

A resume (Europeans generally prefer to call it a *curriculum vitae*) is a candidate's sales brochure. It is necessarily self-serving and should be viewed in that light.

What resumes tell about job-seekers run the extreme from those that are scrupulously conscientious about presenting an honest picture, to those prone to exaggeration, at best; inaccuracies and misstatements, at worst. Our research indicates that roughly 30 percent of resume writers lie on paper, not including lies-of-omission. Many present a reasonably inflated picture of the product—themselves—from which the interviewer, guided by his or her experience, will exercise appropriate judgment.

Since a resume is the traditional beginning of the active hiring process—and a mistake in hiring for an overseas assignment is especially costly—a careful read is warranted. This includes not only a close examination of what's written, but requires that the reader be on the lookout for what's *not* there, and to wonder why.

Experienced judges of resumes are always on the lookout for candidates whose careers have taken a consistent and positive path. The succession of jobs a candidate has held should demonstrate growth, an ability and willingness to take on increasingly demanding assignments, and should further show that such enhanced responsibility has been given to the candidate.

We're all familiar with the term "self-starter," an attribute that every employer likes to see in employees. It becomes especially desirable, however, when hiring someone for an overseas assignment because, in the majority of cases, that individual will be functioning far removed from the direct supervision of the U.S. corporate hierarchy.

But don't be too quick to rush to judgment when an otherwise solid resume indicates a deviation from a steady and upward career track. Sometimes, such detours indicate a logical step.

One example of this involved the senior director of freight sales for a major airline. Dead-ended in a department that accounted for only 10 percent of the airline's business, he sought the advice of superiors as to how he might advance his career while, at the same time, help the company meet its objectives. They told him he needed solid, operational experience on the passenger side of the business. He decided to take a downgrade to fill an opening as manager of operations for the airline at New York's John F. Kennedy International Airport. After two years in that assignment, he was named a regional vice president. Today, he is chairman of the board of a major airline. His resume, if read while he was serving in the JFK assignment, would indicate to some a backward step in his career which, of course, does not tell the whole story.

While an indication of an individual's quest for personal achievement is important, of equal importance is a demonstrable sense of company-mindedness. Has the candidate helped meet corporate objectives in his or her previous employment? If so, the resume is likely to include such items as, "boosted sales 10 percent above department objective," "maintained zero defect levels throughout calendar year," or "controlled costs below prescribed objectives."

Every resume should be read with a careful eye for specifics. Pay particular attention to a candidate's job descriptions, and be committed to verifying their accuracy through careful reference checking, on those who are seriously in the running.

Specifics indicate a command of the person's job, just as specifics about achievements indicate real situations, as opposed to vague descriptions, that often connote puffery.

Job descriptions and achievements should be in sync with responsibilities. For example, it is unlikely that middle-level managers have supervised vast armies of employees, or have exercised control over huge budgets. That kind of exaggeration should raise red flags, and become the subject of subsequent interview questions.

Corporate allegiance versus job-hopping is another factor to be weighed. While many companies espouse the policy of promoting from within, an increasing number of employees in today's tumultuous business climate believe it is only possible to make substantial career leaps by switching companies.

A succession of jobs does not carry the onus it once did, especially if change of jobs follows a pattern of career growth.

Bear in mind, however, that in staffing Europe, there is a greater investment in employee retention than there is for domestic assignments. Such employees will be harder to replace, and their European experience will make them more attractive to the competition, either while they are in Europe, or after they've returned home.

While an indication of experience that meshes with specific job requirements is important, don't overlook the bright candidate who trains well. This consideration speaks to the age-old human resources dilemma: Do you hire the candidate with a great deal of experience but who may be set in his or her ways, or do you opt for the candidate who meets the minimum job requirements, but who has the potential to be trained properly from the outset?

Because staffing Europe involves candidate attributes that go beyond those for purely domestic hiring, more general experience in areas other than called for by the core job description should be considered. These might include experience in the complex and unfamiliar realms of European finance or computer languages, background that demonstrates the valuable character traits of flexibility and diplomacy and, of course, foreign language proficiency. With these characteristics already in place, it may be worth the added expense to train the candidate in some of the specific job skills being sought.

Membership in outside organizations could assume added significance when evaluating resumes of Euro-candidates. An employee who has taken the initiative to join professional or cultural organizations may be the sort of person who will more easily adjust to the socio-cultural requirements of working and living abroad. Furthermore, membership—even better, leadership—in prestigious international organizations will help the candidate construct networking relationships that could prove helpful to success in Europe and, by extension, work to the benefit of the corporation.

Be wary of "heap" resumes, i.e., those created by "resume mills." They indicate a lack of initiative on the part of a candidate, and perhaps a lack of confidence.

Judge a resume's focus. If the candidate is cranking out prototypical resumes in a generic, laundry-list fashion, this does not indicate the kind of leadership potential you may be seeking.

Be alert for the "functional" resume—one that follows a functional, rather than chronological format. This often means periods of unemployment. While the reasons for this may be valid—such as maternity leave, several years off to raise a family, or time out for academic pursuits—they may also indicate more ominous problems, including a pattern of terminations the candidate is seeking to mask.

Candidates lacking solid professional background and experience often try to cover up by making general, vague statements on their resumes. Phrases such as "familiar with," "have knowledge of," "have taken courses in" do not indicate achievement.

Some human resources professionals suggest reading resumes from the bottom, where less meaty, less appealing but sometimes more honest material is often placed.

Gaps that indicate a lack of initiative, an inability to focus on career objectives, or a history of problems in interpersonal relationships can be subtle, and difficult to identify. A close reading between the lines will often uncover them. A successful European operation will demand highly focused employees who have demonstrated ability to work well with others, especially since they will be operating in a venue of unfamiliar customs, language and work rules.

Interviewing

The one-on-one, face-to-face interview has always been the most critical element in the hiring process. Candidates have put their best faces forward on their resumes. If what appears on paper is impressive enough, an interview is warranted. Now, not only can the right questions be asked based upon what the resume says, the more subtle, less tangible aspects of the candidate can be probed and evaluated.

Employment interviews can be as much of a challenge for interviewers as for candidates—at times even more so. Few people enjoy passing judgment on others; fewer still are comfortable with being judged. But that's exactly what must come out of an interview. Candidate and interviewer alike have to make judgments because, when it is all over, jobs must be filled and careers advanced.

In a relatively short period of time, it must be determined through interviews whether a candidate will ably represent a company in a foreign environment, and help achieve its objectives. It is a tall task. The stakes are high for both parties. For the company, the wrong choice can mean a weakened organization. For the employee, the wrong job thousands of miles from home can derail an otherwise promising career.

Given these considerations, interviews should be carefully planned, and include a procedure to ensure that key questions are asked of the candidate, and answered. Every employment interview should be held in an appropriate setting. The interviewer's office is an obvious choice, but only if interruptions can be kept to a minimum. Candidates deserve an interviewer's undivided attention. From a company's perspective, a distracted interviewer is less able to formulate sound judgments when it's time to choose a person to fill a key overseas position.

If it is not possible to avoid interruptions during the normal workday, consider a change in the time when interviews are conducted. Appointments before or after business hours may work better for the interviewer, as well as for candidates who have their own job commitments.

The physical setting, whether an office or not, should help put candidates at ease. Unless, for some reason, the company is interested in a candidate's ability to perform under intimidating circumstances, a war-room type setting, with more than one interviewer firing questions, is not conducive to an open, two-way interchange destined to elicit useful information.

The interview should follow a pre-determined sequence that helps keep it on-track, and avoids unproductive rambling. At the same time, it should not be so rigidly constructed that candidates are unable to deviate in order to get across points they consider important, and to express their individuality.

Along with a physical setting, a good interviewer knows how to enhance a relaxed atmosphere through initial conversation. Some "lighter" questions about a candidate's interests can serve to relieve opening jitters. For reasons only they can give, there are interviewers who feel that candidates should be kept off-guard and apprehensive. All this results in is a person, undoubtedly nervous from the outset, who is unable to present an accurate picture of himself or herself. An employment interview is not an interrogation.

At the same time, an interview is not a casual chat. When interviewers are not prepared, and allow precious time to drift into unfocused banter, little, if anything can be accomplished.

Candidates should be given room to breathe, to think, to express themselves without undue interjections by the interviewer. Some interviewers, particularly inexperienced ones, feel a need to talk a great deal about the job and the company. This serves neither the interviewer nor the company. The candidate should have the floor, prodded by questions that have been carefully considered in advance. In the case of candidates being considered to fill European positions, close attention should be paid to clues to their personality, especially their ability to mesh easily with others.

Do they have proven ability as team players? Are they flexible? Do they demonstrate during the interview a diplomatic sense, a sensitivity to other's needs and views? (One way to help ascertain this is to question others with whom they've come in contact while visiting the company—a receptionist, an administrative assistant, the human resources people who conducted pre-screening.)

In line with this, a word to candidates: We've seen good ones lose out because they were impolite or cold to those they considered "not important." Every person with whom a job candidate comes in contact is important.

Our research indicates that the first person interviewed is seldom offered the job (less than 20 percent of the time). The last person interviewed is hired more than 50 percent of the time. It's highly implausible that in more than half the cases, the last candidate through the door was the best qualified. What seems more likely is that the last person interviewed was simply the one the interviewer remembered best. Taking proper notes throughout the entire interviewing process, no matter how many candidates, helps correct this counterproductive phenomenon.

Interviewing to staff Europe can never be taken lightly. Unfortunately, many managers pressed for time and anxious to fill empty jobs hire on instinct, trust their intuition, make crucial decisions based upon unfocused conversations with candidates and rely upon subjective feelings. That's a bad approach in any staffing situation, but where Europe is involved, it causes costly, disruptive mistakes.

At some point for those candidates who have risen to the top of the pack after multiple interviews, a more detailed explanation of the job should be provided. At the same time, it's important to probe these candidates' understanding of the ramifications of an overseas assignment. Will they be able to handle the exile syndrome, the out-of-sight, out-of-mind aspects of working abroad, away from core company operations back in the United States?

Are these finalist candidates seriously interested in advancing the company's objectives in Europe, or is this relocation more of a personal adventure and career-builder?

Don't sugar-coat the position for these candidates. Explain what they can realistically expect in the way of corporate training, and what on-the-job expectations will be. Be forthright about the timing of moves, and what working conditions may be like, especially in start-up situations. If a candidate does not fully and honestly understand what is expected, there is the increased risk of the company ending up with a disappointed, frustrated and disgruntled employee on its hands in Europe.

How much does the candidate want the job? While arrogance may be a negative, enthusiasm never is. Make every effort to understand the difference. When qualifications are similar, go with the candidate who most wants the job.

End interviews on an up-note. Let good candidates know that you were impressed with them. Highly qualified candidates for positions in Europe will be hard to find. Don't allow the good ones to leave without knowing that they are seriously being considered. We've seen many good candidates lost to companies because the hiring authority operated from some "rule" that says you should never display enthusiasm until you are ready to commit. Offering a job is one thing; indicating to good people that you are sincerely interested is another. Be honest—don't build false hopes. But, if you've found candidates who seem right, let them know that you think highly of them, and will be in touch without delay. Having said that, follow through.

Some candidates will be ruled out immediately after the initial interview. Notify them as quickly as possible to allow them to pursue other opportunities. Treat rejected candidates with honesty and dignity. Leave the impression that your company is a good place to work. These rejected candidates can be good sources of leads for future candidates.

After each interview, write a summary of what transpired, including initial reactions to the candidate. Notes taken during the interview will help in preparing a summary, but shouldn't be relied upon to capture the essence of how things went. The few minutes spent writing a summary while the interview is still fresh in the interviewer's mind will prove extremely useful when, after seeing many people, it's time to make a decision.

How well-prepared was the candidate? Were there inconsistencies between the resume and the candidate's responses to questions? If so, were they clarified to your satisfaction?

Did the candidate say things that particularly impressed you—or that troubled you, at least to the extent that follow-up questions during a subsequent interview are warranted? If there were inconsistencies between resume and what was said during the interview, make a note to focus on those things when references are checked.

With the current dearth of qualified Euro-execs, interviewing companies should keep in mind that the best candidates will be in demand, and will be as selective in choosing a company as companies are when choosing an employee. In this case, the company, as well as the candidate, must be concerned about putting the best foot forward.

One of our European offices reported to us about a client company that insisted upon handling the hiring process long-distance. It allowed our office to do all the pre-screening and early interviews in Europe, but then, to our surprise, the client conducted the final interview by telephone from the United States. The candidate was so unimpressed that a company would think so little of the position that it did not conduct a face-to-face interview—not even at the point of making a final decision—she asked us to withdraw her name from consideration. This company lost a top-notch person. Worse, she went to the company's primary competitor.

Reference Checking

Always a delicate part of the hiring process, reference checking has become more difficult today for a number of reasons. At the same time, it remains a critical element in determining whether a candidate is everything he or she purports to be.

The major difficulty in obtaining useful references is, of course, legal. There have been a spate of lawsuits seeking damages from former employers for providing what candidates consider unfair, or inaccurate information. In most cases, employers in today's litigious climate will do little more than confirm dates of employment. This is especially true in the United States. Many European countries are less litigious than we are, and written references, pro and con, are more common. Whether that will continue to be the case remains to be seen.

Because obtaining useful references has become increasingly difficult, two things have happened.

First, many companies—and individuals within them—no longer pursue references with diligence. This is a mistake. Second, companies that are aware of the critical necessity of thorough reference checking, but faced with difficulties in obtaining them, are meeting the challenge by seeking new and innovative ways of going about it. In many instances, they have taken on the role of "private detective." In fact, more companies than ever are utilizing the services of private investigative agencies that specialize in checking hard-to-check references.

In "kinder, gentler" times, when obtaining references was easier, reference checks would be routinely run on any candidate whose resume looked good. That is no longer possible, or smart. Companies committed to careful reference checking under today's difficulties are narrowing down the list, checking only those candidates who are seriously in the running.

In the past, asking for written references was the most common, and useful approach. It doesn't work today, except in Europe where the candor is refreshing.

Many candidates arrive at the interview carrying with them a number of glowing references written by former employers and colleagues. Like resumes, they are part of the selling package being used by the candidate, and should be judged accordingly. They do serve a purpose, however, in that they give the employer a list of names to pursue in an effort to probe a little deeper into whether these people really hold the candidate in such high regard. More on that later.

Interestingly, written references carried into an interview by a candidate in Europe are viewed with even less enthusiasm than in the United States. In Europe, a candidate presenting written references is viewed, to some extent, as lacking confidence. I don't necessarily read it that way, but U.S. candidates interviewing with European firms should, I think, leave the pre-prepared written references at home.

Because obtaining a written reference in the United States is virtually impossible, that leaves the second of three approaches—calling former employers on the telephone.

Former employers might be more likely to discuss negative aspects of a candidate over the phone than in writing, but don't count on it. While slightly harder to prove, a negative reference given verbally is just as damaging, and actionable, as one offered in writing.

Still, the telephone can be useful, particularly if the person checking references carefully tunes in to not only what is said, but the *way* it is said. The words may be positive and nice, but the tone in which they are delivered could be something else.

A careful reading of a candidate's resume, and an effective interview, should raise questions to be asked when checking references. Ask references for clarification of claims made on a resume. Query former employers on some of the same questions you asked a candidate during interviews: To the candidate: "Did you have an easy rapport with your colleagues at your previous job?"

To the former employer: "Did John (or Mary) have an easy rapport with colleagues while working for you?"

Chances are you'll receive little response when seeking references from a human resources department, which after all, must function under company rules that are written to preclude legal action. But if an attempt is made to reach those individuals to whom the candidate actually reported, chances of candor are increased.

Any employer committed to thorough reference checking, which we encourage every client to be, should use every conversation with a candidate's former employers to expand the number of people who might have something useful to contribute about the person's background and work history. Job seekers, quite understandably, give as references only those people they feel confident will provide a positive picture.

Include colleagues at the company in this expanded list, and vendors with whom the candidate might have dealt on a regular basis. Call people with whom you are familiar through professional organizations, and who might have had dealings with the candidate. In other words, exhaust every possible avenue before making a final decision on sending someone to an important job thousands of miles away.

The third—and best way to gain an accurate look at a candidate's past—is by visiting references in-person. This is time consuming, and demands a certain gumshoe commitment. For high-level jobs, it is well worth the effort. By sitting with former employers, not only can you benefit from nuances of voice, you have the added dimension of observing them. Like a photograph, an expression can say more than a thousand words.

There are subtleties to be considered when speaking to former employers. A previous job may have been characterized by a distinct personality conflict between supervisor and employee. That can lead a former boss to say nothing but negative things about a departed employee. If that represents an isolated incident in the candidate's working past, and you gain a sense through talking with the employer that the negative reference being given is not fair, include that in your formula for judging the candidate.

As in all interpersonal dealings, we can only make final judgments about people based upon what we have been able to learn about them. A visceral response to someone with whom we wish to become friendly usually suffices. Not so in staffing a company, particularly a company looking to place outstanding people in a challenging overseas position. A candidate may present him or herself nicely, be beautifully dressed and have a pleasant personality. Those are all to the good. But unless a conscientious attempt is made to find, and to put into place as many pieces of the candidate's puzzle as possible, the chances for a mistake in hiring are magnified.

There is always a feeling of considerable relief when, after going through the long and demanding process of finding candidates, a choice has been made. The perfect person has been found to fill a key overseas job.

But, it's not over yet, especially when the candidate you've chosen is being pursued by a number of other companies. Making the job offer demands thought as well. That's the subject of Chapter Six.

Before we get to that, let's look at the hiring process from the candidate's perspective. How should those looking to develop careers overseas with American companies approach employers who can make that happen?

Advice to the Candidate

From the outset, men and women seeking jobs with U.S. companies in the New Europe should understand the hiring criteria will be more stringent than for many domestic jobs. This is not to say that companies filling domestic positions settle on less qualified people. The difference is that while companies staffing domestically seek candidates with high professional credentials, there are additional considerations because of the unique demands made upon U.S. nationals working abroad. At least, there should be. If U.S. companies build such additional demands into their hiring standards, it behooves all Euro-candidates to make sure they match them.

Preparation is crucial. Going after any job demands preparation. For most U.S. nationals, working in Europe involves a number of unknown factors. This dictates that preparations begin by researching the European marketplace. It isn't enough to simply proclaim, "I think I would like to get a job in Europe." That might be the first step, but a careful look at the European marketplace—as well as at yourself—could uncover factors that mitigate against following through on that decision.

Working abroad isn't for everyone. One of the things I've tried to accomplish in this book is to give, especially in the earlier sections, an overview of what the myriad cultures of Europe are like. Overseas assignments provide many benefits, but there are also negative factors.

There are people who simply will never be comfortable living in a foreign socio-cultural environment, and who have to accommodate work habits of those who have not been brought up in the U.S. business structure. And, U.S. companies will not be able to simply recreate a domestic operation and run it the way they have in the United States, no matter how successful they might have been.

Research should include narrowing down the number of companies that present a viable and expanding European presence, and to which the interested candidate might apply. Know your market before submitting yourself to it. A good analogy is a writer who sends stories to magazines that do not publish such material. This wastes the writer's time, as well as that of the editor who must read the material.

- Know whether Europe really is for you.
- Know which companies are likely to be looking for good people to staff European operations and therefore might be receptive to your inquiry.

A word here about loyalty and ethics is appropriate.

When companies choose employees to send to Europe for key positions, they expect these people to perform to their maximum potential. Employers are also incurring a significant expense. The cost of relocating an employee overseas is substantial. While I am a firm believer in the right—indeed the obligation of individuals to make personal choices that will enhance their careers—I also urge people seeking employment overseas to respect the commitment and expense involved on the part of the company, and to dedicate themselves to whatever length of service is necessary to accomplish the prescribed task. Those who see jobs as a method of enjoying some time abroad, and who take jobs for that purpose, cheat their employers. No U.S. company in this intensely competitive global marketplace can afford to have such people representing them.

Candidates for overseas positions who are committed to this brand of loyalty and ethics, and who can project it to prospective employers, will have already enhanced their hireability.

Prepare a better resume. There is an adage in the personnel field that a resume will never get you a job, but will lose you many. As you might have judged from reading this book, companies are going to be especially careful about whom they hire to represent them in the EC. Resumes are going to be read with extreme care. Obviously, an individual who does not take the time, and expend the effort to produce the best possible resume, free of typographical and grammatical errors, and with each word chosen carefully, will be quickly dismissed as a potential employee. Your resume is your foot through an employer's door. Make sure it's done right.

Be honest when preparing your resume. Because the stakes are high, companies staffing Europe will check references with even greater care than when filling domestic positions. Don't be one of that 30 percent who lie on resumes. Not only might you be found out, you could also end up in a job that you are incapable of handling, not in your home town but in Brussels, Madrid or Copenhagen.

While I'm on the subject of honesty, let's touch upon another reason for it. The corporate motto at Robert Half International has always been

"Ethics First." The past decade of business behavior, in which ethics too often were forgotten, is exactly that—a decade past. The ethical pendulum is swinging back, and the decade of the '90s will see a greater premium placed upon ethical behavior in business. Success in Europe will depend upon a commitment from both sides to a strong sense of ethics and honesty.

In determining material to place upon a resume, it will be necessary to identify those experiences in one's background that particularly apply to the challenge of working and living overseas. Courses that might have been taken purely for pleasure, and that enhance one's sensitivity to language, diplomacy and international awareness, will now carry more weight.

Experience with foreign aspects of business, however minor they might have been during a previous job, now take on renewed importance. Exposure to community and social programs that brought you in touch with people from other nations—programs like student exchanges when in high school or college, international activities of service clubs and fraternities, and involvement in college groups that focused upon interaction between people of other nations—will all hold you in good stead.

If you've devoted enough time to analyzing the overseas business environment, and have identified those companies that are poised to take advantage of them, you can target your cover letters appropriately. I use the plural because one version of a cover letter is never enough. As you uncover job opportunities that could lead to your goal of working in the EC, you'll find that each involves certain specific requirements. A serious candidate for overseas employment should be willing to tailor the cover letter to accompany each resume to match the demands of the hiring company. Sending out one standard form letter to cover all opportunities makes as much sense as sending a "To Whom it May Concern" letter to every employer queried.

Looking for a job is hard work. Creating the right resume, and cover letter, is all part of the demanding job of finding a job.

Stress achievements and contributions on your resume. Be specific; flowery language and excess verbiage is usually translated by human resources professionals into an attempt to cover up a lack of specifics.

Rehearse for interviews. The secret to a successful interview is preparedness. This takes many forms. Candidates who confidently approach a job interview do so not only because their credentials are in order and have been honestly portrayed on their resumes, but also because they have learned as much as possible about the company, its product or service, the people in it, and its success in Europe, past and projected. This takes hard work. It's inevitably worth it.

In situations where a candidate has gone through a personnel recruiting firm, that organization will provide much of this information. But the same information is available to anyone willing to ferret it out.

Study the company's annual stockholder reports. Scour the files of newspapers and magazines for articles that have been written on the company. Ask questions of your network of colleagues, some of whom might have worked for the company, or others who have tangential knowledge.

But don't be content to learn only about the company. If it functions within an industry that is not familiar to you, do the same sort of homework to learn as much as you can about it.

What is the company's status in its industry? Who are its major competitors, and are they probing Europe for expansion possibilities?

Demonstrating this level of knowledge says many things about a candidate during an interview, all of it positive.

What questions will an interviewer ask? Many will be based upon what you've said on your resume, and in correspondence you've had with the company. I've heard some of our placement professionals talk about candidates who have been searching for a job for a considerable length of time, and have not looked at their resumes for months. They actually forget what's on them, and flounder when questioned about specific items.

Never assume that one answer to a question will suffice. Most answers elicit a second question, and often a third or fourth. Be especially prepared to answer those questions you hope won't be asked.

If your presentation through the interview phase has been honest and forthright, you won't have to worry about being tripped up.

But there's more to preparing for a job interview. The interview is another opportunity to sell yourself, and that means getting across points you consider important, even if the questions asked do not directly address themselves to those areas. Decide the points you consider most important in presenting an attractive picture of yourself, and practice working them into answers to any question. Like a guest on a television talk show with something to sell, you'll have a limited amount of time to make the case why it's *you* that should be hired. Turn that time to your advantage.

Don't be afraid to pause and think before answering. Although you will have rehearsed the selling points you wish to get across, present them in a thoughtful manner. Rehearsed answers delivered as canned replies are always transparent. Work with audio and/or videotape at home, or with a friend. The more familiar you are with what it is you wish to say, the more natural it will sound.

Every interview can be a learning experience. If the one you've just come out of doesn't result in a job, the next one might.

Do a post-interview analysis.

What went wrong, and what went right? What questions were asked that you didn't anticipate, and that might be asked during the next encounter with a prospective employer?

Did you demonstrate a sense of flexibility and diplomacy, an appreciation of other cultures, an ability to roll with the punches and to adapt?

In most interviews, the candidate is asked whether he or she has any questions. Expect this, and have your questions as carefully prepared as were your answers to questions you anticipated being asked.

In an initial interview, try to avoid asking questions about tangible benefits, including salary. Chances are you have a reasonable understanding of what the salary parameters are (perhaps having been given them by a recruiting firm). The initial interview is the time to ask about the potential for growth, and what contributions you can make to the company.

What are the company's plans for the future in Europe, and how might you fit in with those? What sort of team will you join?

Will you have an opportunity to learn, and to interrelate with operations of the company other than your own department? Will you be able to benefit from company training to enhance your capabilities to function, to contribute and to grow?

No matter how an interview goes, assuming you're still interested, follow it up with a note of thanks in which you express an even greater interest in the company and the position. Virtually every job seeker knows to do this, but many fail to simply because they forget, or don't take the time.

Finally, as with your resume, be honest in your reply to an interviewer's questions. The stakes are too big for both you and the company to make a mistake based upon faulty, or deliberately inaccurate information.

Check your references. Every reference you intend to give should be contacted first, and his or her permission sought. Choose carefully.

Unless you're certain that the person is enthusiastic about you, and will demonstrate that enthusiasm, leave him or her off your list.

Our placement professionals counsel companies to not pursue references unless a candidate is seriously being considered for a job. Candidates should extend the same courtesy to their references. A succession of calls to references is not only annoying, it can be counterproductive. A good reference may start out portraying you in glowing terms, but by the time the tenth or twelfth call has come in, enthusiasm is bound to wane.

A conscientious employer, anxious to mitigate the chance of hiring the wrong person for Europe, will undoubtedly contact references not provided by you. Try to anticipate who they might me, and the reactions they're likely to give. If there are skeletons in your closet, consider whether to broach them during the interview, rather than have someone deliver a negative comment about you when a prospective employer calls.

Ask for the job. Every successful salesperson knows that you must "Ask for the Business." Because job candidates are, in effect, selling a product the same axiom holds true. They must ask for the job.

If, after research of the company, the industry and the job being offered, you are convinced it is right for you, express that. Tell the hiring authority that you are enthusiastic about the position, are excited about the potential it offers you and that you want it.

Six
Making the Job Offer

> The key to economic success is GEMS (Global Employees, Mobile and Skilled). The challenge for HR professionals is to attract, retain and invest in GEMS.
>
> *HR Magazine*
> January 1991

The hiring process parallels any free market situation; the buyer-seller relationship prevails. If a candidate is viewed as a "product," and that product is in demand, it can be sold at a premium, especially if supply is short.

That is certainly the case with staffing Europe, at least now and into the foreseeable future. It is no longer the case where a company has an opening, many apply, and the company chooses the person it wishes to hire without having to sell itself. Companies looking for the best of America's men and women to successfully staff operations in the EC will have to do some marketing of their own.

Choosing the right person from a field of candidates can never be done with 100 percent certainty. But, if the search has been conducted in an organized and orderly manner, if the basic rules of smart hiring have been followed, and if the criterion upon which a choice has been made reflects upon a solid plan and carefully conceived job description, then the chances of making a mistake are significantly lowered.

Obviously, the decision-making process can be extended. Sometimes, this is prudent. Some companies, especially where overseas positions are being filled, are bringing in finalist candidates for what amounts to an all-day assessment program in which skills and behavior are judged against a series of exercises. These can include problem-solving aptitudes, interpersonal relations, communication skills, flexibility, adaptability and trainability. Increasingly, personnel service firms with international experience are being asked to construct such exercises, and to provide input into the final evaluation process.

But these situations are the exception rather than the rule. In most cases, a small group of individuals who have been charged with staffing the company's European operation will make a decision. The wisdom of their choice will depend, of course, upon what they bring to it. Hopefully, at least one person will have a firm grasp of the milieu in which the candidate will be asked to function. If that's not the case, the chances of making a misguided decision are magnified.

There is a tendency on the part of some management to hire people like themselves. This often results in a "cloning effect" that is seldom advantageous to companies. The potential downside is enhanced, however, where staffing Europe is involved. Men and women who will successfully represent U.S. interests in the EC will, of necessity, possess attributes that are not generally looked for when hiring domestically. A clone of a company's domestic management, as good as that management might be, won't necessarily be right for an overseas assignment. Accurately judging a candidate's less tangible assets—those necessary for functioning effectively in Europe—will go a long way in making the right hiring decision.

If a U.S. company ends up in the enviable position of having a field of excellent candidates from which to choose, it behooves management to not lose the runners-up. Often, a search for a specific individual to fill one job results in identifying a number of good people who can benefit the company in other capacities. A candidate might not be quite right for the position you're filling, but could enhance another division of the company.

Our placement people see it happen time and again. We're asked to fill a position for a client. Through our network of offices, domestic and international, we identify a number of people with the requisite credentials, and present them to the client. The client hires one individual for the specified opening, but then makes job offers to others who were in the running, and who had impressed management, even though specific positions aren't open. The result? A company strengthened in a number of areas through the process of filling one position.

Once a decision has been made, how does the management to whom the chosen candidate will report sell the company to that individual? Outstanding candidates undoubtedly have other companies—probably competitors—that view them in the same positive light.

The answer goes beyond tangible packages that can be offered. Naturally, a company has latitude with pay, benefits and other monetary career incentives. But that won't be enough for top Euro-candidates. A competitor might stretch its budget and top the salary offer you are able to make, but if a candidate is swayed only by money and perks, it's probably just as well that he or she goes to work elsewhere.

For candidates who are visionary about themselves and their careers, who view each step as a learning and growth process, and who take particular pleasure in making a contribution to an employer, other factors come into play. Whether a company has in-place programs and policies that appeal to an employee beyond salary and benefits will determine whether it is able to project the opportunities sought by such candidates. If a company hasn't paid attention over the years to motivating good people, to helping them learn and to grow, and to recognizing outstanding effort and achievement, it's too late once the perfect candidate is sitting across the desk, has been offered the job, and begins asking a series of questions that can't be answered with conviction.

Is the company firmly committed to doing, and expanding its business in Europe? A good candidate will want to know that.

Has the company considered the difficult challenges of keeping employees happy when thousands of miles away from headquarters?

Is it attuned to the personal needs of men and women asked to serve overseas, including family considerations (subject of a subsequent chapter)?

Are overseas employees considered an integral part of the company, or are they viewed as "those people over there?"

Is the long-term promotion potential equally as available to employees working abroad as it is to those in the company's stateside operations?

The better prepared the hiring management of a company is to give positive and enthusiastic answers to these, and other questions, the more likely it is to prevail in having the chosen candidate join the team.

In line with this, a company that is not only enlightened in employee motivation, but which has projected it through its public relations efforts over the years, will have already established itself as a "good place to work." That's one reason why the *rejection* of candidates must be handled with the same care as the hiring of them.

Everyone who ever comes into contact with a company—employees, vendors, professional and civic organizations, and rejected candidates—carry out into their communities the way they feel about the company. If a company's good reputation precedes a candidate who is applying for employment, much of the sell has already been accomplished. Conversely, if the reputation is bad, candidates whose services are in demand will be wary of working there, no matter how positive a face is put on during the hiring process.

The question of *commitment* to the New Europe does not necessarily mean that a company must have a long history of expansion there, although that certainly helps. One example of a long-term commitment to Europe is the Pall Corporation. Pall entered the European marketplace in 1962 by acquiring a small engineering firm in Portsmouth, in the United Kingdom. The decision to locate in the United Kingdom was risky because one of Pall's principle objectives was to market on the continent. The United Kingdom was not part of the fledgling European Economic Community; in fact it was part of the rival EFTA.

"My conclusion was that there could be no lasting European Common Market without Britain," says the company's vice chairman, Abraham Krasnoff. "We would risk it."

Pall has never regretted its decision. The company was right, of course, about the United Kingdom's entry into the EC. By the time it had, Pall had 40 percent of its sales in EC countries through subsidiaries built in France, Germany, Italy and Spain—as well as in Austria and Switzerland. Furthermore, the chief executive of the small engineering firm acquired by Pall in 1962, Maurice Hardy, rose to become chief executive of the parent company. In the case of the Pall Corporation, convincing a candidate of its commitment to the European marketplace isn't difficult.

On the other hand, there are now U.S. companies, and will be many more in the future, who have not established themselves as major players in Europe, but who are determined to do so. These companies that don't have proven track records in Europe can convince candidates of their commitment to Europe by showing enthusiasm and vision. They can bring the candidate up to date on planning by talking about steps that have been taken to launch an enhanced European presence, or about projects in the works; and by sharing information about financial commitments, marketing strategies, manufacturing and distribution plans. Of course, this is not to say that corporate secrets should be exposed; the candidate may decide not to join the company and go to a competitor. But if the right sort of people are going to cast their lot with a company, they are going to have to be convinced based upon an honest presentation that their commitment to working abroad is matched by the company.

Furthermore, candidates worth their salt will be keenly interested in the company's plans for employee repatriation. Before staffing of Europe can be considered, this area should be thought out, and appropriate policies written.

Those things said, making the job offer involves two givens:

- You can never be absolutely sure you have made the right choice.
- Those who hesitate may lose a good person.

The source from which candidates come to a company will influence somewhat how the actual job offer is handled, and what problems might arise.

Candidates, employed or unemployed, who are recruited from outside the company, perhaps present the fewest problems.

If they're employed, they will naturally have to give adequate notice to their current employer. If they don't feel this necessity, be wary. Chances are they'll fail to extend your company the same courtesy when it comes time for them to leave you. This is especially important when the candidate is working overseas. To leave to go to another company on short notice creates a vacuum in a U.S. company's EC operation that cannot be filled quickly.

Those candidates who have the requisite credentials for top EC positions with American companies will undoubtedly have developed a keen sense of their self-worth. We generally counsel candidates with whom we work to put off discussing salary considerations as long as possible because once a company has committed itself to an individual, it is reluctant to lose that person, and to have to start the search process all over again.

Knowing this, some prime Euro-candidates will use the situation to boost their salary demands. Wanting the highest possible salary for a given position is certainly understandable. But there will be those highly prized candidates who will carry this game beyond reasonable boundaries.

In some cases, they may have a legitimate offer from another company and are looking to top it. Depending upon the latitude the hiring authority has been given, salary can be a matter of negotiation, but that

115

is each company's individual decision. Whether the candidate does, or doesn't have such an offer will probably never be known, but some astute questioning might reveal the truth.

Looking at this situation from the other side of the desk, it behooves companies to establish salary and benefits parameters as early in the interviewing process as possible to avoid reaching the end of the arduous process, choosing the right person, and then losing that individual over a salary impasse.

The question of salaries and benefits is discussed in some detail in the next chapter. For now, suffice it to say that if the salary range has been based upon a solid understanding of prevailing salaries for good people working overseas for U.S. companies, and if the discussion of it with the chosen candidate has been handled properly from the outset, there shouldn't be any surprises when it's time to make the offer.

Sometimes, when a company has identified the perfect individual to fill a position in an EC country, and is then faced with a reluctance on the part of the chosen person, these companies will oversell the potentials of the job and company. While this might be a normal tendency, it should be avoided. If a candidate does not wish to work for a company based upon what it represents, it is better for that individual to work elsewhere. Both company and candidate will benefit.

How much time should a candidate ask for to mull over his or her decision?

That depends upon the candidate's reason for needing the time. With some, they may be hoping for an offer from a competing firm that is more attractive.

Others may have just been testing the waters, and intend to use your offer to attempt to better their lot at their current place of employment, a practice that is not only unfair to everyone involved, it often backfires on these people. Our research indicates that companies who acquiesce to such ploys usually lose the employee anyway after a brief period.

Most candidates, however, simply need some quiet, reflective time to consider whether they are making the right decision. This need should be respected, even encouraged. But a reasonable amount of time should be agreed upon, and adhered to.

It should be stressed to candidates in this situation that while their need to ponder the offer you've made is understandable, you have an important job to fill. Reinforce again that this is the person the company has chosen, that he or she is expected to play an important role in the company's European success, and that the sooner both parties can get started, the better.

In many instances, a job offer will be made pending a check of references. It's our opinion that it is better to identify front-runners as early as possible and check their references before making a job offer.

As I indicated in Chapter Five, the number of candidates whose references are checked should be kept to a minimum. Obviously, if you wait until you've narrowed down the field to one person, that consideration is taken care of. But because reference checking can take a long time in certain situations, it could cause such a delay that the risk is run of losing an excellent candidate.

Another problem with checking references at such a late juncture is that because the company doing the hiring is anxious to move ahead, it might devote less time and energy to the critical task of verifying the veracity of the leading candidate.

One way to head off unpleasant surprises at the job offer stage is to ensure that every candidate is aware from the outset that an offer will not be made until references are thoroughly checked. In fact, one interviewing technique that many of our people use is to couch questions this way: "I want to ask you some questions, and would like you to answer them the way you think your references would answer them about you." This is a subtle, but pointed method of reminding candidates that what they have presented on their resumes, and what they say during interviews, will be verified. If nothing else, it prompts those who have been less than honest to drop out of the running.

For top-level jobs, and especially when relocation to a member state of the European Community is involved, the question of employment contracts will be raised. If highly qualified people are considering leaving a satisfying current job to join your company overseas, they're going to want as many assurances as possible. Who can blame them? They can see themselves leaving a wonderful job, uprooting family, leaving friends, and heading for a foreign environment which, if things don't work out, they may have to deal with as unemployed U.S. nationals overseas.

As with salaries, the question of entering into employment contracts is one of individual corporate philosophy. In general, employment contracts are weighted more heavily in favor of the employee rather than the company. The employee is guaranteed a certain length of service, or an agreed-upon amount of severance should the employer wish to end the relationship, which takes a great deal of the risk out of making the move.

For the company, while an employment contract might bind a new employee for a specified period of time, no contract can ensure hard work, dedication, ethics, loyalty and all the other intangible aspects of human behavior. In general, employment contracts should be entered into only if a job candidate demonstrates a keen sense of integrity, and has a background that confirms it.

The Internal Hire

Ideally, some of the best Euro-candidates will be found within a U.S. company seeking such people. The advantages of hiring from within are the same in staffing Europe as they are when filling a domestic position. The individual is a known commodity, and has a good working knowledge of the company, its goals and methods of doing business.

Whenever someone is moved from one position to another within a company, however, it is done to strengthen one department, but results in a gap in the department from which the employee was recruited. A company has to carefully weigh whether it will be easier to fill a Euro-position by going outside, or whether the slot left open by virtue of an internal transfer can be more easily filled. These kinds of moves require good internal coordination, as well careful analysis by the human resources department.

Promoting from within a company is always desirable because it significantly boosts morale. Employees realize that their career aspirations can be met without having to look elsewhere. But while a company may be rich in talent domestically, it faces the same questions about internal candidates as it does about external ones. For example, do employees currently with the company possess those subtle, intangible, and additional attributes that are necessary for working and living in a foreign environment? Probably no more so than candidates who can be identified outside the organization.

Companies with a firm, long-term commitment to Europe—and we know some who are already doing it—will develop internal programs to teach the requisite skills of diplomacy, foreign languages and EC rules and regulations to men and women currently on the payroll. This negates the need to go outside in search of Euro-candidates. Whether this represents the trend of the future, or an approach that is ultimately short-sighted, remains to be seen. The salient goal is to staff Europe with men and women who will effectively and successfully advance a company's goals there. This challenge will undoubtedly be met, with U.S. firms using a variety of techniques. Simultaneously, a whole new approach to human resources and hiring might evolve.

Foreign Hires

As noted earlier, foreign nationals—those from the country in which a U.S. business will be located, as well as third-country nationals—will be important elements of any management mix, and should be treated with the same dignity afforded U.S. hires. While that statement may seem unnecessary and even patronizing, we are sometimes constrained by national tunnel vision that leads us to do things *our* way, ignoring the wisdom of seeing things *their* way.

It's easy to lapse into such insensitivities as mentioned in Chapter Five where a company sought to conduct the final phase of the interview process over the telephone and, in the process, lost the candidate. If hiring of locals for a European operation is being handled by management on the scene, allow it to make the final decisions. Among many benefits, it serves as a vote of confidence cast by the parent corporation.

For major hires, a face-to-face meeting with the appropriate executive or executives should be axiomatic, whether in Europe or in the United States. A message cannot be delivered about corporate commitment to European operations if a cavalier image is projected when hiring foreign nationals.

Most EC countries have rules and regulations under which employees may be dismissed. It is imperative that a U.S. company's representatives understand that the termination of local nationals cannot be simply a corporate decision made back in the States.

For example, in Belgium, an employment contract can be terminated by mutual agreement, at the expiration of an agreed-upon lapsed period of time for an assignment or for "compelling reasons."

While the first two circumstances are relatively straightforward, the third requires some explanation. EC legal drafters describe it as "a circumstance or incident which makes continuation of employment for one of the parties to the contract so difficult that employment may be terminated upon immediate notification of the reasons without notice given."

It doesn't take a law degree to see the room for interpretation here, and the potential for problems, including prolonged legal snarls with an employee who contests the problematic "circumstance or incident."

There are similarly restrictive regulations in other EC countries. While we should not be preoccupied with the problems of termination when staffing is the immediate goal, we should be conscious that someone we "are taking a chance on" may end up being around a lot longer than we'd like, even if his or her performance is unsatisfactory.

Advice to the Candidate

Assume nothing. Don't count your chickens before they hatch. That may be an old saw, but it is appropriate here. The unemployment lines are graced by otherwise intelligent professionals who left a solid job—however much they may have become disenchanted with it—to assume a new position for which they "were a lock."

You have the job only when it has been offered in no uncertain terms, and without reservation or qualification, when hands have been shaken and, in the case of relocation to Europe, when the offer has been committed to paper (not necessarily a contract but a written confirmation that the job is yours).

By the time you have passed the resume and curriculum vitae tests, and worked your way through the interviews and assessment sessions, it should be clear that you are being judged by a different set of parameters than would have been applied for a purely domestic position. Your prospective employer is undoubtedly aware of what is at stake in selecting personnel for Europe. There could be second-guessing in some quarters of the company, and further calls for evaluations.

Keep up your job search, and stay in the hunt with other employers that have shown interest in you.

Take a final, intensive look at the company. Be sure you haven't been so caught up in the romance of an overseas assignment that you have overlooked the potential for a mismatch. If you have any lingering doubts about the company's commitment to its European operation, or its plans for you within this context, now is the time to have your questions answered.

Tough, intelligent questions will be expected of you—even appreciated—by those for whom you are about to go to work. But once those questions have been answered to your satisfaction, make a decision, and make it known.

Be prepared to negotiate. There may be room to negotiate pay and benefits. You should know what you are worth in this new job market; if you don't, find out. Check executive recruitment ads, talk to your recruitment firm, and query your networking contacts.

A prospective employer will be dealing within the limits of salary ranges and benefits packages, but there is always slack in these parameters, especially if the company is anxious to acquire your services. That's why it's wise to delay salary and benefits discussions as long as possible, ideally until you've been chosen.

However, don't overplay your hand. The company is still judging what kind of employee it thinks you will be, and will not be impressed at this late stage by someone who is making unreasonable demands.

Beware the hard sell. Just as companies are wary of potential employees who oversell themselves, candidates should adopt a similar philosophy. Granted, companies will be in intense competition for solid Euro-candidates, but a company that tries to pressure you into an acceptance may be having problems beyond the strains of basic competition.

There may be legitimate reasons for this: approaching deadlines, the need for staff members to be on-site to supervise developments in a physical plant and/or the purchase of equipment, or the exploitation of pressing market opportunities. Accepting all that, the decision you are about to make will have a dramatic effect on your career. You have a right to ask probing questions, and to ponder—for a reasonable amount of time—your decision.

Get it in writing. In order to eliminate, or to at least minimize ambiguities, ask your prospective employer to put the job offer in writing, and to spell out in as much detail as possible the position, salary, overseas differentials, benefits, relocation assistance, training orientation and start date. An employer should not be reluctant to do this. If it is, ask why.

Give the appropriate notice. Burning bridges never does anything positive for a career. A decent amount of notice should be offered to a current employer even if you are parting on less than the best of terms.

Every employer deserves the respect of an appropriate period of notice. How long it should be depends upon corporate policy, and the position you now hold. The way you leave a job should demonstrate dignity and professionalism. Your stature in your profession and its industry will depend upon your actions over the years, and how you are perceived by others, including former employers. There are many success stories of executives returning to their former companies in more senior positions because they left on the right terms.

Accept defeat graciously. If you are not offered the position, be a good loser. This also falls under the category of not burning bridges. I've made the point repeatedly that top-notch potential Euro-executives will be at a premium. A missed opportunity today could develop into a job offer tomorrow.

If your chemistry with the prospective employer was right, maintain contact even though you lost out. Stay in touch. Your ability to take defeat with diplomacy may pay a dividend down the road or, in some cases, even in the short-term. If you are rejected but were seriously in the running, call the employer a week or two after being told the job had gone to someone else. It happens: a company settles upon an individual, dismisses other candidates, and then runs into a roadblock with the person hired. A better offer comes through at the last minute or, in the case of an overseas assignment, minds are changed about making such a major and disruptive move. Often, companies in this position are reluctant to get back in touch with the other good people. Make it easy for them. Call, thank your contact once again for his or her consideration, and indicate you're still interested in the job in the event it were to open up again. If nothing else, you've touched base again with a new member of your professional network. At best, you might be invited in because the person you lost out to decided to stay put.

Seven
Pay and Benefits

> (T)he Community has no intention of sacrificing fundamental workers' rights on the altar of economic efficiency.
>
> Jacques Delors
EC Commission President

While understanding global business is critical for senior management in today's corporate environment, many major U.S. corporations have come to discover that providing such experience does not come cheap. Relocating executives to Europe can cost a company multiples of what pay and benefits amount to for a domestic assignment. If the relocation is primarily to provide promising executives the opportunity of European experience, then the benefit of that exposure must be weighed against the cost, often double what it takes to maintain an individual in a domestic division.

Before discussing the details of compensation and benefits packages for overseas assignments, we should understand that certain basic rights of workers is a subject of major concern in the EC.

At the European Council meeting in December of 1989, the heads of member states adopted the "Community Charter of the Fundamental Social Rights of Workers," to be applied to all workers in the EC, regardless of national origin.

Among key provisions of concern to employers are those covering employment and remuneration, which:

- Assure every worker an equitable wage and a decent standard of living;
- Guarantee that wages may be withheld only in accordance with national law, while nonetheless enabling workers to continue to enjoy the necessary means of subsistence for themselves and their families;
- Allow every worker equal access to free public placement services;
- Provide workers with a weekly rest period and paid annual leave;
- Guarantee an adequate level of social security benefits.

Within the framework of these basic tenets, let me re-emphasize that the paramount consideration for U.S. companies staffing Europe is assembling the best possible team. The costs incurred in assembling this team are important, but should not be the driver in the decision-making process, especially if it results in settling for less-skilled people. Having said that, let's examine the options.

In staffing a U.S. operation in Europe, there are essentially three sources from which to draw: local nationals, U.S. nationals, and third-country nationals. Each calls for different compensation and benefits packages.

Local Nationals

In almost every case, hiring a local will be less expensive than bringing in employees from the other two categories. Expenses associated with relocation will not be a factor, nor will overseas differentials for housing, education or taxes. However, locals with the requisite skills and/or experience may not be easy to find, and the cost of training such people must be factored into any compensation and benefits equation.

U.S. Nationals

Without equivocation, relocating U.S. citizens to help manage a European operation will be expensive. Many factors must be considered, all of them adding to overall labor costs.

With superior Euro-executives at a premium, a salary considerably higher than for a domestic hire will be necessary to entice exceptional people to accept overseas assignments. These high salary expectations play out against a background of widely differing pay scales among the various member states of the European Community, and can result in intrinsic morale problems unless delicately handled.

Beyond salary, there are additional costs to relocate a U.S. employee to Europe, as well as a family if applicable:

- A differential to cover additional taxes that the employee will have to pay to the country in which he or she lives and works. In some cases, this can be greater than the employee's base salary.
- Housing allowances.
- Cost of living allowances (where they add markedly to an employee's expenses).
- Travel allowances (where a considerable amount of road time is involved in canvassing other countries of the EC, or to allow the employee and family to return home on a regular basis).

If a family is involved, there may be the additional expense of assisting a spouse to find employment, or with children, the reimbursement of educational expenses. (More on "The Family Fit" in Chapter Twelve.)

Third-Country Nationals

If a manufacturing operation has been established in a low-labor cost location, such as Ireland, Greece or Portugal—but the company's principal markets are in Germany, Italy or France—a sales staff that understands the geographic market, speaks the language or languages there, and has the contacts needed to open doors, provides obvious benefits. But, staffing U.S. companies with people from other EC countries incurs additional expenses similar to those when relocating U.S. citizens. There are likely to be the same tax differentials, relocation expenses, and family and education costs.

Furthermore, it can no longer be assumed that base salaries for relocated U.S. citizens will be higher than those paid citizens of certain EC member states. A German national will more than likely cost up to 20 percent more than an employee with similar qualifications from the United States, while a Belgian national could cost almost twice as much.

On the plus side, nationals from EC states provide the benefit of their ability to move more freely throughout the EC, as well as the obvious local knowledge they can contribute.

Surveys have shown that third-country nationals, not unlike their counterparts in the United States, are most apt to move to another country for reasons of career opportunity and financial reward. The career-building experience of working in another country is also high on their list.

The principal deterrents for them are family concerns, an inability to communicate in the host country language and apprehension about cultural differences.

• • •

Let's now examine some specific cost factors involved in compensation and benefits packages when staffing Europe.

Relocation

The cost of relocating is a non-recurring expense, but must be dealt with when moving employees and families to a European assignment and, in most cases, when they are repatriated. In addition, there are cost factors beyond the obvious expenses of moving household goods. Since there are innumerable variables, involving everything from the size of an employee's family to the distance to be traveled, I won't attempt to assign dollar figures. As a rule, however, from one quarter to a third of an employee's base salary for the first and for the final year of an overseas assignment can be anticipated.

Beyond travel expenses and the movement of household goods, the following should also be budgeted for:

- *Sale of current residence*—Real estate fees and administrative expenses involving the sale of the employee's present dwelling, or satisfying lease requirements on a rental property, are often covered by the company, particularly if it is going to attract the best crop of Euro-executives. There may also be the tax impact of a capital gain on the sale of an employee's property. And, many companies agree to absorb the costs of disposing of an employee's vehicle(s).
- *Temporary living*—Most companies cover hotel or apartment expenses while employees seek something permanent in their new European setting.

- *Relocation allowance*—Permissible out-of-pocket expenses incurred during the transition period of the relocation—e.g., meals, local transportation, telephone calls—are generally part of an overseas compensation package.

Housing Differential

If the cost of housing abroad is significantly greater than in the employee's home country, this differential will have to be covered to attract top executives. Another factor arises when there is a significant increase in the cost of essential goods and services, especially if such differences are precipitated by swings in foreign exchange rates. Downward shifts in the buying power of the dollar in Europe have occurred during the past decade. Such swings can have a dramatic impact upon the quality of life of American employees abroad.

As mentioned earlier, however, American management must be sensitive to resentment that can build with European employees when American-born managers and supervisors, supported by differentials, live a more affluent lifestyle than their European counterparts, perhaps even than their superiors.

Educational Expenses

The experience of attending a local school in an EC country can prove valuable for children of U.S. citizens working there. But in the majority of cases, particularly with younger children, most will attend an English-language, or U.S.-curriculum school.

"American schools" are located in most major cities in Europe and, as is the case with all non-public education, they charge tuition. Since the quality of education available to children is invariably a leading concern of employees relocating abroad, companies often cover the costs of private schooling. Where such schools are lacking, the cost of a boarding school in the United States or other country, and periodic visits from the children might, of necessity, be part of a compensation package. (More on this subject in Chapter Twelve.)

Taxes

Often the most significant cost factor assumed by American corporations placing foreign nationals in Europe is the additional burden of local taxes. Again, it is difficult to place a dollar value on what this expense is likely to be because of the many variables involved.

Variations in tax rates between countries are affected by definitions of taxable income. Benefits such as housing, cost-of-living allowances, foreign-service incentives, or company-reimbursed travel may be considered taxable. When they are, they have a spiraling effect on the cost of doing business. Employees will have to pay additional taxes for these benefits, and the employer may, in turn, have to compensate them.

Some companies limit the number and extent of such benefits and allowances to reduce the tax burden. The problem is that these perks help attract candidates, and cause them to choose one firm over a competitor.

Candidates for overseas positions will naturally be interested in how their absence from the United States will affect their income tax situation there. In general, U.S. expatriates can exclude up to $70,000 of annual earned income. In order to achieve this benefit, however, they must establish that their place of doing business is in a foreign country, and must also establish a primary residence there. They must also work outside the United States for 330 days out of any 12 consecutive months, live in a foreign country for an entire tax year, and indicate that they intend to stay there indefinitely.

But while $70,000 of income may not be taxed in the United States, U.S. citizens working overseas will have to pay taxes to the host EC country which based upon a $50,000 salary, would result in $14,000 in taxes in Great Britain, $5,000 in Japan and nothing in Saudi Arabia.

Social Security Benefits

The Social Security Administration has negotiated bilateral agreements with foreign governments to eliminate or minimize dual coverage by social security programs for U.S. employees working abroad. These agreements save employees additional payments each year that could add as much as 75 percent to their compensation package.

The United States has been party to such agreements since 1978. Through 1990, bilateral agreements were in effect in the EC countries of Belgium, France, Germany, Italy, Portugal, Spain and the United Kingdom. Agreements also exist with non-EC countries such as Norway, Sweden and Switzerland.

It should be pointed out, however, that where an employer makes up the difference in additional social security exposure for an overseas employee, it is considered additional taxable income in most countries. This perpetuates the spiral effect; the more an employer pays for an employee's additional social security coverage, the more tax exposure is created by this additional income.

Aside from eliminating dual taxation by home and host countries, agreements also seek to fill gaps in benefits protection. Employees who might be impacted are those who spend time outside the United States, but who find they have not worked in the host country long enough to qualify for its benefits—or have minimized their U.S. benefits by not having worked recently enough at home.

Where such bilateral agreements exist, the two primary considerations are the territorial rule, and the detached-worker rule.

- *Territorial rule*—This holds that an employee is subject to the social security laws of the country in which he or she works.
- *Detached-worker rule*—This is the principal exception to the territorial rule, and applies in many cases for U.S. companies staffing Europe. Employees are generally considered temporarily transferred to the country in which they work if the assignment is for five years or less—in which case they are still covered by U.S. Social Security regulations. The rule applies whether the transfer is to a company-owned operation, or to a wholly or jointly owned subsidiary.

A certificate of coverage is usually required to gain exemption from another country's social security taxes. Those certificates, as well as other pertinent information on social security agreements, can be obtained from the Office of International Policy, Social Security Administration, P.O. Box 17741, Baltimore, MD 21235.

Health and Medical Insurance

There are country-to-country disparities in health and medical insurance programs. In some, the insurance company pays medical bills directly. In others, the patient must pay at least a portion of the bill.

The EC administration sees "harmonizing the Community's health insurance systems as likely to be extremely difficult." By the early 1990s, there were no significant plans to do so.

Since any kind of consistent policy in this area is not likely in the near future, health and medical insurance will become a matter of individual assessment on a country-by-country basis, combined with applicable corporate policies.

The situation is even less optimistic in non-EC countries of Western Europe, where a dramatic aging of the population has created a trend away from government subsidies of health and medical programs, and in the direction of the private sector. In general, Europeans have a longer-term perspective on the jobs they choose. Many consider their employment a position for life. Consequently, they have traditionally been more attentive to health and retirement plans than their counterparts in the United States. As European business goes global, and a younger generation of Europeans is exposed to how business is conducted in other countries—particularly the United States—these new employees are likely to expect less in the way of back-ended compensation, and more in front-ended gratification.

Lower Wage Rates for Local Employees

While it may make good business sense to take advantage of lower wages in certain sectors of the EC, U.S. companies should be aware of recent developments in this area.

For one, as I've previously noted, the larger labor unions are concerned about the impact of low-wage EC nations upon job opportunities for workers in more developed areas. Unions are forming international alliances to combat this form of job flight. Simultaneously, the administration of the EC has singled out such "social dumping" as a matter of great concern.

"Competing against each other to attract relocating businesses, regions have introduced more and more sophisticated inducement packages over the past few years," says a recent EC report. "Many of these packages are in contravention of the EC Treaty, and the Commission has viewed their development critically."

The EC offered the following advice in its booklet, *1992—The Social Dimension*:

> Of course there will be investment in those countries where labor costs are lower, where social security is cheap and where employees—and thus also the machines—work long hours . . . [but] the work factor [is] not the only criteria governing a company's choice of location. Financial conditions, training opportunities, availability of information and speed of access to information [is] also crucially important. The risk that a

company might choose to set up elsewhere therefore should be viewed in perspective.

Alien Worker Considerations

Most nations—including the United States, of course—have laws to protect the local workforce against what is viewed as unfair competition for jobs by workers who are used to lower wage scales—the so-called alien worker, or "green card" rules.

Such regulations exist throughout the EC. In most cases, in order for an alien staff member to assume a position in the host country, the employer must show that the employee is uniquely qualified to fill that position and that it would be difficult, if not impossible, to find a candidate locally.

For example, according to information provided by the Netherlands Foreign Investment Agency:

> Residence permits and employment licenses . . . will be issued if the employee's presence in the Netherlands serves Dutch economic interests and personnel with equivalent qualifications not readily available from the Netherlands or from another common market country.

In Spain, the residence and work permits are granted on the same document for five-year renewable periods. However, during periods of high unemployment in Spain, these work permits are difficult to obtain, especially for lower-level positions. It is easier to garner permits for senior management, especially when such management is necessary to set up an operation that is perceived as beneficial to local employment.

In Germany, the alien residence permit is not issued unless there is evidence "that the cognizant Labor Office has assured (the potential employee) that, provided he otherwise qualifies for the alien's residence permit, he will be issued a work permit." The issuance of that permit "is governed *inter alia* (among other things) by the present situation and development of the labor market."

Work permits in France are difficult to obtain for lower and even middle-level management positions, but easier for senior executives, particularly those whose roles are essential to the employment of French nationals, as is often the case with the start-up of a new business venture.

In Belgium, a differentiation is made in the paperwork itself. Work permits are issued for salaried, or wage-earning employment. The "professional card" is issued to managing directors of companies incorporated in the country.

While Denmark adheres to procedures similar to those in the rest of the EC, the country prides itself on being among the top of the list of those countries that issue temporary expatriate work permits.

The Investment Office of the Royal Danish Consulate reports:

> Work and residence permits are usually granted to management staff of subsidiaries or branches of foreign companies in Denmark, their spouses and children. Permits are also granted to applicants in possession of special skills, expertise, or capabilities which are either lacking or in short supply in the Danish labor market. Such permits [however] may be limited to the period of time needed to transfer the skills in question to the local labor force.

Work permits sometimes involve such limits. Spain, for example, has three types: seasonal—for up to nine months, renewable only after 12 months have elapsed between each nine-month permit; specific profession, activity or geographic area—for one year and extendable for an additional year; any profession or geographic area—five years, renewable indefinitely.

Training

The EC charter of workers' rights states:

> Every worker of the European Community must be able to have access to vocational training and to benefit therefrom throughout his or her working life. In the conditions governing access to such training, there may be no discrimination on the grounds of nationality.

Aside from the dicta of directives or charters, ongoing training is simply a good idea. It will prove beneficial to expatriate U.S. nationals in the areas of language, local business practices, and local technologies, among a wide variety of possibilities. It will be a motivating factor for local nationals who are in the process of developing extended allegiance to the company. And, it will demonstrate to third-country nationals that they are valuable assets, whose ability to contribute is important to the corporation.

Vacations

In most European countries, vacation is one of the great rites of summer. Many factories shut down completely during the month of August, and cities such as Rome and Paris run on skeletal staffs. It is axiomatic that if you go to Paris in August, the only people you will likely find there will be tourists.

European vacations generally call for at least a month, and can run to six weeks in Italy and Germany, seven weeks in the Netherlands.

U.S. companies who take the issue of vacations lightly, or feel that they can be negotiated down, are in for some rude surprises.

One of our European offices was retained to find management candidates with a strong background in finance for a large U.S. company that was locating a branch there. One of the parameters given our recruiters was the corporate vacation policy: two weeks. We pointed out that four weeks vacation was the norm in the host country.

"Is it part of labor law?" we were asked.

"No," we answered, "it's a tradition."

Company managers decided to stick to two weeks, and had very few takers. They decided to compromise at three weeks, but still did not attract interested candidates.

Eventually, the company relented and offered four weeks vacation per year to start. The position was eventually filled, but it could have been resolved much sooner had the company not tried to impose its stateside vacation policy upon candidates from the host country.

Another benefit expected by many Europeans is a company car, which numerous European companies routinely offer. American management should be aware of these things before creating a job package. Many times, a top candidate will decline an offer and not state the reasons why. It could well have been that the vacation policy, or lack of a company car, was behind their decision.

Advice to Candidates

Despite the fact that a company's compensation plan for Europe may appear predetermined, it's beneficial to make yourself as knowledgeable as possible about what you will face in the EC country to which you will be assigned, and to determine how the company's compensation package addresses the unusual needs of that assignment.

Place your salary in its proper context. Granted, the demand for Euro-executives will be greater than the supply, and companies will be paying a premium for qualified candidates. But you need to evaluate the salary being offered against various factors. Before reaching the stage at which salary is discussed, do your homework about economic conditions in the EC host country. Your salary may turn out to be little more than a matter of keeping pace with an increased cost of living. Understand what a dollar is buying at current exchange rates, and research costs of housing, fuel, market-basket items, and other expenses that, in many cases, could be considerably higher than at home.

The salary and benefits package you and your new employer agree upon is, of course, a matter of your personal decision, and should address the needs of both parties. But because relocating to Europe involves many additional considerations not usually present when being hired in a domestic job, it's important that you understand the ramifications of the move, and the differentials the company is willing to provide to help defray the costs of housing, fuel, food, education, travel and taxes.

Large American companies with a sizable and ongoing European operation will, in most cases, have standardized compensation packages for Euro-execs, and have reduced the elements to writing. In the case of smaller companies, however, especially those starting up in Europe, such details might not have been formalized. In this situation, once all salary and benefits have been agreed upon, ask that the details be put in writing for you. This doesn't have to be in the form of a formal contract, simply a letter that spells out the financial aspects of the job.

Be sure you have a clear understanding of the following:

- If you own your residence in the United States, what help is the company prepared to give you in disposing of that residence? Many companies will assist in the sale of your current home, or will make provisions to guarantee its fair market value should you be unable to sell it before you leave. It should also be ascertained whether the company will help with real estate fees and administrative expenses associated with selling a house, and whether it will help you in some tangible way to deal with the impact of capital gains that might result.
- If you rent, and have to break a lease, some companies agree to cover the loss of security payments or other expenses that result from taking such action.

- To what extent will the company pick up your expenses during the transitional period between leaving your home in the United States, and finding a new and suitable residence overseas? Will you be given a temporary living allowance to cover such expenses as hotel or short-term apartment rental, per diem allowances for meals, vehicle rental and other costs you and your family will incur while seeking to set up your new life in the EC?
- Does the company have a formalized repatriation policy, and has it been adequately explained to you? Will the company cover all expenses related to your returning to the United States on the same level as when it sent you to Europe? Under what circumstances will the company not assume the expense of bringing you home?
- Should you leave the company while in Europe and take a job with another U.S. firm doing business there, will you be expected to pay back any of the relocation expenses that have been paid on your behalf? Or, what happens if you're fired? Will the company still pay to bring you back to the United States?
- Is your assignment to the EC of a defined length of time? Companies that are willing to provide pay and benefits for specified tours of duty may not continue those benefits for a permanent reassignment. (For one thing, it is more difficult to justify to local nationals.)
- What happens if you should marry someone from the host country and decide to stay there indefinitely?

Your new company, and its executives who have experience in the host country, should be of help in providing such information. But independent research by you will prove useful when making salary decisions. Contact the trade commission for the host country (addresses and phone numbers are in the appendices), but understand that the information they give out will position their country in its most favorable light. Also check with the EC Information Service: 2100 M St., N.W., Washington, DC 20037; (202) 862-9542.

You can also stay current on what is happening in the host country through the business pages of newspapers, business publications and specific studies published by financial services companies. A word of caution. Because there are wide disparities in pay scales among member states, salary is often a delicate issue with fellow employees. Handle any discussions of the subject with appropriate diplomacy.

No matter what agreement you come to with your new employer on a compensation package, make sure both parties clearly understand it to avoid conflicts in the future.

Section III
Elements of the Workforce

Eight
Achieving an Effective Workforce Mix

> I don't think that language or cultural differences have been a big problem for MCI, simply because of the way we staff the offices. When I fly to Europe, I deal with MCI employees who have lived in the country. They are French or Italian, for example, and they know not only the language but also the customs.
>
> Bert Roberts, President,
> MCI Communications Corporation,
> in an interview
> in the September 1990 issue of *Europe*

As U.S. companies continue to top the list of cross-border mergers and acquisitions in Europe, the integration of human resource elements into this expanding U.S. presence will make the difference between success and failure.

The *Wall Street Journal* reported:

> Responsibilities are rapidly shifting from national to regional or Pan-European units. At the same time, companies want to stay in touch with local tastes. So they need managers who can think big while understanding local nuances. Mastering that tricky mix often means hiring what some companies call Euro-managers: people skilled at dealing with a variety of cultures and at bringing a diverse team together. And that means hiring and promoting more foreigners.

The management of the Arthur Andersen Worldwide Organization, the giant international accounting firm, was aware of this need as far back as the 1950s. Recognizing that many of its large U.S. clients were looking abroad for growth, it began the process of opening its own overseas offices to better serve them.

Its staffing policy from the outset focused upon achieving the right workforce mix. Initially, these offices were staffed, for the most part, with executives from Andersen's U.S. operations—but only until the right nationals were identified, hired and trained in the company's culture and way of doing business. Once a consistency of operations had been established, control of each overseas office was placed firmly in the hands of local people.

This approach continues to form the core of Arthur Andersen's hiring and management philosophy. It stems from the obvious realization that local management best understands local customs, language and the business environment. But there's another dimension that has always been important to the firm. Managers drawn from local ranks have a strong sense of pride in their countries, and a desire to improve economic conditions in them. That additional and powerful motivation is difficult to achieve by using U.S. nationals overseas.

Arthur Andersen's long-standing commitment to the EC has spawned a recently published book, *The Arthur Andersen European Community Sourcebook*. It contains information on each EC member, and includes such topics as currency and exchange controls, population, taxation and the requisites to establishing a business. This extremely useful book also includes extensive lists, sorted by topic and industry, of EC contacts, European associations, publications and other public and private information sources.

As we've discussed in previous chapters, the most effective workforce for U.S. companies in Europe will come from three geographic sources: the host country, North America, and other countries, in this order.

There are advantages to staffing with employees from each of these key sectors; the principal challenge is to strike the most-effective balance. While it is impossible to categorize by geography alone, employees from each of these areas are likely to bring certain intrinsic benefits to the mix.

It must be presumed that locals know and understand their business terrain. They have grown up in it, can read its nuances and idiosyncrasies, have useful contacts and are familiar with entrenched bureaucracies. To draw a U.S. analogy, it would be reasonable to assume that someone who has spent the last 20 years on Wall Street understands the frenetic pace of New York's financial district, has a sense for what impact the rise and fall of business cycles has on the day-to-day attitudes on "The Street," knows how to find his or her way around the various exchanges, has a feel for what competitors are touting or trashing, and even understands that the executive secretary to the CFO of a certain investment banking firm is not someone to be trifled with.

U.S. companies must view their movement into Europe as a process of integration into its business environment. They should not come to "colonize," i.e., reserving senior management positions for U.S.-grown executives, while filling lower-level jobs exclusively with Europeans. Setting up a European operation cannot be viewed as taking a chunk of the United States and relocating it to Europe. From a human resources perspective, the process should be viewed as a marriage, not a conquest.

In addition, once the most effective mix for local management has been achieved, giving that management a sense of autonomy—or, perhaps better said, the authority to make decisions—is important. For managers to operate effectively, they cannot be under the rigid control of decision-makers thousands of miles away.

Obviously, certain major, broad-stroke decisions will continue to be made at regional or corporate headquarters as part of that carefully conceived and thoroughly debated business plan, but local management should be guaranteed some input into that planning process, as well as having day-to-day authority to make decisions.

Donald Nicholls, senior sales and marketing executive in Europe for Pall Corporation, joined that company 30 years ago after eight years as an instrument engineer in the United Kingdom with a large U.S. high-tech company. He left that job principally because the company tried to run everything from its headquarters in the United States.

"They had a huge rule book, written at corporate headquarters and distributed to its offices around the world," he says. "It was a totally centralized operation. They always sent Americans to run the operation in the United Kingdom who basically did not understand how to operate in Europe. After eight years, I could see that my future was not with this company."

During the three decades since Mr. Nicholls's departure, that same high-tech company has replaced 12 of its 13 top senior managers with non-U.S. nationals, including the chief executive for the entire European theater, who is French.

Aside from integrating key management positions in Europe, U.S. senior management back home should make a concerted effort to *listen* to what local European management is saying. In too many cases, when European management tries to educate absentee decision-makers about local conditions and important differences in methods of operation, it is perceived as an excuse for shortcomings, or an inability to meet objectives. Such advice from locals should be taken seriously.

Diplomacy and delicacy will always rate high when working with the local employee population. Without those prized traits, stereotypical perceptions of U.S. management style will be reinforced to the detriment of U.S. companies.

For the most part, U.S. companies are viewed as more aggressive than their European counterparts, with a shoot-from-the-hip management style. (I hasten to add that this is not always a negative perception, especially among the newer breed of European business executive who views the slower-paced style at home as a thing of the past, and who admires companies that are not afraid to take chances.)

Whether the U.S. style of doing business will work in the European environment depends, to a great extent, upon the quality of research that has been done on the local business climate of individual EC nations. For instance, the U.S. management style is more likely to be admired in Belgium or the Netherlands than in Germany or France.

U.S. companies doing business in Europe will also have to deal with the European perception of U.S. business as being short-term oriented, sometimes to the point of operating under what many Europeans view as an almost constant state of crisis management. The European business psyche is more comfortable with business plans that plot a course 10, or even 20, years out. But even they have their limits with forward-planning. They sarcastically term the Japanese management style that works from the ultimate in long-range planning, "The 99-Year Plan."

The U.S. business style isn't the only thing subject to misconceptions. A myth of sorts has developed about the "superiority" of some foreign workers, at least in comparison to the U.S. workforce. I was struck by a story in *USA Today* that commented on the German "super-worker," who by this point in history, has achieved a near-mythological stature. The newspaper concluded that the German worker does not necessarily work harder than his or her U.S. counterpart; the typical German work week is 37.5 hours. It is more a matter of Germany's greater emphasis on skills development.

The report went on:

> Apprenticeship, called the *Lehre* system, is an integral part of German culture. Almost 70 percent of the country's high school graduates enter a company for three years of in-house classes and hands-on training.

Those who can't enter an apprenticeship program because of poor grades might stay in the category of *Hilfsarbeiter* (helper) the rest of their lives. This emphasis on training has given Germany the ammunition to fight its war for premium goods, and has insulated it from competition from Taiwan, Mexico and other low-cost centers.

German workers might not necessarily be better than American workers, but we can obviously learn something from the German system.

To be sure, integrating locals into the workforce mix, which has been going on for decades, has increased in intensity as the EC moves towards its market objectives.

General Motors, for example, has been replacing its large U.S. management contingent with local nationals since the beginning of the 1980s. An Italian runs the biomedical facility for Pall Corporation in Italy. U.K. nationals run our Robert Half International offices in Great Britain; Belgians fill two of the three top management posts of our operation in Brussels (the other is held by an Englishman).

This approach is by no means exclusive to U.S.-based companies. Britain's giant Imperial Chemical Industries PLC now has a senior executive groups of which half are non-Britons, as opposed to an almost exclusively British-born senior executive cadre just 20 years ago.

The time spent nurturing a local employee contingent to help service U.S. business interests in the EC is time well spent. Chase Manhattan Bank, for example, has been in London for more than a century, and in other European countries for many years. The bank has nourished relationships there with its local workforce.

"We are not trying to be all things to all people," Tom Swayne, Chase's senior vice president and Europe corporate finance director, told *Europe* magazine. "It is a business that requires very good local execution capabilities and the flexibility to move one's resources around."

In Zagoria, Spain, General Motors has utilized locals to add a third shift to its assembly plant and, in the process, has created the first round-the-clock auto production operation in Europe, boosting its annual output at the plant to more than 350,000 vehicles.

While locals bring with them connections, as well as an understanding of the machinations of the local infrastructure, there can be negatives, too. Some locals may carry with them long-standing dependence on traditions of political influence in hiring and firing, and the subsequent dependence upon hand-outs and patronage.

In addition, consolidations, mergers, and acquisitions and international joint ventures often create unfamiliar bedfellows that can take some getting used to. For example, as a result of merger activity among major accounting firms during the past decade, those with European business bases have found themselves auditing the U.S. clients of their acquisition partners, and having to teach their foreign-born employees how these companies structure their finances.

The point is, of course, that as in all hiring, the development of an effective mix in a European operation must be approached with neither jaundiced eye, nor rose-colored glasses.

Let's look, then, at some of the more important considerations, and most likely concerns in achieving the best working mix of locals, third-country nationals, and U.S. nationals.

Locals

Surveys show that as many as three-quarters of the most productive American managers and department heads working overseas rate recruiting and training of local managers among their highest priorities. Succeeding at this is not easy. Concerns about loyalty, motivation, competence and training methods in unfamiliar territory predominate.

Like the best U.S.-Euro managers, the best local talent is at a premium. With the ascendency of the EC, improving economies in individual member states, and greater penetration of global markets by European-based companies, opportunities for locals at non-U.S. firms have increased dramatically.

These uniquely attractive opportunities, once the near-exclusive domain of American-based corporations, are now more widely available to top overseas talent. Other foreign-based corporations have exploited cracks in the armor of U.S. companies to attract the best talent. The market for top local candidates has shifted from buyer to seller.

The challenge, then, is to attract the best in local talent, effectively evaluate their potential to contribute, and have the machinery in place to secure their services. There are two ways to help achieve this; even better, a combination of the two:
- Hire a local human resources manager;
- Recruit via an international personnel placement firm.

Human resources manager—If a U.S. company is committed to European operations, and ongoing human resources needs are expected, hiring an on-the-scene human resources manager makes sense. This individual (or group) is potentially a U.S. company's most important overseas hire. For example, Colgate-Palmolive hired a Dane, with a reputation for his pan-European approach, to head its European human resources operation. Among other things, his assignment was to foster mobility among managers throughout the company's European division, including those based in the United States.

Such a human resources manager should understand local talent pools, have connections with sources of candidates and possess experience in local labor practices.

For this person to do the job effectively, he or she must have a clear understanding of what decisions can be made at the local level, and have the authority to make them. How this critical staff member is selected should embrace all the best job description and talent identification principles detailed in earlier sections on the hiring process.

Personnel placement firm—The reach of an in-house human resources operation can be significantly enhanced by securing the services of a solid, experienced personnel services firm with international scope. Choosing such a firm should be done with care.

There are a number of services that operate on a European (even worldwide) scale, and that can apply methods of proven success to finding outstanding talent for specific European positions. They have access to the best available candidates, and usually have long-standing relationships with these professionals.

The ideal combination is to locally have in place an experienced and skilled human resources department, augmented by a personnel services firm that has been established for many years, and that has the people and experience to ensure access to a deep pool of candidates. Beyond the general demands outlined earlier for recruiting U.S. nationals to staff Europe, what are the particular challenges in recruiting local talent?

Assessing a local candidate's ability to perform the tasks outlined in a job description is, of course, one such challenge. But there are others which have added significance where a foreign assignment is involved.

Motivation—Productivity will play a key role in the intensely competitive markets being predicted for Europe post-1992. American companies with the right group of local employees, each motivated to outperform the competition, will contribute substantially to success.

Loyalty—Loyalty, of course, must flow both ways. Desirable candidates deserve to know that the company is committed to a European presence, and will be there for them over the long haul.

Simultaneously, local candidates must be assured that they will be treated on equal footing with their U.S. colleagues, that decisions affecting careers and benefits will be evaluated on the merits and not on the basis of some invisible caste system.

Competence—This word takes on a different significance when hiring locals to staff U.S. EC operations. It is not a matter of the relative levels of competence ascribed to U.S. vs. foreign employees; it should be based more on an understanding of the systems under which employees from other countries have developed their skills. While the character of U.S. training, and the methods of operation within a particular sector of U.S. business will be familiar, European standards in these areas might not be so easily understood.

Aside from benchmarks developed through U.S. managers' experiences and native instincts, greater dependence will have to be placed on local screening procedures that reflect such an understanding.

A note: Europeans, like U.S. nationals, are sensitive to the information that is available on them, especially in this electronic age of computer data bases and high-tech telecommunications. More personal information has been available, on a less restricted basis, for Europeans than for U.S. nationals, and the EC is seeking to add additional restraints. The Commission recently proposed a directive to protect the privacy of individuals by shielding much of this personal information from unauthorized use. The directive, when passed, will make it illegal to transfer any type of personal data without the individual's consent.

Third-Country Nationals

Of the three elements in a European employee mix, it is most difficult to generalize about third-country nationals. They may possess many of the attributes locals bring, plus some additional advantages—as well as some potential disadvantages.

Third-country nationals, like locals, may have excellent business connections if they've worked in the local's country for an extended period of time. Citizens of EC member states are free to move about the Community in search of work, so third-country nationals can be expected to turn up anywhere.

While the tendency grows in the United States to regard Europe as a single market, there is still resistance to this concept at many levels of the European management structure. This is based, in part, upon mistrust among business people from different countries and regions, who for years, have disdained differences in language, culture and regulations between nations that currently comprise the EC or that might be added to it in the future.

Of course, there are outstanding European corporations that have already adapted to the single-market concept, but many companies are still markedly nationalistic, their executives, particularly upper management, home-country oriented.

Third-country nationals who have already demonstrated a willingness to travel (and, by extension, are less likely to suffer from such provincialism), could nicely fill a U.S. company's needs in this regard, perhaps even better than U.S. national or local talent.

Obviously, a principal benefit of hiring third-country nationals is the assistance and expertise they can provide concerning their countries of origin. This will be especially helpful to U.S. companies with operations that span a number of EC borders, and that depend upon these employees for their sales and marketing expertise.

When the migration of third-country nationals is from poorer member states to richer ones, it will generally benefit companies seeking help with their manufacturing, production and distribution operations. In this case, careful attention should be paid to EC and local labor laws not only to function legally, but to avoid the negative ramifications of gaining a reputation for exploitation.

U.S. Nationals

U.S.-born Euro-executives will succeed or fail, depending upon how well they interact with their foreign counterparts in decidedly unfamiliar surroundings. U.S. methods of operation, no matter how successful at home, must now conform to EC directives, host country rules and regulations and, in many cases, ingrained tradition.

While Europeans will be valuable to their U.S. counterparts in the useful local knowledge they provide, U.S. nationals can assist their European colleagues with knowledge of corporate operations and how U.S. business, in general, functions.

For example, while Pall Corporation, for the most part, tries to hire the best in local talent, it builds its filtration plants around the world as virtual carbon copies of its U.S. plants. Obviously, U.S. personnel are helpful in getting these operations up and running, and in training many of the local employees who make up the bulk of the staff.

When the synergy is right—when the various parts of the employee mix contribute to corporate objectives—Europe has been properly staffed and managed.

Every employee in the mix, European and U.S. national alike, will at times bring native biases into his or her business conduct. Ideally, the best methods of each will be adopted by all. In the worst cases, each will become intractable, and walls will go up. Senior U.S. management, charged with the responsibility of developing the best possible working conditions and methods of overseas operation, will have to pay particular attention to ensuring that the latter scenario does not develop. The best way to achieve this is by hiring right in the first place, and by establishing workable and sensible conditions under which a European staff can best function. A proper chemistry must be developed and nurtured. If it isn't there, more time will be spent solving personnel problems than concentrating on meeting corporate objectives.

There was a situation a few years ago in which a major hotel chain entering a foreign market for the first time was so dictatorial about company policy that it paid scant attention to the fact that locals had their own methods of operation developed over years of experience in the hospitality industry.

By the time the hotel opened, a distinctly antagonistic posture existed on the part of most lower-level employees—from chambermaids to bartenders. Daily operations were nightmarish. Business was off because employees who met the public on a daily basis were unhappy, and conveyed their displeasure to the hotel's guests. In the end, it was management that had to account for the significant loss in revenue.

The company was forced to fall back, to regroup and to spend an inordinate amount of time in confrontational meetings with labor unions, followed by employee motivation sessions. While all this enforced diplomacy had some positive effects, long-term damage already had been done. The company may never know the full extent.

Diplomacy in every aspect of personnel relations, especially for a company committed to operating in the international arena, is paramount. An impulse to restrict thinking and, by extension, policy decisions to chauvinistic U.S. thinking is to court potential failure for both the short and long term.

When the "American way of doing business" is imposed upon the European segment of a company's staff, it helps to bring as many of these employees as possible to the United States where the rationale behind decisions can best be demonstrated and explained. At the same time, rotation of European employees through headquarters gives them a sense of being an integral part of the company's international team, men and women on equal footing with their U.S. colleagues.

Expenses involved with employee motivation are often slashed when times get tough because they don't contribute to a company's short-term bottom line. This is understandable; reduced revenue means something has to go and, in most cases, it won't be those hard-core operations that keep the company going.

But when times are better, employees who have been ignored during the lean periods and, as a result, have suffered a decline in motivation, are not primed to take advantage of expanded opportunities.

Hiring "smart" is the key to effectively staffing any company, anywhere. But, if the good men and women who commit themselves and their careers to you lose even a modicum of their motivation through neglect, those same smart hires fail to live up to their potential. That's a bad situation when they're down the hall from you. It's considerably worse when they're thousands of miles away, and have been sent there at considerable company expense.

Tomorrow's global executives will emerge from many sources. Many will be U.S.-born employees whose rise into leadership positions will result, in part, by their experience in the European Community. But if U.S. companies, particularly those without extensive experience in Europe, fail to look to those other elements of their EC mix—locals, as well as third-country employees—for future leaders, a rich resource will have been squandered.

Advice to the New Employee

In your new job in Europe, you will be working as a member of an international mix. Your new employer will depend upon every element of that mix to develop the necessary chemistry to meet corporate objectives. The skills you bring to the EC will not be enough to achieve this. It will take those same less tangible assets you possess that impressed your employer in the first place—flexibility, diplomacy, tact, an appreciation of other cultures and people, wide-ranging interests and a willingness to learn and to grow as a person.

Your new working environment will demand all those things—and more. While the company's objectives may be laid out in its current business plan, *how* the company achieves those objectives will depend greatly upon how you interface with your fellow employees, be they from the host nation, or from other countries of the EC.

Your European counterparts will have things to teach you. Maintain an open mind. If you want to be heard seriously by them, you'll have to listen seriously to unfamiliar methodologies and ideas, and be willing to incorporate them into the overall way of doing business, even if it clashes with what you've learned from your domestic working experience. A truly successful performance by the European team you've joined will require drawing from the best of many approaches, many concepts, and many sources.

Evolving into a position of leadership with your peers will result only partially from imposing U.S. confidence and know-how. Those are important aspects of leadership, to be sure, but they aren't enough. Tomorrow's U.S. leaders in the EC will achieve that position by being able to pull together the disparate human resources of which they are a part. Commit yourself to achieving this and the future is boundless, as well as borderless.

Nine
Temporaries, Part-Timers and Para-Professionals

The competitive success of businesses in the Community in the last decade has been significantly dependent on the flexibility they have been able to show in responding to changing market conditions. Such flexibility has created new opportunities for existing employees to maximize their potential as well as new job opportunities. Temporary and part-time employees and those on fixed-duration contracts are at the heart of many companies' efforts to enhance their flexibility. It is vital that this type of employment continues to be allowed to flourish to safeguard the Community's position in world markets and to meet aspirations of employees themselves.

Union of Industrial and Employers'
Confederation of Europe

I've outlined in previous chapters what may be some of the more difficult generic European staffing problems which any U.S. company will face:

- A scarcity of potential Euro-candidates on both sides of the Atlantic;
- Declining workforce numbers in general among the developed nations of the world;
- The substantial premiums employers will have to pay for top-notch international talent;
- The ongoing need to maximize productivity from those candidates who are hired.

To deal with such concerns, our thinking needs to be expanded to include untraditional sources of talent, some of whose use and value has been misunderstood and, by extension, underutilized.

One example is temporary workers. For too long, they've been considered by some to be a source only of fill-in clerical or warehouse help. That concept is hopelessly outmoded. Temporary workers provide their valuable services in every strata of employment, including the professions.

At Robert Half International, we have a division called Accountemps which for many years, has provided professionals on a part-time basis in accounting, finance and information systems to corporations at all levels.

Many companies large and small—and the number is growing—have found the use of such highly trained and experienced people to be a practical remedy for what often begins as a finger-in-the-dike during crisis situations, then develops into an ongoing solution to one aspect of overall staffing needs.

Another example of an often neglected manpower resource is the use of permanent part-time employees, who can effectively expand a staff to cover tasks where full-time employees are not needed, and consequently aren't cost effective.

And, there are the growing ranks of para-professionals, who provide an excellent source of workers to handle lower-level tasks currently being performed by higher-paid professionals.

Let's take a look at some of these nontraditional solutions to staffing problems, particularly as they apply to Europe.

Temporary Workers

Developing local sources of temporary employees allows flexibility in staffing European operations. To illustrate, let's look at a hypothetical, but realistic situation.

A company is staffing its accounting department, and has decided it needs a highly skilled management-level accountant with a knowledge of local laws, regulations and reporting procedures to prepare detailed tax reports four times each fiscal year. The current small permanent staff cannot handle this additional burden without neglecting the demands of its other assignments. In the periods between these quarterly reports, the workload recedes to its routine level.

The traditional solution has been to hire that additional staff member with the expectation that, as European business expands, he or she will do work beyond those reports. Sometimes that happens; often it does not. The permanent staff might have been unnecessarily expanded, with a new annual salary to pay along with an expensive benefits package.

A better solution in this situation would be the use of temporary help, four times a year. The use of such temporary professional help allows management the flexibility of employing them only during the time they're needed; they become, in effect, a company's pad factor, allowing it to deal with increases and decreases in workload. And of course, the company's relieved of the cost of having to pay unessential staff during slow periods when they are being underutilized. This approach enables the company to better protect its core employees from layoffs or salary reductions in bad times.

Firms that have utilized a temporary workforce in this way have found it instills a confidence in permanent employees that they will be protected from market downturns. It is more difficult for a company staffed completely by permanent employees to offer the same level of assurance. Given the undesirability and difficulty of laying off employees, companies are beginning to plan more strategically.

"Strategic staffing" is an approach to hiring that takes into consideration the larger goals of a company and department. Traditionally, hiring managers with a position to fill have tried to find a new candidate with the exact skills as the prior employee. But the concept of "one job, one person" is gradually giving way to the broader strategy of determining the best way to accomplish an objective. And that strategy may involve hiring two junior permanent people and/or using one or two temporaries during peak work periods. In some cases, it may mean eliminating the position altogether.

Companies are now establishing the right mix of permanent and temporary employees to be better able to increase productivity. Their use of temporary workers generally falls into four categories:

- Buffers—including temporary help for the normal peaks and valleys of business;
- Critical technical skills—accessing people who can put into place new initiatives, such as establishing a new system, or creating an innovative technical procedure;
- Special project needs—for the completion of specific, well-defined tasks;
- Consultants—to provide counsel to permanent employees who then perform the task.

By determining which functions within a company lend themselves to flexible staffing, the company can avoid the expense of constant firings and rehirings, thus becoming "right-sized." For example, positions with fluctuating workloads, chronic overtime, or high turnover are probably ripe for more extensive utilization of temporary workers.

Right-sizing enables a firm to stay "lean and mean" without jeopardizing the ability to perform all the duties necessary to maintain quality performance.

The level of professional accounting skill applied to the quarterly reports project described earlier would be every bit as good as the accountant hired on a permanent basis. Accountants provided on a temporary basis to handle such assignments as our hypothetical quarterly reports would have a background in this type of work, be familiar with EC regulations and reporting procedures, understand the necessary forms and be able to work with minimal supervision.

Top personnel services agencies that provide qualified men and women on a temporary basis, especially those that specialize in certain professions, keep files that indicate strengths, areas of expertise and overall experience of the professionals they represent. This facilitates matching the professional with the job, rather than with the company, an increasingly valuable asset in this era of function-specific, as opposed to company-specific needs.

A further benefit of utilizing temporary employees is the opportunity it affords a company to take a close look at a professional, who might one day be the right person for a permanent assignment with the company.

Some surveys show that as many as 25 percent of temporary workers get permanent jobs through their temporary assignments. In this situation there is an agency conversion fee to be paid, but both company and employee will have had an opportunity to get to know each other. Hiring permanent staff in this manner gets rid of much of the guesswork. While some temporaries choose not to work full-time, others are between jobs and are seeking permanent work. If an opportunity develops to upgrade a temporary assignment to a permanent one, many of these professionals are inclined to take advantage of it because they too know the company and whether they'll be happy there.

Furthermore, when a member of permanent staff leaves, filling the position with a temporary worker allows a company to take a step back and evaluate whether the function really needs to be filled again on a full-time basis.

This kind of creative use of temporary employees is proving increasingly valuable in Europe, particularly for start-up operations where the size of departments needs to be kept lean until the business develops.

But care must be taken not to exploit such employees. While the use of specialized temporary help is becoming more of an institution within companies, temporary workers in most nations are excluded from most, if not all, the benefits available to permanent employees. But be aware that there has been international labor union pressure on the EC to include them.

Many argue that providing at least some benefits to temporary workers is a social or moral obligation. For example, our firm and others in the United States offer the option of voluntary enrollment in a health insurance plan for our temporaries. (While health insurance is not as critical an issue in the EC because of the existence of various national plans, it is an important benefit for many U.S. temporary workers.) The EC currently has a directive before the Council of Ministers concerning the employment of temporary professionals.

The EC's intentions with the directive are:

> To protect temporary and fixed contract workers by ensuring, as far as possible, that they enjoy the same rights as permanent employees; to protect the permanent work force by preventing the misuse of temporary labor and to ensure that only reputable agencies can engage in the supply of temporary workers.

The directive would impose the following restrictions:

- Temporary workers from an employment agency could be used only in connection with a temporary reduction in the workforce, or a temporary or exceptional increase in activity;
- Temporary workers could not be recruited or used to perform the duties of employees on strike; and
- Before having recourse to temporary workers, companies would have to communicate in writing pertinent information to employee representatives.

Our earlier, hypothetical example, would fall under the first provision. While temporary employment provides an excellent opportunity to get a look at possible permanent additions to staff, including promising young people, the EC is concerned with growing unemployment and underutilization of its youth, and will keep a close watch on cases where temporary employment is used in ways they deem exploitative.

A guide published by the EC's "European Foundation for the Improvement of Living and Working Conditions," designed to provide advice for youth who are leaving home to venture out into the workforce, put it this way:

Flexibility has become a key to describing changes in the nature of employment conditions, recruitment strategies and the broader reshaping of the sphere of work. Translated into everyday experience, this has meant the growth of more casual and insecure forms of employment, with part-time and fixed-term contracts replacing long-term, permanent jobs.

Many young people have not only had to contend with rising unemployment but also with a deterioration in the terms and conditions of work which is on offer. For those who do not experience unemployment on leaving school or college, the alternative may be a succession of casual jobs, on short-term contracts or on state training schemes.

During any given day, more than a million temporary workers are on assignment throughout the European Community. Many of these workers are not in a position to take any other form of employment, nor do they necessarily want it. Individual member states of the EC have become more aware of the important role the temporary workforce plays in their business environments, and are beginning to react to the need for them as an alternative solution to specific employment needs.

For example, France, which had traditionally discouraged the use of temporary help, has loosened restrictions in this area in recent years. As long as such workers, or employees on short-term contracts of less than 24 months, "are not used to fill permanent jobs linked to the normal activity of the firm, companies no longer need to justify the need for temporary contracts or to request authorization," according to *Delegation a l'Amenagement du Territoire et a l'Action Regionale* (DATAR), the French agency responsible for providing assistance to foreign investors. Consequently, the use of temporary workers by the end of 1989 was up about 25 percent over just five years earlier.

By the end of the 1980s, the United Kingdom, France, the Netherlands and Germany were the heaviest European users of temporary help, all behind the United States where the utilization of temporary workers has always been substantial. Finally, knowing where to draw upon a cadre of talented temporaries can assist in dealing with some of Europe's business traditions. As noted in Chapter Three, substantial segments of business and industry in some EC countries literally shut down for entire blocks of time in the summer, and sometimes around the winter holidays. If your company needs to carry on with more than a skeletal staff during those periods (if for no other reason than to interface with headquarters or regional offices in the United States), temporary workers can fill those gaps, too.

Permanent Part-Time Employees

Aside from their traditional use in lower-level, non-executive functions, part-time workers, like temporary workers, can play a role on the professional level.

Back to our accounting department example. While accountants working on a temporary basis have solved the problem of the spike in quarterly workload during tax reporting periods, there is still a good deal of repetitive work required on a day-to-day basis that is tying up a substantial portion of time for higher paid professional staff—$40-an-hour staff members doing $20-an-hour work.

The solution is part-time staff. The pool of talent in Europe available for this type of work is substantial, especially because many women with professional degrees and experience choose not to work full-time during their child-rearing years.

In the United Kingdom, for example, 45 percent of employed females work part-time; in Denmark, 42 percent. And recent polls show that as many as two-thirds of women outside the workforce would be interested in some form of part-time employment.

There is a similar situation with retirees, who wish to supplement their income with part-time assignments. Such talent pools can prove a tremendous resource if factored into overall staffing plans.

For example, Pall Corporation utilizes some of its top retired line supervisors in part-time staff positions to benefit from the wisdom they have gained during years in the company. Their input into formulating future plans is highly valued.

Also, in the age of personal computers and modems, part-timers are able to telecommute or perform much of the work at home. In the case of child-rearing mothers, such electronic networks work for both parties; a staffing problem is solved—at least minimized—and the company has a contented staff member. In addition, a valuable prospective full-time employee is being groomed should a part-timer elect to return to the workforce on a full-time basis.

At the other end of the experience spectrum are college students looking for real-life experience while attending school. Again, aside from helping to solve an important staffing problem, employing bright and ambitious college students on a part-time basis helps companies examine their work over an extended period of time.

Part-time help is often the most practical solution to job-specific assignments that do not require full-time staff. A few years ago, a flight kitchen at San Francisco International Airport won a contract for exotic, expensive food service on an airline from the Orient. The caterer determined that it could make only a minimal profit by hiring additional full-time staff, but could increase profits substantially with part-time help. These part-timers became the core of the caterer's expanded full-time team when the airline later expanded its U.S. service.

As with temporary help, it is important to play by both the rules of the host country and of the EC. Concern for possible inappropriate use of part-time employees has surfaced on both the labor and management sides of the EC labor relations table. Management is fearful that proposed guarantees of salary and benefits will reduce the cost-effectiveness of such labor, while labor sees part-timers as eroding the base of available full-time employment opportunities.

An EC directive, now before the Council of Ministers, seeks to codify the treatment of such employees. According to the EC:

> This proposed directive is intended to encourage part-time employment by assuring equitable social security and salary rights for part-time employees, and to prevent discrimination against these workers. Its provisions stipulate the conditions according to which employers in the EC may hire part-time workers. It is based on the following principles:
>
> - Equal rights between full/part-time workers;
> - Personal rights for part-timers regarding remuneration, holiday pay, layoffs and retirement pay;
> - Written agreements between employers and part-time employees;
> - Priority for employees wishing to change internally from part-time to full-time work and vice versa;
> - Accounting for part-timers in the total number of company employees.

Obviously, a company's commitment to permanent part-time employees will be greater than it is for temporary workers, but if their respective roles are clearly defined, each of these categories can be used effectively.

Para-Professionals

Para-professionals, like temporary help and part-timers, can free up more highly skilled professionals to address the more complicated functions they were hired to perform. In the case of many service industries, this practice can maximize the more expensive billable hours such professionals command from clients.

A $300-an-hour attorney spending time on the telephone tending to administrative protocol with the EC bureaucracy is not being used effectively. Even if such time were billable, it would still be unfair to the client to waste professional time in such a fashion. Such an assignment can be handled effectively by a paralegal, a fully trained and usually college-degreed professional.

Designing job descriptions and putting into place the supervisory apparatus for para-professionals, requires an allocation of time and resources. But such an investment is a one-time expense, with an ongoing payback in the cost-effective use of human resources.

However, in order to fully realize that payback, para-professionals must be utilized effectively. This often means a shift in thinking on the part of superiors, who are sometimes unwilling to trust to para-professionals certain tasks they feel can be properly performed only by fully credentialed staff.

For example, many hospitals now have nurse practitioners on staff. These people have the training and licensing to perform routine examinations, and to dispense certain pharmaceuticals. Utilizing them as a resource allows hospitals to maximize the skills—and revenue potential—of their physicians. Yet, many are still reluctant to fully utilize nurse practitioners.

In effect, staff managers should be educated about the potential of para-professionals, and encouraged to demonstrate confidence in their abilities.

Managers who bring para-professionals into their departments, but who have not utilized them before, should be particular not to isolate them into a kind of sub-category in the chain of command. Their needs will be not unlike those of more highly paid professionals. A career path for para-professionals should be in place, along with clearly defined incentives to properly motivate them if they are expected to make valuable contributions to a company's EC business objectives.

Advice to the Candidate

Temporary workers. Our offices in Europe report that it is all but impossible for an American national to find employment as a temporary worker there. Given the alien-worker rules, and the priority afforded locals and former full-time employees of firms, the chance of finding such work is slim.

Some U.S.-based companies with long-term operations in Europe may be able to offer opportunities for temporary work to the spouse or grown children of employees, but these opportunities will be rare, and should not be anticipated when budgeting for an upcoming family move to Europe.

Part-time employees. Ongoing, part-time work will be similarly difficult to find, except perhaps in those cases where the individual possesses rare skills or totally unique experiences that cannot be duplicated locally.

Contract workers. Fixed-contract work is a possibility, again where the employee has a unique skill. Start-up companies where specific tasks will be required on a one-time basis are most likely to seek this type of arrangement.

Para-professionals. Para-professionals will likely have as difficult a chore educating European employers as to what they can contribute, as they often have with companies in the United States.

Your best opportunities in Europe will be via employment in the United States with companies that have, or intend to have, operations in the EC. Once employed there—and having proven your worth—it might be possible to work from the inside to gain the European experience you wish to have.

For all people who do manage to find employment in the EC as temporary workers, part-time employees, or as para-professionals, the same rule applies. Approach your responsibilities with all the zeal and commitment as any member of the full-time permanent staff. By being on the scene, you enjoy an advantage not available to others seeking full-time jobs with the company. Many fine permanent jobs in Europe have resulted from temporary, or part-time assignments.

Ten
Women

> Women may have missed the industrial age, but they have already established themselves in the industries of the future.
> *Megatrends 2000*
> John Naisbitt &
> Patricia Aburdene

CEOs. Prime ministers. Cabinet secretaries. Chiefs of scientific research and high-tech manufacturing. Senior executives at financial services firms. Women have been turning up with increasing frequency in executive positions that would have seemed unlikely a few decades ago.

Resources for women abound.

There is an international organization—Women's World Banking—which helps women around the globe get started in business. It is funded by a number of governments, plus foundations and organizations from all over the world. Its president, Nancy Barry, a graduate of the Harvard Business School, told the *New York Times*, "The business we are in is to provide various products and services that increase the access by women to credit." The organization's scope is wide ranging and it operates in 40 countries.

The trend toward employment of women in a broad spectrum of jobs, including higher levels of management, is unmistakable, unstoppable and long overdue. The EC reports that during the past two decades, employment of women is up throughout the Community and that "this is due in particular to the steadily increasing number of women seeking work."

More than 55 percent of all women in EC member states between the ages of 14 and 59 have a job.

The EC has sought to institutionalize women's rights as an article of its "European Social Charter," which guarantees them equal pay for equal work, and assures equitable treatment in terms of access to job opportunities, social protection, education, vocational training and career-path opportunities.

However, the EC administration is quick to point out that directives alone will not suffice to alter ingrained attitudes about women in the workplace.

> Since the 1980s, an action program has been under way to promote equal opportunities for men and women in the Community," the administration states in one of its recent reports. "This program gives special weight to education for girls, combating unemployment among women and promoting vocational training. This concern for equality has led the Community to take a stance and, where necessary, support action in a number of areas.

However, the EC emphasized, "If the goals set are to be attained, the ideas and attitudes of many Community citizens will have to change."

While the EC's newly adopted "Charter for the Fundamental Social Rights of Workers" reinforced the need that "equal treatment for men and women must be assured," and "equal opportunities for men and women must be developed," it went even further, adding, "measures should also be developed enabling men and women to reconcile their occupational and family obligations."

Demographic realities will apply pressure in favor of women. The workforce in the industrialized world is growing at far slower rates than in the past, and estimates are that as much as two-thirds of the increase over the next decade will be women entering the workforce or returning to it after taking family leave.

Even with this kind of pressure, and the progress that results, there is much to be accomplished. Although women represent about 40 percent of the EC workforce, they account for more than half of its unemployment numbers. For the most part, conditions under which women work still differ from standards achieved by their male colleagues. Access to jobs traditionally held by men has been limited, and training is often restricted in these areas.

Prevailing national customs have provided a hurdle as well. The woman's traditional role in many EC countries as homemaker has limited her opportunities, to varying degrees, depending upon country or region.

In Spain, only about one-third of the female population in the 16–64 age group is part of the workforce.

On the other hand, the *Denmark Review* reports that the percentage of women in the Danish workforce has almost doubled over the past 30 years. It goes on to say:

> While there were 48 women for every 100 men in employment in 1958, the ratio had risen to 84 women for every 100 men by 1989, and women provided almost the entire increase of 650,000 jobs during the period. According to Danmarks Statistik, the national bureau of statistics, the Danish labor force numbered 2,899,000 at the end of 1989, comprising 1,571,000 men and 1,328,000 women. . . . The role of women as a significant force in the labor market has grown steadily over the period. While about half the women workers were part-time employees in the late 1970s, 63 percent of the female workforce were doing full-time work in 1989.

In Germany, on the other hand, women are restricted by provisions of a number of labor acts, with just over half of those in the 16–64 age group in the workforce. According to the Federal Office of Foreign Trade Information:

> Women are prohibited from working at certain jobs. They are also protected by maximum hours regulations and may not be employed at all between the hours of 8 p.m. and 6 a.m. The Maternity Act of 1968 protects pregnant women and nursing mothers by prohibiting both their employment in certain occupations as well as their discharge for maternity-related reasons. In particular the pregnant woman is not permitted to work neither six weeks before nor six months after the birth delivery. At the same time, she is entitled to further full wage payment.

The Netherlands' Foreign Information Service provides a frank assessment of the gender disparities in its country and the steps being taken to rectify them. While admitting that "the percentage of married women in employment in the Netherlands is still low compared to other countries," it points out that "diverse women's organizations in the Netherlands have worked for equal rights for women during the last 80 years."

Virtually all ministries in the Netherlands have committees concerned with women's rights, and the Foreign Information Service points to an ongoing commitment in this area:

> The central objective of equal rights policy in the medium term is to transform a society in which the division of roles between men and women is still largely institutionalized into a pluralist society where everyone has the opportunity of an independent existence, irrespective of sex or marital status and in which men and women have equal rights, opportunities, freedoms and responsibilities.

With more women of child-bearing age entering the workforce, the increasingly prevalent situation of pregnant professionals is causing some attitudinal issues.

The *Wall Street Journal* reported on cases where attitudes of co-workers ranged from a positive, "some men seem to warm up for the first time when an assertive colleague becomes pregnant," to a very negative, "resentment in the form of 'we think you should be doing more.'"

Where disparities in treatment of men and women do exist, women have legal recourse via EC directives.

During a period of more than a decade since such anti-discrimination directives were introduced into EC law, they have been utilized infrequently because women must show that male counterparts are earning more for work of equal value. This burden of proof has discouraged many cases. However, where cases *have* been litigated, they have resulted in changes.

The United Kingdom, in particular, has been directly impacted by EC rulings. A decision by the EC Court of Justice in the case of *Hedlen Marshall v. Southampton Health Authority* held that it was discriminatory to mandate different retirement ages for men and women.

Earlier, the Court of Justice had ruled that the U.K.'s Equal Pay Act of 1970 was not in compliance with Commission directives. It mandated equality provisions concerning work for which equal value is attributed in all aspects and conditions of remuneration.

The U.K.'s original Equal Pay Act mandated equal pay based upon job evaluations. If none existed, the employer could structure pay scales accordingly. The government, therefore, had to introduce regulations that permitted job comparisons even where no formal evaluations had been instituted.

The EC has also placed emphasis on member states making provisions for child care during business hours, and has formulated programs for parental leave. Efforts have been underway for years to standardize maternity leave throughout the EC, with proposals zeroing in on a 14-week/80 percent pay minimum standard and an anticipatory scaling up of maternity leave salary to 100 percent of base pay.

Within some individual states, however, the present directive would be a non-issue, since they are at, or above, the standard.

Luxembourg, Greece, Germany and Belgium have 14 weeks or more at 100 percent pay.

Denmark, on the other hand, has 28 weeks at 90 percent pay for blue-collar workers, but 28 weeks at just 50 percent pay for white-collar.

For Ireland and Spain, the pay rate would have to be scaled up from 70 and 75 percent respectively.

The result of the body of EC legislation, and the growing number of court rulings, has placed a greater burden on employers to critically examine their pay and benefits structures to ensure they are in compliance, not only with local law, but with EC directives. Beyond the court costs involved in litigating discrimination cases, an employer with a large number of lower paid female employees, who loses such a case stands to suffer a substantial loss in potential damages—not to mention the image problem resulting from negative publicity.

With education and skill levels rising among women around the world, most European companies are realizing that finding top talent is hard enough without limiting the field through sex discrimination.

Simple arithmetic demonstrates that the inclusion of skilled females in the workforce should double the pool of potential employees. In an industrialized world facing declining birthrates, that alone should be incentive to consider women for all levels of employment.

Advice to the Candidate

Sex discrimination is illegal throughout the European Community. Still, there is always the potential of *de facto* discrimination. Customs, traditions and social histories dating back thousands of years may create situations of preference for a male candidate, especially when the hiring decision is made by someone from "the old school."

The best way to approach a job search for a position in the EC is to assume that you will be judged on your merits as a candidate—expect no more than a male counterpart—and demand no less.

Section IV
Fitting In

Eleven
Keeping European Staff Motivated

Treat people as if they were what they ought to be and you help them to become what they are capable of being.

Johann von Goethe

Once a European operation is up and running, how well it performs will depend, to a great extent, upon the ongoing motivation of its working team. Motivation levels, in turn, may depend upon whether the staff feels it is part of a well-integrated organization.

"There is a tremendous failure rate of American executives overseas," the *Wall Street Journal* reported in a story on the results of a study conducted by the Columbia University Business School. The report went on to cite "employers for failing to train managers or provide them and their families with the support needed to cope with challenges abroad."

On the other hand, the same edition of the *Journal* ran a separate piece that reported "overseas exposure is desirable, if not indispensable, many firms say."

This dichotomy points out how important it is not to lose sight of the needs of the individual while simultaneously plotting the course of the company. Expatriate employees need a clear understanding of their career-path opportunities before leaving on an overseas assignment. At the same time, a company must reinforce for its employees their importance in the long-term picture. Constant contact and communication is the key.

There will also be important concerns for family and other non-work related social matters while overseas. The matter of the socio-cultural fit outside the business community is dealt with in the next chapter.

In order to alleviate such concerns about adhering to unfamiliar procedures, try working with colleagues from different business backgrounds and cultures. This will help reconcile the potentially disturbing out-of-sight/out-of-mind syndrome. Clearly defined goals need to be set for overseas employees. An effective use of in-house media is necessary to assure the maintenance of ongoing personal contact between foreign-based staffers and their American-based counterparts, and to continually reinforce the importance of European contributions to the company's business objectives.

From a motivational perspective, therefore, let's examine in greater detail the following areas:

- Sharing the business plan
- Defining career opportunities
- Utilizing in-house media
- Maintaining personal contact
- Reinforcing European contributions
- Motivating locals and third-country nationals

Sharing the Business Plan

Since Euro-executives will not enjoy the same level and frequency of contact with the home corporate offices as U.S.-based executives do, understanding the company's business plan provides important guidelines for what is expected of them, and establishes benchmarks for how progress will be measured.

Few would dispute the importance of such plans to the senior management of a European operation. However, *every* management staff member should be provided with an outline of the plan and what is required of all departments.

For new American ventures in the EC, objectives will undoubtedly include start-up goals, a timetable for the construction, the hiring of staff and the launching of operations.

Operational objectives might include defined levels of productivity, inventory and product flow to meet anticipated levels of sales activity.

Marketing objectives might include achieving realistic penetration of traditional demographic markets, the creation of exploratory market niches and clearly delineated expectations of market share growth.

While these objectives and countless others are shaped by a company's management at its headquarters in the United States, the input of European-based employees will help define the goals in real terms.

But, besides assuring that resulting plans make practical sense, there's another advantage to inviting EC operations staff to contribute to shaping company objectives. When employees, particularly those far from headquarters, have a hand in planning, they consequently understand what the company hopes to accomplish and what their expected role is to help turn plans into profit. When employees know where they're going, and how they're expected to get there, morale invariably rises. Company directives written thousands of miles away, instead of being viewed as alien missives, become constructive additions to the overall business plan. All business plans need to be reviewed and revised regularly to reflect the changing realities of overseas operations. Once again, to make such changes without consulting the men and women who implement them and, where the EC is concerned, understand local demands and problems, is to ignore valuable contributions. The result? Less effective revisions of plans, and employees who begin to feel they are cut off from decision making and, by extension, are less important than those closest to the corporate headquarters.

Defining Career Opportunities

Understanding what career opportunities are available to Euro-employees should begin early in the hiring process. From that point forward—and throughout the careers of the best performers—self-actualization, and the potential to move up through various levels of the corporate pyramid, will be key motivational elements, as they've always been.

As noted in earlier chapters, there will be great demand for Euro-executives, with the consequent competition for their services. If top executives with international experience understand the career path opportunities available to them within their chosen company, that company will have a better chance of hiring them, retaining them, and benefitting from the sizable investment that has been made in their careers. We all tend to work harder and with greater enthusiasm when the goals are clearly defined and the rewards for reaching those goals are visible and reachable.

Utilizing In-House Media

The out-of-sight/out-of-mind syndrome is a factor to consider for employees in field operations for any company with a far-flung empire. The natural perception is that when promotion opportunities or choice assignments open up, those closest to the seats of power will receive first crack at them or, at the very least, have the inside track by virtue of being able to cultivate important intra-company relationships at the higher echelons.

With those on a European staff, this problem can be exaggerated. If an EC operation is small, it can sometimes end up being shuffled into the background by higher priorities back home. A European operation that received a disproportionate share of corporate attention during its inauguration may feel it has become the forgotten stepchild as the corporation returns its attention to its traditional business sectors in the United States.

While it would be difficult, if not imprudent, to maintain a disproportionately high level of attention towards European operations over an extended period of time, a structure should be in place to ensure that staff members working there do not feel that their labors are going unnoticed.

To ensure that such an isolationist attitude does not develop requires ongoing lines of communication, some traditional and others that are more sophisticated.

Employee communications—The various forms of employee communications play an important motivational role for all companies. Like a community newspaper, they keep employees at every level and in every location apprised of the names and faces that are making news throughout the corporate community. For European staffers, they play a dual role:

- They provide information about what others are doing at headquarters and in other field locations.
- They provide a format to showcase, for the rest of the system, how the European offices are doing, with the attendant positive motivational results.

The most common form of employee communication, the one with which most of us in business are familiar, is the employee publication. The best of these play a crucial role in both disseminating information to employees, and as a motivational tool.

Information contained in them should always be highly credible. While it is important to inform employees of key decisions and the thinking behind them, blatant propaganda and thinly disguised sales pitches, tend to have a negative effect over time.

Aside from the traditional monthly employee newspaper, there are other communications media that may prove particularly valuable for geographically distant operations:

- *Management newsletter*—Published monthly, or in some cases even weekly, these four-to-eight page newsletters provide useful information for management on such topics as major corporate decisions, company or industry trends and forecasts, labor negotiations and the company's position on relevant topics. Without regular access to high-level staff officers, this medium can provide important insight otherwise unavailable to those in the field.
- *Video reports and messages*—With the widespread acceptance and use of the video medium, companies have a valuable communications and motivational tool at their disposal. For European offices, this medium offers the ability for high-level executives to deliver important company position statements, with all the attendant visual aids—charts, graphs and video footage—which help make those decisions comprehensible even when not delivered in person. This is not only an important way to stay in touch, but it reinforces the importance that the company places upon keeping EC employees informed about decisions and events coming out of corporate headquarters.

For particularly important occasions, a teleconferencing hook-up with corporate stations around the world creates a sense of urgency and of wanting to share critical information at the moment it is being disseminated. The use of teleconferencing historically has had a significant motivational impact upon all employees, especially those in distant locations.

- *Daily "newswire"*—Some companies have found it useful to maintain regular daily contact with overseas operations. This is particularly true for such entities as airlines, oil companies and financial service firms who do business in a volatile international business environment. While the departments most closely involved with fluctuating prices, rates, supplies or inventories usually stay current as a matter of course, staffers who are not part of this pipeline may find a daily wrap-up useful in the conduct of their business. Such a newswire is easily disseminated by fax machine. It should have a recognizable format, and be transmitted at or near the same time each day, not only to differentiate from routine memos, but so that employees on the receiving end come to anticipate its arrival. (A regular publication schedule for weekly and monthly newsletters should also be established and adhered to.)

The more extensive the media network is, the easier to take proactive stances and reactive positions, especially in situations where timing is crucial.

Maintaining Personal Contact

Along with an effective use of employee communications media, there will always be a need for face-to-face meetings. The two should complement each other. Ongoing personal contact between foreign-based staffers and their U.S.-based counterparts is important, not only as a good business practice but for motivational reasons.

It's been my experience that while personal contact with employees serving overseas is often undertaken by top levels of management, it is sometimes lacking further down the chain of command where it is needed as much.

Contact between domestic and foreign line managers (as frequent as is economically feasible) allows for diverse geographical sectors to hear first hand about new developments, operating techniques and improvements instituted by colleagues functioning elsewhere. At the same time, such contact allows managers at home to develop a *feel* for how things are going in Europe, rather than relying only upon written reports and telephone exchanges. In addition, it fosters beneficial camaraderie with European counterparts that can prove to be highly motivational for expatriate U.S. managers working in Europe. And it affords overseas employees the opportunity to have their specific questions answered, which is not always possible with employee media.

Visits by U.S. management to EC operations should not take on the character of an inspection, and should be kept separate from regular corporate avenues for auditing and quality assurance purposes. If visits by American management always assume a critical posture, they will be awaited with dread rather than being anticipated positively.

Of course, corporate traffic doesn't have to be limited to eastbound movements across the Atlantic, nor should it be. Return visits by European staff should be factored into their overseas assignments to allow them to feel that their personal input is valued by the company and that their voices are being heard and heeded.

Reinforcement of European Contributions

Accomplishments of EC offices should be the subject of official company recognition whenever possible, and particularly noteworthy achievements the subject of official visits by high-level corporate executives. Simultaneously, stories in the employee media should spotlight these achievements.

Awards and incentive programs might include special categories for Europe, and company-wide annual conferences used to spotlight the resulting awards. European staffers should be utilized as speakers at these conferences.

As we all know, office politics can be a particular problem in overseas operations where the lines of communications are thinned by distance. Left unchecked, rumor mills can be detrimental to all aspects of a company's operations. A company's commitment to a sustaining program of communications with its EC employees is the best deterrent against them. At the very least, regular dispatches from headquarters that have achieved a reputation for veracity can help mitigate negative rumors.

Motivating Locals and Third-Country Nationals

As I've indicated in previous chapters, particular care must be taken to maintain equal treatment and recognition of local employees and third-country nationals. Because some U.S. companies, particularly those new to doing business in the European Community, will not have much experience dealing with these two European employee groups, there may be a tendency to view all programs from the perspective of what benefits the U.S. employees. This should be avoided, of course, or a we vs. they division can develop among the European staff.

All levels of recognition should be administered equally, including trips, vocational training, seminars, conferences and long tours of duty back to the home office. To the local national, the opportunity to interface directly with key departments and important personnel at corporate headquarters may be as important, perhaps even more so, as it is for U.S. employees abroad.

Arthur Andersen Worldwide Organization, whose hiring and management philosophy abroad has always stressed the utilization of local employees, is equally committed to fully involving them in all aspects of the company. All foreign professionals receive identical training at the company's training centers, at annual worldwide partners' meetings, and at other company-wide forums. The Big Six accounting firm's culture and management strategies are shared with all. And, all partners, foreign and American, share income on a global basis. As Arthur Andersen's Chief Executive Lawrence A. Weinbach has stated, "We decided from the beginning of our international expansion that we would not be just an American company. Everyone is to be treated equally, regardless of geographic area."

. . .

More than likely, many of the tools and programs needed to properly communicate with overseas staff are already in place. It may be necessary, however, when staffing Europe, to expand headquarters' staff with people experienced in employee communications in order to make sure this vital aspect of doing business overseas is properly addressed and carried out.

A sense of corporate isolation can have a lethal effect on an overseas operation. The greater the emphasis is on keeping overseas staff motivated, the greater the likelihood of success. A highly motivated staff reinforces a company's reputation for being a good place to work which, of course, impacts favorably on all staffing programs over the long term.

Advice to the New Employee

Stay current on the company. It is important that you not only pay close attention to your direct responsibilities, but that you use every avenue available to keep abreast of the company as a whole. Employees who are content to "do my job," and who leave it at that, usually find their success potentials limited. You are not only part of a division or office, but you contribute to, and are impacted by, the company's overall operations and goals.

Be a regular reader, listener and viewer of employee media. Information on major corporate decisions, personnel changes, new developments and techniques, major technical breakthroughs and important discoveries should be part of your ongoing information gathering process.

But steer clear of rumor mills and office politics. Interpersonal relationships will be important to the way you fit into your new company, as well as to your psychological well-being. Becoming embroiled in internecine squabbles will be detrimental to your ability to function effectively and could ultimately damage your future with the firm.

Maintain personal contact. To the extent that it is appropriate, keep the lines open to colleagues and counterparts in other offices throughout the system, particularly those in regional and headquarters' operations.

This is not to suggest violations of the chain of command. Rather it is a way to keep current, to learn and to develop a network of people with similar goals and experiences. Developing and maintaining such a network takes effort and time. It's well worth it.

Contribute to employee media. Keep the corporation abreast of what you and your department are doing. Stories in the employee media will let people—including decision makers who will determine your future—know what is happening in your area of responsibility, and the activities with which you're involved that contribute to the company. I have met many people, including managers and executives, who do not take advantage of this opportunity to put their best faces forward and at the same time advance corporate objectives. Employee media is extremely important vehicles for transmitting useful information and for sharing ideas. When your department has done something that may prove beneficial to other departments, you owe it to them to share it.

I've often heard department heads ask why other departments get so much exposure in the company's employee publication.

The answer is simple. They contribute to it.

Twelve
The Family Fit

[T]he failure rate of Americans abroad—due to family stress, bad performance, or unhappiness with the foreign posting—ranges from 30 percent to 50 percent. Nancy Adler, a professor on the faculty of management at McGill University, [says], "unfortunately, we [the United States] are the leader in the world in expatriate failure."

Steven Dryden
Europe magazine, September 1990

As we saw in Chapter Seven, dealing with the family of an employee, or prospective employee, can be one of the most vexing problems in staffing Europe. Helping to relocate a family, including finding suitable housing and schooling for the children, can prove daunting, so much so that some firms—quietly, of course—opt for hiring the single candidate for overseas assignments rather than confront those issues ("quietly" because they are probably violating anti-discrimination laws).

There is little question that not having to deal with a spouse and children can save countless hours of a company's staff time, to say nothing of many thousands of dollars in logistical costs. But, relying on recruitment of single candidates is obviously not the solution, even if it were possible to circumvent the law. Family issues must be confronted if quality candidates are to be found and hired.

Overcoming the logistics of relocating a family to Europe deals with only the front end of the problem. If the spouse and/or children are not happy once they're settled in the host country, the new employee will be discontented, and that will probably mean a disruption of performance.

Good sense dictates that a company can be saved considerable woe if it is prepared to offer sound advice, as well as tangible assistance to help employees' families comfortably settle in. Here are some of the concerns that must be addressed.

The Working Spouse

In a world in which two-income families have become the norm, it is difficult for many couples to do without a spouse's wages once they have created a lifestyle dependent upon both incomes.

Relocation of a family to Europe is not likely to change the desire or the need for a second income. The cost of living in much of Europe is as high as it is in the United States. In some sectors—housing in particular—more money often buys less value. Also, most couples will want to partake of the social and cultural benefits Europe has to offer, and that cannot be easily done with a decrease in family income.

"Working spouses remain a problem," the *Wall Street Journal* reported. "Many governments *won't let them* pursue careers." [Emphasis added.]

What does this mean?

Once again, we are confronted with the alien-worker problem.

While the transfer of an employee may be viewed as intra-company (which addresses the problem of obtaining appropriate work permits), a spouse will not, in most cases, be in the same situation. A husband and wife are not considered a tandem by most host countries' labor regulators, and placement of a spouse will not be easy.

What can a company do to help?

Involvement can range from no involvement at all, to playing an active role in trying to match a spouse with an appropriate overseas position. This necessitates a considerable expenditure of time and effort, which may not be fiscally possible for most companies. But, every company can demonstrate sincere concern, and can offer some form of tangible help by putting employees' spouses in touch with a personnel services firm experienced in placing candidates overseas.

To put the process in perspective, let me share some of the knowledge we've gained through our years of doing business in Europe, and offer some tips on how best to utilize the services of an international placement firm.

Start as early as possible. As soon as a candidate has accepted a European assignment, ascertain if he or she will need help finding overseas employment for a working spouse. If so, point out that the company is interested in helping achieve this, but that effort is likely to take a good deal of time. By informing both candidate and spouse that the process has begun, it allows them to face the relocation with greater confidence and enthusiasm.

Once actively seeking an employment opportunity overseas, the spouse becomes a candidate in his or her own right, subject to the same screening and interviewing procedures that take place at any efficient placement firm. The candidate's needs and wants must be determined, as well as what attributes are present that are potentially marketable in the targeted European destination.

The originating office in the United States will then contact its appropriate European office, which will try to match the candidate's background and skills with open job orders, and to begin surveying clients that historically have sought people with backgrounds similar to that of the candidate.

So far, the process is not unlike what would occur in the placement of any candidate relocating between two areas of the United States. But now, the processes diverge.

A good international placement firm additionally should provide guidance in how candidates can be positioned to satisfy local alien-worker requirements—to position the candidate as unique, and thus not easily duplicated locally.

For example, our Robert Half International offices in Brussels have had success with spouses who have worked in the U.S. offices of large international accounting firms, most of which maintain offices in the Belgian capital. Because they are familiar with the demanding audit reporting requirements and government regulations in the United States, they offer a uniquely marketable skill to clients of these accounting firms—a skill not in great supply among the local population.

In one example, a top executive at a giant American multinational food firm was reassigned to Brussels. Our office there was able to place her husband, who had a marketable background in banking. Because the spouse worked in a technical area of banking which was relatively new to Brussels, there was not a cadre of locals possessing this skill from which to draw. It would have been considerably more difficult to place someone on the commercial, or public-contact side of banking, since those positions could easily be filled by employees from the local population.

Even when government regulations can be satisfied, there is the difficulty of convincing a prospective EC employer to hire candidates whose tenure will be limited by a spouse's tour of duty. A spouse's special knowledge and skills may help mitigate this.

Of course, there is the possibility of finding a position for a spouse at the firm where the husband or wife will be working in the EC. This, however, is fraught with potential problems. By hiring a spouse, a tandem has been created, increasing the probability of having to fill two jobs when one or the other leaves.

My advice is to avoid this situation. While it may solve a sticky problem on the front end, it is likely to result in ongoing problems throughout a company's relationship with both employees.

Company-sponsored briefings, seminars and workshops for spouses looking to continue working while in Europe not only prove helpful to these people, but are an indication to both employee and spouse that the company cares. Even if job opportunities are limited, especially in the beginning, briefings and seminars can help explore alternative solutions such as freelance possibilities; university courses to enhance academic levels, or to acquire additional training; volunteer or charity work; and the rare temporary or part-time assignment. All this effort is worth it for any company with a commitment to succeeding in the EC. A once-active, once-happy, once-*working* spouse can become very *un*happy if forced into an extended period of inactivity. Bored and unhappy, he or she can seriously impair their working spouse's ability to perform effectively.

If the difficulties of creating family fit situations resurrects thoughts of a singles-only solution, bear in mind that the cultural acclimation of singles is not without its own set of problems. Recent studies have shown that singles can feel particularly isolated on an overseas assignment. They do not have a second set of ears to listen to their problems, or to share in their triumphs. Too, many find the local social situation difficult to navigate for a foreigner.

In any case, the family fit situation should be addressed in a systematic manner as part of any company's overall plan for effectively staffing Europe.

The Socio-Cultural Fit

In 1990, Robert Half International began to survey attitudes in the European workplace vs. those in the United States.

The first survey asked 200 executives at firms in the United Kingdom and the United States to compare the pace with which jobs are completed. More than half the executives on both sides of the Atlantic felt that the work pace in the United States was faster.

To quote Dr. Laurence Peter, "America is a country that doesn't know where it is going but it is determined to set a speed record getting there."

Such an attitude runs counter to the work habits of many Europeans. We believe that while those in the United States honor the newest and fastest way to get the job done, other cultures base their approach more on a respect for tradition, thoroughness and stability.

U.S. companies planning to open offices overseas should understand the differences in work patterns, values and customs of the host country if they expect to be successful in building an effective staff. They also need to understand that those employees transplanted to Europe from the United States will have to deal, on a daily basis, with cultural differences. These will effect not only time spent on the job, but will follow them into their new social setting.

Nor can American companies be able to view Europe as some kind of homogeneous entity, despite the promise of a European community. The differences between the 12 member states make it difficult to generalize, despite EC directives conceived to create common ground.

For example, people in the 12 member states speak from eight to 13 languages, depending upon who's counting, and what local dialects are considered true languages.

There are also geographic anomalies. Greece, an EC member state, sits far to the southeast with no border touching any fellow member state; while Austria and Switzerland, two non-members, ring the northern border of Italy and separate it from Germany and the Benelux countries (Belgium, the Netherlands and Luxembourg).

Vastly improved communications between nations, developed during the past quarter century, have created a large and growing area of common understanding. The increased acceptance of English as the universal language has helped bridge gaps, since many European children take English as a second language. (Incidentally, the widespread use of English in continental Europe appears motivated by business considerations more than anything cultural; the continent's two biggest business partners—the United States and Japan—conduct most of their international business in English.)

In order to succeed, however, U.S. expatriates should be briefed on what to expect in their host EC countries, and how they are expected to act once they get there. While most companies provide formal orientation programs for new employees, I'm sometimes dismayed at how many consider orientation for an overseas assignment as involving little more than a cassette tape of the local language and the most current edition of a travel guide.

An inability to deal with social and cultural differences will have a negative impact upon a new employee's performance and may result in an abandonment of the assignment. Given that a company can spend at least three times an employee's base salary to relocate, accommodate (e.g., housing and other allowances) and repatriate that person in an overseas assignment, the stakes are high, and an inability to sustain an employee's motivation and productivity levels in Europe will prove even more costly.

Unfortunately, some studies show that one out of four U.S. citizens who relocate to overseas assignments return home before the assignment is completed, in most instances because the employee, spouse or another family member cannot adapt to the alien culture. To try to ensure against this, some companies have gone so far as to limit their job searches to individuals who have proven track records in foreign assignments, i.e., they've already demonstrated an ability to manage an offshore operation and have families that have acclimated to a previous overseas posting. That approach, however, seriously limits what is already a shallow candidate pool.

Faced with the high cost of relocating employees and their families and the unacceptable failure rates as evidenced by studies, many of the best run companies have taken steps to assure a smoother adaptation by its overseas employees.

For example, Motorola, who has a heavy commitment in Europe, surveyed its overseas employees to determine if the company was preparing them adequately for their assignments. The answer was no. Furthermore, the survey determined that once in place in Europe, there was little aid available in setting up an in-country residence, locating schooling for the children and introducing new employees into social circles. Motorola made adjustments.

"We're trying to go to a holistic approach," Motorola's director of international personnel administration, James McCarthy, told the *Chicago Tribune*. "It just makes eminently good sense."

Motorola's program now includes language training, a course in cultural preparedness, a pre-assignment visit abroad and in-country assistance for its overseas employees.

The concept of in-country mentors is particularly helpful, not only in assisting new employees to adjust to new surroundings, but also to help redirect any latent chauvinistic attitudes.

As those who travel abroad know, there is often a perception that U.S. citizens have a form of tunnel vision, ignoring the protocols of other cultures and acting as though they never left home.

An additional European view of U.S. citizens is that we do not read other cultures well. They see our actions as part of our overall impatience and drive to get things done, often without stopping to consider possible ramifications.

While most societies are tolerant of an outsider's ignorance of their ways—at least initially—most are justifiably intolerant of an attitude that disparages the host's traditions, and that attempts to change them to accommodate the foreigner's culture. Local patience grows short when outsiders continually misread what is expected of them and conduct themselves inappropriately.

For example, while German business people may tend to expect myriad minute details in a transaction, no matter how painfully recapitulated, the French business person will sometimes grow impatient, even feeling at times insulted with explanations covering information already explained.

Again, while stereotypes may fail the test of specific situations, a company's overseas representatives must make it their business to learn the local mindset and to adjust accordingly.

Fortunately, it has been my experience that whatever arrogant tendencies U.S. citizens may have had in the past they are being tempered by having to deal with other cultures. To assure that staff members continue to advance an improving perception of U.S. nationals abroad, it will pay to launch a pre-assignment, preemptive strike on Europe-bound employees' cultural prejudices, and to provide the wherewithal for them to acclimate.

Language Training

There is little question that English has become the language of preference with the international business community, and many people at the professional level in Europe speak that language. However, fluency in the local language will be of inestimable benefit to any American employee's ability to effectively conduct business there.

Words, as we all know, can convey different meanings. Even though these differences may appear subtle, they can make a large difference in interpretation.

Take the word "diplomatic." To a U.S. national, being diplomatic generally means listening to the other person's side of the story and adjusting accordingly. But, to the British, it means being diplomatic about something you are going to do anyway but, via diplomacy, intend to cover your tracks.

Or take my personal experience with the word "quite." In memos I once sent to our United Kingdom offices, I praised the managers for doing "quite a nice job" on a particular project. To some British staff, however, "quite" has a different connotation than the one it carries here in the United States, the one I intended to get across. It is viewed as being somewhat sarcastic to the British, in effect damning with faint praise.

To make matters worse, I had inadvertently left the word "quite" out of one of the memos, so it appeared as if that particular manager was the only one I had actually meant to praise. Outside the workplace, a staff member's ability to speak the local language will more than likely make the difference between a cultural fit, and an inability to acclimate.

Employees will gain respect from co-workers and social contacts if they speak the language. If nothing else, it indicates a respect for the host country's way of life and traditions. It also indicates that the foreigner—a U.S. national in this case—has taken the time, and made the effort to try to understand what is important to the people who live in the local community.

Making fluency in a foreign language a requirement for employment when recruiting in the United States is, however, counterproductive. Losing the best candidates because they don't speak the language is unnecessarily rigid, given all the language training opportunities available today. It makes more sense to plan for such training of successful candidates, than to have language requirements encumber the hiring process.

On the other hand, there are candidates who will be resistant to language training or have little aptitude for it. The interviewing process should include questions about the candidate's attitudes about and experience with foreign language study to help determine if this will be a problem.

Given the importance of spouses acclimating to the European environment, a company should also consider language training for them. The spouse's fluency will assist a family's assimilation overseas; money spent here will reap considerable, albeit subtle rewards over the course of an employee's EC assignment.

If positions in Europe are to be filled on a regular basis, companies should inquire about an ongoing arrangement with one of many language schools or institutes. There may be economies of scale and discounts for guaranteed levels of traffic. Furthermore, some organizations offer customized training to meet specific requirements, such as where demanding schedules and logistical problems make attending pre-scheduled classes impossible.

The French Institute/Alliance Francaise (FI/AF) in New York offers a full complement of language training in French—from beginner to very advanced courses—as well as exposure to a wide range of French cultural experiences.

Programs can be personalized to include beginner's courses, remedial instruction, crash courses for emergency overseas assignments or advanced studies in business French. The latter includes training in the language as it is spoken in business meetings, conferences and in one-on-one conversations. It examines business idiom and speech patterns—the type of training that is difficult to get in ordinary language training, but that proves vital in the conduct of business. Subject areas cover such complex areas as economic planning, budgeting, trade agreements, banking and other financial services transactions, all covered within group settings and including written exams.

FI/AF will also arrange instruction conducted on the company's own premises for groups, or even individual training for the business person who is too busy to leave the desk.

To prepare a business person and family for the cultural aspects of a French assignment, FI/AF screens French movies and television programs, conducts slide presentations on French art and literature, has a full-fledged performing arts center and an extensive library including books, newspapers and magazines.

You can inquire about such language and cultural training for France, as well as other countries, through the information office of the appropriate consulate in major American cities.

Cross-Cultural Training

Understanding the language of the host country is a step in the right direction, but only one.

Before relocating to Europe, staff members should be given a briefing about the host country. What is it that they should understand about customs, traditions and about the working environment? Subject matter should range from the mundane concerns of everyday life, to the important aspects of conducting business. Where and how do I do my food shopping? How do I get a telephone hooked up? Are there facilities for a disabled child? What about emergency medical services? What are the nuances of business etiquette?

If an about-to-be expatriate family is sent on an orientation visit to Europe, try to allow them an experience as close as possible to the environment in which they will be living. Specifically, arrange for them to stay as guests with an expatriate couple, rather than staying in expensive hotels and dining in gourmet restaurants. After all, they will not be spending three or four years living in a four-star resort.

If you have the benefit of repatriated staffers who have worked overseas, they will be an excellent resource here and should be utilized to best effect. They will be able to offer, on a first-hand basis, information about job requirements and social differences.

Continental Bank, for example, has an offshore support group for outbound and returning employees that has been in existence for more than 30 years.

There are also outside organizations that conduct cross-cultural training.

One such organization, International Orientation Resources (IOR), headquartered in the Chicago area, was itself born out of the problems its founder, Noel Kreicker, had in adjusting to her former husband's assignment as an attorney representing a U.S. firm in South America. Despite the fact that both she and her husband had served in the Peace Corps in the Philippines, a relocation to Colombia with their three small children proved difficult. There was no preparation of any substance prior to their departure, and no in-country assistance once they arrived. Nor had there been advice stateside on housing, schools, even language training, let alone where to turn for mundane, everyday services.

When Kreicker returned to the Chicago area, she hatched a plan to start a company providing the very kinds of services she felt would have smoothed her own family's relocation. In the early 1980s, Kraft, Inc. hired her firm for an assignment and her company was on its way.

Today, IOR clients run the corporate alphabet from Abbott Laboratories to Zimmer Corporation. IOR conducts cross-cultural training in cities across North America and has in-country representation in many of Europe's principal cities. Along with the social aspects of cross-cultural training, there are also intercultural business briefings and even assistance for dual-career families.

"Families about to move overseas need to begin by identifying how the move will impact the dynamics of the family," Kreicker says. "If you do research in the area of cross-cultural transition for expatriate families, you'll find again and again that it is the spouse who most often does not adjust and therefore becomes the source of failure. That was certainly true for me in Bogota."

Kreicker feels that this is an unfair burden for a spouse. She says the source of the problem is that the couple often does not clearly understand the alterations the move may exact upon their family. To help rectify this, the family—together and individually—needs to assess what they expect of the move, then to set goals. The process is hard-nosed. In some cases, couples—and even the employee—will determine that the move is not really the correct one at that particular time, which could drop the company back to square one and another round of recruiting. But that's better than finding out things did not work out *after* relocation.

It is important that the entire family buy into the move before it actually takes place, and that they view it as a joint decision. That cannot happen unless they address their individual concerns and make determinations about their individual needs.

IOR, which has on-site representatives to help with housing, schools and other settling-in concerns, recommends that any U.S. company staffing a European operation attempt to have someone on the scene responsible for such matters.

The Children

A principal concern for all families moving far away from home is the education and welfare of their children. In terms of schooling, the two most pressing questions are usually:

- Will there be English-language education available?
- Will the school be similar in structure and curriculum to those back home, thereby allowing for ease of reintegration into the U.S. system after returning to the United States?

The U.S. Department of State's Office of Overseas Schools provides a listing of educational institutions around the world which "demonstrate American educational philosophy and practice." Aside from this broad-based criterion, schools vary from country to country in terms of individual approach, but most offer instruction from kindergarten through high school. A listing of a number of such schools is provided in the appendices.

A growing problem involves the relative lack of U.S. schools outside larger European cities. This, coupled with the fact that businesses realize greater incentives for locating new operations away from traditional business and industrial centers, may result in more expatriates having to send their children away to boarding schools.

Also, expatriate employees who move about a great deal during their European tour may have problems as their children get older and need the stability of several years in the same school along with the requisite courses and skills necessary to gain entry into U.S. colleges and universities.

This problem, of course, is not limited to U.S. expatriates. Ideas about how to solve it may vary.

For example, while British executives are often willing to send their children to boarding schools back home, many continental Europeans want their entire families close by. Some even accept unaccompanied assignments, living in residences provided by the company during the work week, then spending quality time with their family on weekends and holidays.

One of the benefits of an overseas assignment is the opportunity for interaction with people of another culture, adults and children alike.

For example, Donald Linehan, manager of marketing communications services, Europe, for 3M Corporation, coached in the Brussels Basketball League while he was on assignment in Belgium. He told a meeting of the Association of National Advertisers in 1989:

> I'm working with eight 12-year-olds from five different countries who love basketball and are learning to work together as a team. These kids are playing basketball in local gymnasiums all across Europe. At age 12, they have a competitive spirit and a world view that could be the envy of you and me, and the companies we work for. In their outlook, clothing, music, tastes and aspirations, these kids share more in common with their competitors in the gyms of Europe than they necessarily share with the folks at home who happen to be their countrymen. In this sense, the unification of Europe, and the world, is upon us, with or without target dates like 1992 and directives from the EC.

Tomorrow's crop of Euro-executives may well be found on the basketball courts of Belgium.

Professional Organizations

American companies that encourage their overseas employees to affiliate with as many professional organizations as appropriate do themselves and their people considerable good. Such associations provide excellent opportunities for networking and new business development, while simultaneously fostering relationships that can help their employees integrate into the broader social environment.

Of course, there are familiar faces that seem to accompany U.S. citizens wherever they go. CNN is now available in all countries of the EC—providing a link with home through a well-known and comfortable source when spirits are low.

Advice to New Employee

In terms of actually moving and settling into your new EC position, here are some important considerations:

Make an orientation visit. If your company offers such a program, take advantage of it. If it allows for your spouse and children to accompany you, bring them.

Make the most of such a visit. Try to experience working and living conditions that best approximate what you will encounter once you relocate. Talk to as many expatriate colleagues as possible whose situations parallel what yours will be.

If possible, stay for a period of time with a co-worker and family to avoid being misled about the quality of life represented by luxury hotels and fancy restaurants.

Arrange an orientation tour of those areas in and around the workplace where you may be living. Get a sense of what accommodations will be like, what facilities and services are available and where people tend to socialize.

Visit the school your children will attend. Talk to the administrators and teachers, and encourage your children to interact with other children.

Understand that your spouse and/or children may react negatively to their future surroundings. Pay close attention to their concerns and try to address them, both during your visit and after returning home.

Learn the language. Take full advantage of whatever language training is provided by the company. If none is offered, make your own arrangements to learn the language, even if it means an unreimbursed expenditure on your part. Encourage your spouse and children to take advantage of any language-training opportunities, too. While their interest in doing this will not be as urgent as yours is, convince them that their ability to communicate abroad will enhance their enjoyment of the European experience.

Be enthusiastic about cross-cultural training. There is a growing appreciation for the importance of cross-cultural training for executives relocating to foreign assignments. A key reason for the failure to adapt to a foreign assignment is an inability to understand and to acclimate to the foreign culture. Cross-cultural training better prepares you for that challenge.

The best of these programs are geared to accommodate the needs of the employee and family. They deal with the important psychological issues that may grow into problems, particularly with family members. These include the feeling of loss at leaving family and friends behind for an extended period of time, and the general sense of isolation in a foreign country. Experts that conduct these programs can help your family confront these issues and others, and to develop their own commitment to the move. A happy and enthusiastic relocation to the EC on the part of employee and family alike results in your family's happiness, increases the potential for success and enhanced performance by the U.S. employee in Europe. Everyone wins.

Do your homework. The fact that you are receiving in-house assistance from the company does not relieve you of the responsibility for independent outside study. Continue to read everything of importance on the business, economic, political and social environment of the country to which you'll be moving. A measure of whether you will succeed in your new assignment—from both business and social perspectives—will depend upon your willingness to take command of your own future.

Use your personal network. If you are a member of professional, social, cultural, charitable or religious organizations, seek out their counterparts in your host country. These organizations may become effective sources of information, provide excellent business contacts and allow for the building of new social relationships—all of which will benefit you and your family.

Making a successful transition to an assignment in the European

Community demands of us all the same disciplines as does any challenge. Success never just happens. We make success happen, and this holds true when preparing to experience a major shift in our lives. If we're motivated to make an overseas assignment work, we have an obligation to motivate others who will share with us the risks and rewards. We owe it to ourselves—and to them—to make use of every available resource. In some cases, these resources will be presented to us by our employer. In most cases (and even when an employer makes it "easy"), it will take additional and individual initiative to round out our preparations.

If we fail in our European opportunity, it's easy to blame "them," the way they do business, to claim they don't understand how it's done. But like every situation where the reasons for failure are put upon others, it doesn't hold up. To point to family as a reason for our failure is to unfairly shift the burden of responsibility. An employee and family moves to Europe as an entity. If everyone comprising that entity has honestly made every effort to prepare for the experience, the chances are good that it will work.

If, after you've made every attempt to get ready for Europe, there still exist grave doubts about whether it will work, consider bowing out. For you and your family, failing thousands of miles from home is an unpleasant contemplation. For the company that has invested considerable time and money in moving you there, your failure sets it back in many ways.

A job with a U.S. company in the European Community represents a valuable experience for everyone involved. If it's for you and your family, run, don't walk to find the opportunity.

If it isn't right for everyone, leave it for others and continue building your career closer to home where the opportunities, while perhaps not as "glamorous," are substantial nonetheless.

Thirteen
Retrofit: Protecting Your Investment

With the rapid geographic expansion of multinational corporations, the day of overseas assignments being filled from the same pool of career expatriates is passing into history. As discussed in previous chapters, finding, hiring, holding and maximizing the effectiveness of Euro-executives will involve intensive recruiting, followed by careful nurturing of candidates, and then paying considerable attention to the concerns employees may have about serving a company in the far reaches of the realm.

For many, if not most, one of the greatest concerns of U.S. citizens on assignment in Europe is repatriation.

As we discussed in Chapter Eleven, the so-called exile syndrome may seriously concern candidates for overseas positions as early as during the initial hiring process and, if not addressed properly, could become manifest while on assignment in Europe. If it does, it will adversely affect job performance, which in turn, has the potential for serious negative impact on a company's objectives.

While many companies with overseas commitments invest considerable time and energy in the early stages of an executive's foreign assignment, there is sometimes a slackening of such attention once employees are well into their jobs. In some cases, this unfortunate situation becomes even more pronounced as employees' overseas tours begin to wind down.

Employees embarking on European assignments will want to be assured that they will be kept apprised of developments at corporate headquarters back home; that they will be given serious consideration concerning opportunities arising anywhere in the company's global system while they serve in Europe; and that repatriation will be handled smoothly and efficiently, and with their best interests in mind.

Overseas employees who perceive that they are out of the corporate loop sometimes have a tendency to become preoccupied with their individual well-being to the detriment of their assignments. Veteran overseas managers become aware of this when employees begin to skirt the in-country chain of command to maintain frequent, direct contact with U.S.-based regional or central headquarters; and when they start favoring only those projects that have the potential for short-term, highly visible positive results, perhaps to the detriment of the long-term goals of the company.

These men and women begin to feel a particularly strong need to maintain direct contact with their U.S. superiors, which of course, creates problems with the local chain of command. When this happens, the inevitable result is to push U.S.-born and foreign-born employees into separate camps, seriously polarizing any European management team.

Some companies have preferred to address this need for an umbilical attachment to U.S. headquarters by institutionalizing "godfather" relationships. Regular contact with an overseas employee is maintained through a designated contemporary at the home or regional office. While this approach can be helpful, it should be the result of a planned program, rather than allowed to develop haphazardly and thus create the perception that it violates the reporting relationships in Europe. In all cases, this so-called godfather should not be a person in the expatriate employee's direct chain of command, and should be merely an information source on matters of interest to the overseas employee such as career advancement possibilities, promotion opportunities and new job openings.

A survey conducted jointly by the Department of Management of Boise State University and the School of Business Administration at the University of Washington found that lack of communication about specific job opportunities was the area most absent for those on overseas assignments. The survey was conducted among employees in a range of businesses, the majority of whom held executive, managerial, technical or professional positions. While most found they had far greater autonomy and more authority in their overseas assignment than they did when working closer to headquarters in the United States, they also had apprehensions about the nature of the job they would receive when they were repatriated.

Failure to deal with such repatriation concerns of Euro-executives may well result in having invested the time, money and corporate energy to create top-notch, internationally savvy executives, only to see them bolt to the competition, which of course, has invested none of the above in these people.

"What I am seeing more and more of in the last few years is an increase in the repatriation failure rate," says Noel Kreicker of International Orientation Resources. "After the company makes that costly investment, the employee returns to headquarters and is gone within a year. Some experts say this failure rate is running as high as 40 or 50 percent."

If the actual repatriation failure rate even approaches those estimates, it clearly indicates that Euro-employees are not being given every opportunity to reintegrate into the corporate structure, and that not enough corporations are committed to creating those opportunities for their employees returning from overseas.

All repatriation programs should take into account certain perceptions, real or imagined, that Euro-executives might have regarding their return, and companies should be prepared to deal with them. Among the most significant can be a very real concern about the organizational transition into the corporate hierarchy.

For example, employees may react negatively to a reduction in autonomy that they enjoyed in the European assignment, with the attendant perception that there has been a reduction in status. These same employees may also feel (and it may well be the case) that they have less influence on policies, programs, plans and business decisions than was the case in the smaller universe of their overseas assignments.

Also, there may be a growing sense of negativism on the part of repatriated employees if they feel the experiences and/or new skills acquired in Europe are not being applied effectively in their new stateside positions. The initial days of their new domestic job may appear unexciting and uninspiring when compared to what was perhaps a more glamorous European setting.

A difficult reintegration often results when employees returning from assignments in the EC believe that they have been repatriated as a matter only of corporate convenience and without a real function, and that they have been placed in some kind of holding tank while awaiting a legitimate position. Even if they've completed an assignment of defined duration, this belief can develop, and every effort should be made to prevent it. Plans to reintegrate returning employees where they can be the most useful to the company should be made well in advance of repatriation.

The university survey cited above listed among the chief concerns of repatriated employees:

- *A less attractive, overall financial package than the one enjoyed while overseas.* While employees have been working in Europe, they may have come to expect, even rely upon, such additional benefits as housing allowances, help with educational expenses and tax assistance.
- *A reduction in fringe benefits and perks.* Long vacations, company-subsidized trips home and multiple similar perks could also have become part of the Euro-employee's lifestyle.
- *Sticker shock at the price of having to buy back into the housing market.* The cost of buying a new home may bear little resemblance to what employees sold their houses for when they departed the United States. Re-entering the housing market at the level at which employees enjoyed before heading for Europe may not be possible in a market that has inflated during their absence.
- *A lack of company programs for interim financial assistance.* Employees may look for assistance from the company in getting themselves re-established back home, including such financial help as bridge loans that may have been a part of the package when they were hired for Europe.
- *A lack of financial planning assistance.* Employees may also need sound advice, particularly within the modern, more fluid environments that exist in virtually all aspects of financial planning—from insurance to pension plans.

The returning employee's reintegration into the specific workplace environment may also involve a readjustment on a day-to-day basis. The *National Business Employment Weekly* reported:

> Instead of feeling like they are home, new returnees often feel distant. Their experience with another culture has changed them. While they

were away, the U.S. changed, too. Even their workplace may be different, especially if significant political or personnel changes took place during their absence. The fact that few people recognize this phenomenon makes readjustment even harder. Friends and co-workers don't realize that the transferee needs help. They may be uninterested in the executive's stories about life abroad. They may even treat him or her with envy, wariness or hostility. If nothing is done to help, the manager's work or career will likely suffer.

Counseling will help counteract this situation, along with more frequent meetings between employees and supervisors and co-workers in an effort to gain their understanding. Another principal area of concern is socio-cultural re-entry. The departure from the overseas assignment will involve giving up relationships or, at the very least, place vast distances between friendships. Unlike leaving the United States, with the implied understanding that the family will one day return, the departure from an overseas residence, and a circle of friendships developed there, carries no such implication that employees and their families will *ever* return.

Returning to the United States from an EC assignment will not, of course, require the language training and socio-cultural briefings that were necessary to prepare employees and their families to move to Europe. But there is a need for an organized series of briefings on what to expect once home, and how best to adjust to major changes that have occurred while employees have been gone.

Getting the Most Out of Your Investment

In dealing with the return of a Euro-employee, companies should be committed to re-examining what they'd sought to gain from an employee's assignment overseas, and to evaluate the relative success or failure of the experience.

Repatriation of staff members is really less a process of bringing employees home, and more a matter of moving them into new assignments from which the company can derive the greatest benefit while, simultaneously, enabling employees to feel that they are utilizing their skills and experiences to the best advantage. While there are obviously logistical considerations involved in moving employees about any company's system, staff members should nonetheless have a sense that this movement is well-orchestrated and planned, and that they are not skipping any beats along their career paths.

With the right kind of understanding between company and staff, and the mutual respect that is bound to result, each is best positioned to make the most of the Euro-employee's experience, and to assure a continuing and mutually beneficial relationship.

Advice to the Returning Employee

Returning home from an interesting and challenging EC assignment will, even under the best of circumstances, involve adjustments. Some will be readily apparent and can be dealt with directly. Others will be more subtle, and proportionately more difficult. In any event, it will behoove you to take the time to prepare yourself for the return by seeking out and taking advantage of any counseling or reorientation services offered by your company. You may not feel you need such help, but it obviously can't hurt to expose yourself to these services. Not only might you benefit from them, you can make a contribution to them by adding your experiences and insight.

Understand the differences in compensation. Your domestic pay and benefits package will probably have gaps compared to what you've become used to while serving in Europe. Gone will be allowances for housing and education, subsidized trips back home and tax assistance; in short, any of the special benefits and perks that were the specific result of your European adventure.

On the other hand, your tour of duty in Europe may well have advanced your standing with the company, and the return from a successful EC assignment may be the result of a promotion, with its inherent additional compensation and sense of achievement.

Prepare for the return. While you and your family may have returned home periodically, you should make a special trip back prior to a permanent return to the United States. Use this trip specifically to reorient yourself with what you will need to accomplish when you return. Don't view this trip as a vacation. Instead, use it to house hunt, check out local schools and to soak up the changes, large and small, that have occurred. Even if you are returning to the area from which you left, time has passed and things will have changed.

Reintegrate diplomatically. Just as you approached your early days on the job in the EC, return home with the same demonstration of sensitivity and diplomacy. Share your experiences and newly acquired knowledge humbly and with a sense of sharing, rather than flaunting it. Your working relationships back in the United States will necessitate the same give and take as they did in Europe.

If you find yourself having problems reintegrating with your new co-workers, discuss the situation openly and honestly with them and your supervisors. One of the objectives of going overseas was to develop a more well-rounded employee, not to create a person without a country. The proper attitude, along with a little time, will ease the reintegration.

Employ your new knowledge. Your experience in the European Community will have provided you with an invaluable opportunity to grow professionally. You return as part of a relatively small group of U.S. men and women who proved themselves capable of handling the rigors and challenges of working overseas, and who now can claim hands-on experience. That places a premium on your services. Obviously, you now have a great deal to offer other companies in search of people like you. It was the company that sent you to the EC, however, that gave you this opportunity—and paid for it. You owe, I believe, a heightened sense of allegiance to that company in order to help it continue with its future success in the EC and in other areas of the world.

Naturally, each of us has a parallel obligation to our own careers. If the opportunities you seek simply are not available with your present company, you will look outside it, and rightly so. But that determination should be seriously and thoughtfully made. Too often, we look elsewhere for career opportunities when the best of all are right where we are.

Welcome back!

Epilogue
The Other Europes

Fourteen
Non-EC Europe

> The underlying arrangement now envisioned is that EFTA will conform to the basic EC internal market principles of removing barriers to the free flow of goods, services, people and capital (and the major supporting EC bodies of law in areas such as competition policy and product standards) in return for a formal, institutionalized role in EC decision making. The sticking point is whether EFTA's role in this process would be truly participatory or merely advisory.
>
> Europe 1992
> International Division
> U.S. Chamber of Commerce

The EC, of course, does not comprise all Europe. Three other "Europes" exist outside its embrace: the nations of Western Europe that form the EFTA economic alliance; the former Communist-dominated nations of Eastern Europe; and most recently, the republics that once were part of the Soviet Union, but that now seek new configuration.

Within these three spheres, there is considerable economic life and business opportunity. Each also presents its own set of unique challenges.

Some nations from the first two of these geopolitical zones have expressed interest in joining the EC, but the membership list is closed until after the 1992 single-market unification. In the interim, however, the nations of these groups will go about their businesses. A brief overview might be helpful in rounding out the picture of Europe. (The dissolution of the Soviet Union is too recent to warrant speculation as to how its breakaway republics might interface with the EC.)

EFTA

In response to the formation of the European Community in 1957, the non-EC nations of Western Europe formed, at a 1960 convention in Stockholm, the European Free Trade Association (EFTA). The original signatories were Austria, Denmark, Norway, Portugal, Sweden, Switzerland and the United Kingdom. Denmark, Portugal and the United Kingdom have since left and joined the EC, while Finland, Liechtenstein and Iceland have since joined EFTA.

The formation of the two economic blocs represented, to a degree, fundamental differences in how the member states viewed the future of Europe.

EC members, for the most part, saw Europe as a supranational union of states, tied to each other politically as well as economically.

EFTA members saw the future as more of a loose confederation of states, maintaining their traditional political independence and trade affiliations with other key sectors of the world.

Nonetheless, each organization has become the other's most significant trading partner. More than a quarter of the EC's exports are to EFTA member states (greater than exports to either the United States or Japan); while almost two-thirds of EFTA exports are destined for EC nations.

Although the EC's economic clout has overpowered that of EFTA during the intervening decades since each was founded, the remaining six members of EFTA boast economies that are among the strongest in Europe (their per capita income of $19,000 is significantly higher than the EC's), and there have been important steps wedding the two organizations in key trade areas.

A series of agreements in the early to mid-1970s were instrumental in bringing the two organizations closer together. In the Luxembourg Declaration of 1984, the member states of the EC and EFTA declared their intentions of creating a European Economic Space (EES), which would allow nations of both to participate in certain aspects of the single market concept. Since then, progress has been made in eliminating technical barriers; reducing border formalities; facilitating the movement of capital; and cooperating on educational programs, environmental issues, company law, consumer protection and matters of social policy.

EC Commission President Jacques Delors even proposed what he called a "concentric circles" concept that would include the EC, EFTA and the nations emerging from the former Communist-dominated Eastern Bloc. (The breakup of the Soviet Union had not occurred when Delors made his proposal.)

The movement towards cooperation through concepts such as the EES has had a high degree of general acceptance, but not without reservations on both sides.

One of the principal concerns involves the poorer members of the EC, who have expressed concerns about EFTA members gaining what they view as a free ride by virtue of preferential access to the benefits of the EC's internal market, with little if any, of the financial burdens of membership. Some of the more conservative members of the British Parliament have even dubbed EFTA the EFRA—"European Free Ride Association."

From the opposing perspective, some EFTA countries are hesitant to take on the additional financial burdens of membership, which they do not see as benefitting their countries. The *Wall Street Journal* reported:

> Rich non-EC countries, meanwhile, aren't all that thrilled with the [regional development] fund. Switzerland and Sweden, for example, want closer ties to the European Community and even contemplate joining one day. But so far they have hesitated, partly because joining means shelling out huge contributions to the regional development fund, which wouldn't much help them.

Key members of the EC Commission have pointed out to EFTA members, however, that there is a significant difference between becoming part of an EES holding action, and becoming full-fledged participants in the internal market, with privileges available only to EC member states.

There are other concerns among EFTA members, as well. Dr. Kurt Meier, chairman of Worort, a Swiss employers' association, pointed out the following in an interview in the Swiss publication, *SHZ:*

> The EES contains the elements of a broader-based and better-structured partnership between the countries of the EC and EFTA. The aim is to create conditions in which something like a true single common European market would be achieved, offering maximum greatest possible freedom in the exchange of merchandise, services and capital, as well as for personal travel across frontiers.

He stopped short, however, of proposing a complete assimilation:

> [C]ommon and reciprocal EES rulings should be strictly limited to the regulation of frontier-crossing border traffic. Matters that are not connected with the prevention of discrimination in such traffic should be dealt with in the EC in accordance with the provisions of the Single European Market agreement—and in EFTA countries in conformity with national legislation. This would obviate EFTA interference in matters of internal concern to the EC.

Irrespective of concerns, areas of collaboration increased. The EC asked for ongoing "association relationships" with EFTA and some form of "structured partnership," with areas of common decision making. While a good deal of the language was hedged with terms such as "mutual right to be consulted" and "constructive co-determination," both organizations appeared dedicated to the achievement of some form of common economic zone.

Some EFTA members are forthright about the importance of the EC to their economies. Austria, for example, in an "Information and Service" brochure targeted at companies seeking to establish businesses in its country, reported:

> The EC as a commercial partner is of greater importance than the EFTA. Whereas the percentage of trade with EFTA countries was not more than 11 percent, trade with EC countries amounted to approximately two-thirds of the Austrian foreign trade... Austria succeeded in increasing exports to the EC countries to 63 percent.

While the result may be the eventual elimination of EFTA—Austria has applied for membership in the European Community; Finland and Norway have expressed intentions of joining—EFTA's demise is hardly a foregone conclusion. For example, the demands of membership in the EC run counter to national policy in Switzerland, particularly with the prospect of the EC assuming greater political significance as the Cold War disappears. According to a report published by the Union Bank of Switzerland's Department of Economic Research:

> On the basis of an inquiring into the effects that joining the EC would have on government policy and Switzerland's neutrality, the Federal Council has adopted a clear position by ruling out EC membership as an objective of Swiss integration policy in the present circumstances.

The report cited such potential problem areas as: Switzerland's long history of neutrality; conflicts with the country's parliamentary powers, form of direct democracy and federalist system; and its autonomy in trade, agricultural and labor market policies.

The report admits the potential for a serious downside to non-membership, the most significant being the country's exclusion from the EC's decision-making processes by which it is significantly affected. It concluded:

> Switzerland's future position in the process of European integration will depend to a high degree on the general willingness of the EC to cooperate with third countries.

The negotiations between EFTA and the EC reached a climax in October of 1991, when each side put aside years of bickering and concluded an agreement they called the European Economic Area, which in effect created a link between the two trading blocs in one "common market." While the two sides ostensibly would keep their individual identities, the agreement would abolish barriers to products, services and the movement of people.

The agreement would have to be ratified by each of the EFTA countries, including Switzerland, where a referendum would be required to approve this assault on more than 700 years of fierce independence. Meanwhile, the individual members of EFTA which had already indicated an interest in joining the EC said they still intended to pursue membership, although the EC has said it will not entertain new applications until after December 31, 1992.

Meanwhile, the potential is there for even more dramatic business growth among EFTA member states, especially those non-EC members who are in "bridge" positions between the Community and the emerging Eastern Bloc.

Finland, for example, has been an economic bridge between Western Europe and the former Soviet Union since the end of World War II. The country has a barter arrangement with the USSR, at least in its former state, from which it imports almost all of its oil, and a significant amount of business has always been conducted between the two nations. While Finnish officials have indicated they intend to apply for membership in the EC before the end of the decade, until then, and perhaps even after, there may be opportunities for U.S. companies to conduct business with

Finland and, by extension, with the independent republics that have emerged from the Soviet Union's demise.

The choice of an EFTA country location as opposed to—or in addition to—an EC location is a business decision best addressed by a careful assessment of opportunity vs. risk. The potential for business development is certainly there. Incentives, similar to those available in EC member states, are also available to foreign investors seeking to establish operations in EFTA. Modern transportation and communications systems exist within them at levels equal to, and sometimes greater than, those of EC nations. Similarly, there is considerable red tape that must be dealt with when relocating employees, obtaining work permits and settling them into their new environments.

The inclusion of EFTA in a company's business perspective enlarges the European market to more than 380 million people—from what once was an EC market universe of 324 million—and to billions more in potential sales. There are myriad areas of business overlap between the two federations, each offering an opportunity to extend market penetration beyond the borders of the country where a company chooses to locate.

But no matter what the differences between theaters of operation, good, solid recruiting and hiring principles apply universally. Achieving an optimum employee mix will be as important in Switzerland as it is in the Netherlands. Acclimatizing of employees to life in Sweden will not be markedly different from the socio-cultural adjustments that must be made for staff members relocating to France.

The Eastern Bloc

The breakup in the homogeneity that once characterized the Communist Eastern Bloc in Europe brought about a sense of exhilaration. The culturally rich states of Eastern Europe would once again make their individual and valued contributions to the continent.

Once the cheers had faded, however, more practical concerns about the roles each would play have taken center stage.

That there are great differences between the countries of the Eastern Bloc became apparent almost immediately. East Germany was absorbed so quickly by West Germany that it almost seemed as if the previous four decades of schism, and some of the most tense moments in modern history, were a form of illusion. Democracy movements in some countries became manifest immediately; in others, there were struggles. The

Soviet Union, itself, saw a union of more than 70 years dissolve into a chain of republics. The differences were predominant; the similarities subjugated.

"I get telephone calls from prospective business partners who tell me they can help me in Eastern Europe," says Donald Nicholls of Pall Corporation. "When I do, I ask them, 'what country are you talking about?' Often, the answer is something like, 'you know, Eastern Europe.' I immediately dismiss these people as not knowing what they are talking about."

Eastern Bloc attempts to catch up with free market economies in the West, which have had a 40- to 70-year head start, will be difficult. Along with democratization and steps to establish free-market economies, most experienced negative GDP growth in the early 1990s along with double-, and in the case of Poland, triple-digit inflation levels.

Evidence of the extent of the problems could be read in the headlines in the *New York Times* during one four-week period, after the euphoria of political independence had subsided:

"First Sale of State Holdings a Disappointment in Poland," and

"Czech Conversion to a Free Market Brings the Expected Pain, and More."

The stories detailed how Polish investors were unenthusiastic about the sale of stock in five large state-owned corporations, and how a free market economy was adding multiples to the prices of consumer goods at Prague grocery stores.

During that same period, enthusiasm on the part of western companies for doing business in the Soviet Union had waned. Whether the new loosely-knit republics will change the ease of doing business within their borders remains conjecture.

"Opening your own operation in the [former] Soviet Union will involve dealing with the entrenched bureaucracy," explained Leif Lundstrom, vice president of Route Sector North for Finnair, whose airline was, in 1956, the first Western carrier to begin service to the USSR. "Tending to the ordinary practical matters can be difficult. Such things as getting office space, work permits, telephone and electric lines, office furniture, even office supplies, take time. You can't pack two suitcases, book a hotel room and expect to have an office set up in a week."

Lundstrom recommends business relationships with local attorneys, accountants and administrative consultants before beginning to make plans for ongoing business operations.

"These are usually former government officials who still have many connections," he says. "They can swim in those waters where you could not."

He also cautions patience.

"*Perestroika* never really penetrated deeply into the real world where you need to get things done," he says. "There was always a layer of middle management that was left with no guidance. They don't dare make decisions because they are not sure who will be in power from one day to the next, and are not sure if they will be condemned or praised for their decisions."

There are, however, some significant pros to go with the cons of doing business in the Eastern Bloc.

Czechoslovakia offers a highly educated workforce. Hungary boasts high-level telecommunications and a well-established financial services sector.

On the other hand, Bulgaria, Romania and especially Yugoslavia are beset with serious, ongoing political problems.

But help is on the way.

The EC concluded bilateral agreements with most emerging nations of Eastern Europe, as well with the former Soviet Union. It then entered the second phase of this freer trade posture with negotiations of cooperative agreements on a country-by-country basis.

The European Investment Bank approved loans to Poland and Hungary in late 1989, after the European Council decided to assist Eastern Bloc countries in developing market-oriented economies. In addition, 40 countries, including the United States, the members of the EC, and the former Soviet Union, among others, established the European Bank for Reconstruction and Development (EBRD) to "promote private and entrepreneurial initiative in the Central and East European countries." The bank was capitalized to the tune of 10 billion ECU ($12 billion U.S.) and headquartered in London, with Jacques Attali, senior advisor to French President Francois Mitterrand, as its first CEO.

Nor was the private sector sitting on the sidelines, despite dire predictions about economic growing pains.

"The challenge of establishing market economies in Eastern Europe," General Motors Vice Chairman John F. Smith Jr., told an audience at Duke University in 1990, "involves shifting the entire pattern of resource utilization by pricing goods to reflect their scarcity, eliminating massive state subsidies and creating the real possibility of bankruptcy and unemployment."

He warned against being overly cautious, however, asserting that GM had put its money where its mouth was, entering into an agreement to do business in Hungary.

"In fact, Western companies wanting to do business in Eastern Europe need to get in now or risk being locked out," he said. "They will have to invest and establish operations there, and they will have to export out of Eastern Europe. There will be real opportunities, but those who go for them will need to earn their way over the long haul."

American Express has been doing business in Eastern Europe for more than 30 years. It sees great potential for its travel-related services. While historically much of the business had been inbound travel, the company expects the outbound growth curve to move up the graph.

"In the longer term, the demand for outbound travel services is expected," Thomas Holtrop, vice president, public affairs and communications for Amex's office in London, told *Europe* magazine. "The latter will be determined by the hardening of Eastern European currencies."

Perhaps the most telling symbol of the U.S. charge into Eastern Europe was the planting of the Coca Cola logo in East German soil. The company, which was handing out free samples to East Germans pouring through those now-famous holes in the Berlin Wall, almost immediately thereafter reached an agreement to put a facility on the east side of the wall. It expects to move 100 million cases a year by 1995.

Where Eastern Bloc currencies remain suspect, enterprising companies hammer out creative barter arrangements. Pepsico, for example, has taken payment from Poland in wooden chairs, which it uses in its Pizza Hut operations in the United States.

Where is all this movement East headed?

According to the U.S. Chamber of Commerce's International Division:

> The unanswered question is: Will West European leadership allow East European products to circulate freely in the Community in order to help the economies of their impoverished Eastern neighbors, or will domestic political backlash at the member state level inevitably force the Community to take a more protectionist stance?

From the perspective of this text, the question is how to staff operations in the Eastern Bloc, and with whom? The questions are even more vexing where the former Soviet Union is involved.

The answer is difficult; perhaps a more accurate word would be elusive. Given the fluid nature of the political situations in each of these countries, along with ventures into free market economies that range from a cautious testing of the water to an unrestrained swan dive, it is impossible to generalize with any degree of confidence.

For example, there were estimates just before the breakup of the Soviet Union that as many as 40 million people would be unemployed there as it made the painful transition to a market-based economy. Its new structure does not change things, at least for the short-term. The Soviet way of doing business is entrenched; the new republics will undoubtedly forge change only over many years.

Among the most daunting of tasks will certainly be the development of new systems within the emerging republics, and the adoption of rules and regulations to permit freer movement and greater mobility of the workforce; less-regulated programs of pay and benefits; a complete rehabilitation of training systems; and an institutionalized program to guarantee the rights of employees.

Part of the process will be re-educating the workers themselves.

"Soviet workers must understand and believe that the turn to the market economy is made forever," Gregory Raiter, a Soviet human resources expert told *HR Magazine*. "The return to the old, administrative and centralized economy is impossible."

To deal with the potential problems, well-planned staffing procedures should form the foundation of an American human resources program, with local modifications to fit case-by-case situations. Here are some basic guidelines:

Do your research. Staffing an operation in Eastern Europe demands intensive investigation before you can even begin to determine what will be needed in the way of human resources. Help from such organizations as the U.S. Chamber of Commerce, other business and professional organizations, offices of the target country's industry or trade commission and American firms already doing business in the country will be invaluable.

Involve your human resources team at the outset of initial planning. Face-to-face contact between your personnel staff and their counterparts at other U.S. corporations doing business in the target country will provide your professionals with a better understanding of what challenges they must overcome, and how they can begin to design workable staffing programs.

Operate from a sound human resources plan. Finding and hiring U.S. men and women capable of functioning within the East Bloc calls for objectives and strategies beyond what was needed to staff EC operations. Primary among them will be the need to develop and deploy employees who are experienced in performing under minimal supervision, and in unsympathetic business environments. Perhaps the best equipped will be those who have proven themselves in the EC, and who are then sent into countries of the Eastern Bloc for what might be considered an advanced degree in business diplomacy.

In terms of local recruiting, identifying the best in-country assistance, and working within the parameters of local customs and law will be paramount. In some cases, hiring procedures may be defined for you, with little chance of circumventing them.

Recruiting in the now defunct Soviet Union provided a good example:

"You could not put an ad in *Pravda* and announce you were hiring," says Finnair's Lundstrom. "If, for example, you needed a secretary who spoke English, German and Russian, you contacted the official personnel agency and they sent someone. You could send that person back, and they'd send someone else. You were not simply given 10 people to choose from."

The mix will be critical. While we have sung the praises of the proper employee mix throughout this book, that mix will be most critical in the uncharted territory of Eastern Europe. Much of what will be needed to compete effectively will have to be built from the ground up, or totally rehabilitated from existing physical plants and resources. To do that effectively will take top-notch local talent, working in concert with U.S. experts in company procedure. The effective integration of this mix of human resources will determine whether these difficult challenges result in success or failure.

"You had to have people who spoke Russian in the USSR," Lundstrom says. "Even though many of the younger Soviet managers spoke English, I would not [have] entered into any sort of business arrangement there, without people who were fluent in Russian."

Motivation Is Crucial

There will be tremendous opportunity in Eastern Europe among populations that have been starved of participation in the good life to the west, which they have had only glimpses of since the end of World War II. While ineffectively run operations will flounder amid the problems of growing a business in many of these countries, well-run U.S. companies will be recognized as such, and will reap the rewards.

215

A motivated staff will make the difference. A company that is well managed will gain a reputation in the local community as the place to work, while at the same time, it develops a nationwide market for its products or services. That company, and others like it, will continue to attract the best personnel; the cycle feeds upon itself.

Perhaps the most succinct description I've read about the potential for Eastern Europe appeared in an article by Robert Lyle, an international financial correspondent, in *Washington Flyer* magazine.

> What is important, however, is the simple fact that a sizeable number of people on this globe didn't want to be left out any longer and decided to do something about it.

The best managed and staffed U.S. companies will determine how to most effectively utilize all that potential human resources energy to their benefit.

Fifteen
Afterword

The winds of change blowing through Europe are part of an evolution that has been going on for hundreds of years. What is encouraging about this evolution is that it is driven by the desire to construct a confederation maximizing the economic well-being of EC citizens. It is not propelled by the desire for political conquest.

During the great political restructuring taking place in Europe at the close of the twentieth century, the desire on the part of its populations to participate fully in the good life has become manifest in the development and growth of companies, which will provide the goods and services to make that participation possible.

We in the United States have been participating in our own version of that process, with few interruptions, for most of our 200-plus years. Because we have gone through similar experiences, a U.S.-European business partnership is natural and certain to lead toward a mutually profitable alliance.

Challenges, problems, differing opinions and bureaucratic red tape notwithstanding, the movement appears headed towards a more unified planet, under the aegis of a new world order, a new community of men and women. Business will be the engine that powers this new machine into a better life. Business people will be the drivers. Selecting, motivating, retaining and promoting the best of these people will separate the successful companies from the less successful. Any firm anywhere in the world, can only be as good as the people who make it work. That's why it's been a commitment during my career to focus upon the human dimension of business, to help companies large and small not only identify, hire and retain the best and the brightest talent, but to motivate them to reach their potential, and the potential of the companies they serve.

The European Community—the New Europe—offers a remarkable opportunity for business growth. At the same time, it is a vista in which U.S. men and women can expand their knowledge and professional experience, while growing as individuals and learning to embrace the concept of a more unified world.

I hope *Staffing Europe* has been of assistance in helping companies and individuals chart their course into this New Europe, and I wish you all good fortune in the years ahead.

Appendices

IMPORTANT EC HEADQUARTERS

EC Information Service
2100 M Street, N.W.
Washington, D.C. 20037
(202) 862-9542

Council of Ministers
rue de la Loi 170
B-1048 Brussels, Belgium
Tel: 32-2-234-6111

European Commission
rue de la Loi 200
B-1049 Brussels, Belgium
Tel: 32-2-235-1111

European Parliament
Centre Europeen
Plateau du Kirchberg
L-2929 Luxembourg
Tel: 352-430-01

Economic and Social Committee
rue Ravenstein 2
B-1000 Brussels, Belgium
Tel: 32-2-519-9011

The Court of Justice
Palais de la Cour de Justice
L-2920 Luxembourg
Tel: 352-430-31

European Investment Bank
Boulevard Konrad Adenauer 100
L-2950 Luxembourg
Tel: 352-4379-1

U.S. Mission to the European
Communities
Bouleard du Regent 40
B-1000 Brussels, Belgium
Tel: 32-2-513-4450
Fax: 32-2-512-5720

INVESTMENT INFORMATION OFFICES

BELGIUM

Embassy of Belgium
Investment Section
3330 Garfield Street, N.W.
Washington, D.C. 20008
(202) 333-6900

DENMARK

Embassy of Denmark
Office of the Commercial Counselor
3200 Whitehaven Street, N.W.
Washington, D.C. 20008
(202) 234-4300

F.R. GERMANY

Federation of German Industries
1 Farragut Square South—6th Floor
Washington, D.C. 20006
(202) 347-0274

GREECE

Embassy of Greece
Office of the Economic Counselor
1636 Connecticut Avenue, N.W.
Washington, D.C. 20009
(202) 745-7100

FRANCE

French Industrial Development Agency
610 Fifth Avenue—Suite 301
New York, New York 10020
(212) 757-9340

IRELAND

Irish Development Agency
140 East 45th Street—41st Floor
New York, New York 10017
(212) 972-1000

LUXEMBOURG

Board of Economic Development of Luxembourg
801 Second Street—13th Floor
New York, New York 10017
(212) 370-9870

Board of Economic Development of Luxembourg
1 Sansome Street—Suite 830
San Francisco, California 94104
(415) 788-0816

ITALY

IMI
Capital Markets USA Corp
375 Park Avenue—Suite 1501
New York, New York 10152
(212) 754-0100

NETHERLANDS

Netherlands Foreign Investment Agency
One Rockefeller Plaza—11th Floor
New York, New York 10020
(212) 426-1434

Netherlands Foreign Investment Agency
11755 Wilshire Boulevard
Los Angeles, California 90025
(213) 477-8288

PORTUGAL

Portuguese Trade Commission
1900 L Street, N.W.—Suite 401
Washington, D.C. 20036
(202) 331-8222

SPAIN

Embassy of Spain
Commercial Office
2558 Massachusetts Avenue, N.W.
Washington, D.C. 20008
(202) 265-8600

National Institute of Industry
1155 Avenue of the Americas—Suite 2800
New York, New York 10036
(212) 765-0550

UNITED KINGDOM

British Trade & Investment Office
Inward Investment
845 Third Avenue, 11th Floor
New York, New York 10022
(212) 593-2258

Embassy of Great Britain
Trade Section/Inward Investment
2221 Massachusetts Avenue, N.W.
Washington, D.C. 20008
(212) 462-1340

Chambers of Commerce and Trade Associations of the EC Member States in the United States

BELGIUM

Belgian-American Chamber of Commerce
Empire State Building
350 Fifth Avenue, #703
New York, New York 10118
(212) 967-9898

Belgian-American Chamber of Commerce
233 Peachtree Street, N.E., #204
Atlanta, Georgia 30303
(404) 588-9380

Belgian-American Chamber of Commerce
P.O. Box 66087, AMF O'Hare
Chicago, Illinois 60666
(312) 437-4240

DENMARK

Danish-American Chamber of Commerce
825 Third Avenue, 32nd Floor
New York, New York 10022
(212) 980-6240

Danish-American Chamber of Commerce
5353 West Dartmouth
Denver, Colorado 80227
(303) 980-9100

Danish Trade Office
1475 N.W. 77th Avenue
Maimi Lakes, Florida 33014
(305) 556-5666

FRANCE

French-American Chamber of Commerce
509 Madison Avenue, #1900
New York, New York 10022
(212) 371-4466

French-American Chamber of Commerce
1250 24th Street, N.W., #600
Washington, D.C. 20037
(202) 775-0256

French-American Chamber of Commerce
425 Bush Street, #401
San Francisco, California 94108
(415) 398-2449

French-American Chamber of Commerce
6380 Wilshire Boulevard, #1608
Beverly Hills, California 90048
(213) 651-4741

French-American Chamber of Commerce
1540 Texas Avenue
Houston, Texas 77002
(713) 224-9381

French-American Chamber of Commerce
Three Center Plaza, 4th Floor
Boston, Massachusetts 02108
(617) 423-6265

French-American Chamber of Commerce
55 East Monroe Street, #4500
Chicago, Illinois 60603
(312) 263-7668

French-American Chamber of Commerce
141 Sevilla Avenue
Coral Gables, Florida 33134
(305) 443-3223

French-American Chamber of Commerce
600 West LaFayette
Detroit, Michigan 48226
(313) 964-2423

French-American Chamber of Commerce
c/o Fabula
650 Poydras Street
New Orleans, Louisiana 70130
(504) 523-1385

French-American Chamber of Commerce
Suite 1125, LB 37
4144 North Central Expressway
Dallas, Texas 75204
(214) 821-7475

French-American Chamber of Commerce
Foshay Tower, #904
821 Marquette Avenue
Minneapolis, Minnesota 55402
(612) 338-7750

French Industrial Development Agency
610 Fifth Avenue, #301
New York, New York 10020
(212) 629-6380

French-American Chamber of Commerce
One Georgia Center, #1860
600 West Peachtree Street
Atlanta, Georgia 30308
(404) 874-2602

French-American Chamber of Commerce
c/o Reed, Smith, McClay & Shaw
Mellon Square
435 Sixth Avenue
Pittsburgh, Pennsylvania 15219
(412) 288-3131

GERMANY

German-American Chamber of Commerce
666 Fifth Avenue
New York, New York 10103
(212) 974-8830

German-American Chamber of Commerce
3250 Wilshire Boulevard, #1612
Los Angeles, California 90010
(213) 381-2236

German-American Chamber of Commerce
465 California Street, #910
San Francisco, California 94104
(415) 392-2262

German Representative for
Industry and Trade
One Farragut Square South
Washington, D.C. 20006
(202) 347-0247

German-American Chamber of
Commerce
3475 Lenox Road, #620
Atlanta, Georgia 30326
(404) 239-9494

German-American Chamber of
Commerce
104 South Michigan Avenue,
#600
Chicago, Illinois 60603
(313) 782-8557

German-American Chamber of
Commerce
Two Houston Center, #3418
909 Fannin
Houston, Texas 77010
(713) 658-8230

GREECE

Hellenic-American Chamber of
Commerce
960 Avenue of the Americas,
#1204
New York, New York 10004
(212) 629-6380

IRELAND

Irish Export Board
10 East 53rd Street, 28th Floor
New York, New York 10022
(212) 371-3600

Irish Export Board
350 North Orleans Street, #848
Chicago, Illinois 60654
(312) 467-1891

Ireland-U.S. Council for Commerce and Industry
460 Park Avenue
New York, New York 10022
(212) 751-2660

ITALY

Italian-American Chamber of
Commerce
350 Fifth Avenue
New York, New York 10118
(212) 279-5520

Italian Trade Commission
499 Park Avenue, 6th Floor
New York, New York 10022
(212) 980-1500

Italian Trade Commission
3050 Post Oak Boulevard, #1090
Houston, Texas 77056
(713) 626-5531

Italian Trade Commission
233 Peachtree Street, #2301
Atlanta, Georgia 30303
(404) 525-0660

Italian-American Chamber of
Commerce
Pierre Giorgia Luciani
1801 Center Park East
Los Angeles, California 90067
(213) 203-0253

Italian Trade Commission
401 North Michigan Avenue, #3030
Chicago, Illinois 60611
(312) 670-4360

Italian Trade Commission
1801 Avenue of the Stars, #700
Los Angeles, California 90067
(213) 879-0950

LUXEMBOURG

None in the United States

THE NETHERLANDS

Netherlands Chamber of Commerce
One Rockefeller Plaza, 11th Floor
New York, New York 10020
(212) 265-6460

Netherlands Chamber of Commerce
233 Peachtree Street, N.E. #404
Atlanta, Georgia 30303
(404) 523-4400

Netherlands Chamber of Commerce
303 East Wacker Drive, #412
Chicago, Illinois 60601
(312) 938-9050

PORTUGAL

Portuguese-U.S. Chamber of Commerce
590 5th Ave, 3rd Floor
New York, New York 10036
(212) 354-4627

Portuguese Trade Commission
590 5th Ave, 3rd Floor
New York, New York 10036
(212) 354-4610

SPAIN

Spanish Chamber of Commerce
350 Fifth Avenue, #3514
New York, New York 10118
(212) 967-2170

UNITED KINGDOM

British-American Chamber of Commerce
275 Madison Avenue, #1714
New York, New York 10016
(212) 889-0680

British-American Chamber of Commerce
1640 Fifth Street, #224
Santa Monica, California 90401
(213) 394-4977

British-Florida Chamber of Commerce
2520 Ponce de Leon Boulevard
Coral Gables, Florida 33134
(305) 444-6267

British-American Business Association
1133 15th Street, N.W., #1000
Washington, D.C. 20005
(202) 293-0010

British-American Business Association
c/o Winchester Properties
410 17th Street, #750
Denver, Colorado 80202
(303) 298-9347

British-American Commerce Association
1601 Elm Street, #4450
Dallas, Texas 75210
(214) 979-0574

British-American Chamber of Commerce
3150 California Street
San Francisco, California 94115
(415) 567-6128

British-American Chamber of Commerce
P.O. Box 18738
Tampa, Florida 33679
(813) 874-8617

British Trade & Investment Office
845 Third Avenue, 11th Floor
New York, New York 10022
(212) 593-2258

British-American Business Association
601 Jefferson Street, #320
Houston, Texas 77002
(713) 759-9499

British-American Business Group
6472 East Church Street
Douglasville, Georgia 30134
(404) 658-8700

New England-British Association
265 Franklin Street, #1000
Boston, Massachusetts 02110
(617) 439-4894

Overseas American-Sponsored Elementary and Secondary Schools, Assisted by U.S Department of State.

(Source: Office of Overseas Schools, Room 245, SA-29
U.S. Department of State
Washington, DC 20522-2902
(703) 875-7800)
Numbers in parenthesis indicate enrollment and grades offered.
N = Nursery, K = Kindergarten, PK = Pre-kindergarten, JK = Junior-Kindergarten, PG = Post-Graduate.

Austria, Vienna
Director—(723, N-12)
American International School in Vienna, Inc.
Salmansdoerferstrasse 47
A-1190 Vienna, Austria
Tel. 43-1-44-27-63
Fax. 43-1-44-37-69

Belgium, Antwerp
Headmaster—(418, PS-12, PG)
The Antwerp International School
Veltwijcklaan 180
2070 Ekeren, Belgium
Tel. 32-3-541-6047
Fax. 32-3-541-8201

Bulgaria, Sofia
Director—(75, PK-8)
Anglo-American School of Sofia
c/o American Embassy Sofia
Department of State
Washington, D.C. 20521-5740
Tel. 359-2-57-02-67
Telex 22690 am emb sof

Czechoslovakia, Prague
Director (115, PK-8)
International School of Prague
c/o American Embassy Prague
Department of State
Washington, D.C. 20521-5740
Tel. 42-2-311-2044
Fax. 42-2-311-7771

England, London
Headmaster—(1,180, K-12)
The American School in London
2-8 Loudoun Road
London, N.W. 8 ONP., England
Tel. 44-71-722-0101
Fax. 44-71-586-6885

Finland, Helsinki
Headmaster (113, K-9)
International School of Helsinki
Stahlberginkuja 1
00570 Helsinki, Finland
Tel. 358-0-684-8166

France, Paris
Headmaster—(780, PK-12)
American School of Paris
41, rue Pasteur
92210 Saint-Cloud, France
Tel. 33-1-4602-5443

France, Paris
Director—(412, PK-12)
International School of Paris
6 rue Beethoven
75016 Paris, France
Tel. 33-1-4224-0954
Fax. 33-1-4527-1593

Germany, Berlin
Managing Principal—(1, 314, K-13)
John F. Kennedy School, Berlin
Teltower Damm 87-93
1000 Berlin 37, West Germany
Tel. 49-30-807-2701
Fax. 49-30-807-3377

Germany, Dusseldorf
Director—(473, PK-13)
International School of Dusseldorf
Leuchtenberger Kirchweg 2
4000 Dusseldorf 31, West Germany
Tel. 49-211-40-7056
Fax. 49-211-4080774

Germany, Frankfurt
Headmaster—(1, 193, K-12)
The Frankfurt International School
An der Waldlust 15
6370 Oberursel 1, West Germany
Tel. 49-6171-202-0
Fax. 49-6171-202-384

Germany, Hamburg
Headmaster—(581, PK-12)
International School Hamburg
Holmbrook 20
2000 Hamburg 52, West Germany
Tel. 49-40-880-2066
Fax. 49-40-881-1405

Germany, Munich
Headmaster—(728, N-12)
Munich International School
Schloss Buchhof
8130 Percha/Starnberg, W.G.
Tel. 49-8151-2606-0
Fax. 49-8151-2606-49

Greece, Athens
Superintendent—(1, 345, JK-12)
American Community Schools of Athens
129 Aghias Parakevis Street
GR 152 34 Halandri
Athens, Greece
Tel. 30-1-6393-200
Fax. 30-1-6390-051
Telex 223355 ACS GR

Greece, Thessaloniki
Director—(146, K-12)
Thessaloniki International High School and Pinewood Elementary School
P.O. Box 21001, 555 10 Piles
Thessaloniki, Greece
Tel. 30-31-301-221
Fax. 30-31-668-118

Hungary, Budapest
Director—(171, K-9)
American International School of Budapest
c/o American Embassy Budapest
Department of State
Washington, D.C. 20521-5270
Tel. 36-1-1758-685
Fax. 36-1-1758-993

Iceland, Reykjavik
Head Teacher—(26, K-6)
American Embassy School
c/o American Embassy Reykjavik
Reykjavik, Iceland
Tel. 354-1-18-209

Ireland, Dublin
Headmaster—(968, 1-112)
St. Andrew's College
Booterstown Avenue
Blackrock, County Dublin
Republic of Ireland
Tel. 353-1-88-27-85
353-1-83-16-27

Italy, Florence
Headmaster—(166, PK-12)
The American International School of Florence
Via del Carota 23/25
50012 Bagno a Ripoli (FI)
Florence, Italy
Tel. 39-55-64-00-33

Italy, Genoa
Director—(110, PK-8)
American International School in Genoa
Via Quarto 13/c
Genoa, Italy 16148
Tel. 39-10-38-65-28

Italy, Milan
Director—(422, N-13)
American School of Milan
P.O. Box No. 55
20090 Opera, Milan, Italy
Tel. 39-2-5760-1546
Fax. 39-2-5550-0274

Italy, Rome
Headmaster—(393, PK-12)
American Overseas School of Rome, Inc.
Via Cassia, 811
00189 Rome, Italy
Tel. 39-6-366-4841

Italy, Rome
Headmaster—(161, 9-12, P.G.)
St. Stephen's School
3, Via Aventina
00153 Rome, Italy
Tel. 39-6-575-0605
Fax. 39-6-514-6007

Italy, Trieste
Director—(203, PN-11)
International School of Trieste
Via Conconnello 16 (Opicina)
34016 Trieste, Italy
Tel. 39-40-211-452

Italy, Turin
Headmaster—(208, N-12)
American Cultural Association of Turin
Vicolo Tiziano 10
10024 Moncalieri (Turin), Italy
Tel. 39-11-645-967
Fax. 39-11-640-7810

Malta, Valletta
Headmaster—(174, K-12)
Verdala International School
Fort Pembroke
St. Andrews, Malta
Tel. 356-332-361
356-334-544
Fax. 356-622-232

Netherlands, Amsterdam
Director—(472, PK-12)
International School of Amsterdam
Post Office Box 7983
1008 AD Amsterdam, The Netherlands
Tel. 31-20-422-227
Fax. 31-20-428-928

Netherlands, Rotterdam
Director—(116, K-8)
American International School of Rotterdam
Hillegondastraat 21
3051 PA Rotterdam, The Netherlands
Tel. 31-10-422-51-37
31-10-422-53-51

Netherlands, The Hague
Superintendent—(586, PK-12)
The American School of The Hague
Rijksstraatweg 200
2241 BX Wassenaar, The Netherlands
Tel. 31-1751-40113
Fax. 31-1751-12400

Poland, Warsaw
Director—(201, K-9)
The American School of Warsaw
c/o American Embassy Warsaw
Department of State
Washington, D.C. 20521-5010
Tel. 48-22-42-39-52
Fax. 48-22-42-56-20

Romania, Bucharest
Director—(105, N-8)
American School of Bucharest
c/o American Embassy Bucharest
Department of State
Washington, D.C. 20521-5260
Tel. 40-0-33-21-20

Spain, Barcelona
Director—(246, N-12)
American School of Barcelona
Avenida Pearson 34
08034 Barcelona, Spain
Tel. 34-3-204-1271
34-3-203-7635
Fax. 34-3-200-1434

Spain, Bilbao
Director—(244, N-9)
American School of Bilbao
Apartadoi 38
Las Arenas (Vizcaya), Spain
Tel. 34-4-668-0860

Spain, Madrid
Headmaster—(634, PK-12)
American School of Madrid
Apartado 80
28080 Madrid, Spain
Tel. 34-1-357-2154
Telex EAM E 49621

Switzerland, Bern
Headmaster—(152, K-12)
International School of Bern
Mattenstrasse 3
3073 Gumligen, Switzerland
Tel. 41-31-52-23-58

Turkey, Istanbul
Principal—(318, PK-9)
Istanbul International
Community School
P.K. 1 Arnavutkoy
80820 Istanbul, Turkey
Tel. 90-1-165-1591
Fax. 90-1-165-0580

C.I.S., St. Petersburg
(4, Elem.)
Branch School
c/o American Consulate General
St. Petersburg
Department of State
Washington, D.C. 20521-5440
Tel. 7-812-274-8235

C.I.S., Moscow
Director—(327, K-10)
Anglo-American School of
Moscow
c/o American Embassy Moscow
Department of State
Washington, D.C. 20521-5430
Tel. 7-095-255-0326
7-095-131-8700
Telex 413160 USGSO SU

Yugoslavia, Belgrade
Director—(134, K-8)
International School of Belgrade, Inc.
c/o American Embassy Belgrade
Department of State
Washington, D.C. 20521-5070
Tel. 38-11-651-832
38-11-652-619

Yugoslavia, Zagreb
Director—(24, K-8)
The American School of Zagreb
c/o American Consulate General
Zagreb
Department of State
Washington, D.C 20521-5080
Tel. 38-41-426-980

Regional School Associations
European Council of
International Schools (ECIS)
Mr. Michael Maybury, Executive
Secretary
21B Lavant Street
Petersfield, Hampshire, GU32
3EL
England
Tel. 44-730-68-244
Fax. 44-730-67-914

East European Schools
Association
Mrs. Joan Byrne, Executive
Secretary
c/o American International
School of Budapest
American Embassy Budapest
Department of State
Washington, D.C. 20521-5270
Tel. 36-1-1758-685
Fax. 36-1-1758-993

In addition to the schools listed in this section, there are a large number of U.S. or international schools not assisted by the Office of Overseas Schools. Location, names, addresses, and other information regarding these schools may be obtained from ECIS.

Index

Advertising Age, 77
Advertising for job candidates, 75–78
Advisory councils, 21
Aging population, 18, 130
Alien worker considerations, 131–32, 180
American Banker, 77
American Express, 213
American Telephone and Telegraph Company (AT&T), 49
Apple Computer, 47
Arthur Andersen (accounting firm), 139–40, 176
Asahi Chemical, 37
Atlantic Monthly, 78
Austria, EFTA member state, 13, 18, 206, 208
Awards and incentive programs, 175

Banking industry, 33
Barron's, 77
Belgium
    coal and steel production problems, 10
    EC member state, 36–39
    employment contracts, 119
    parental leave programs, 165
    social security bilateral agreement, 128
    Treaty of Rome signatory, 12
    work permits, 131–32
Berlin Wall, collapse of the, 12
Bilateral agreements, social security, 128–29
Boise State University survey, 196–97, 198
Bostock, Roy, 29
Boston Globe, 76
Broadeners, 17–18
Brussels, EC headquarters, 13, 36
Bulgaria, 212
Business overview, general
    Belgium, 36–38
    Denmark, 39–40

France, 41-43
Germany, 44-45
Greece, 45-46
Ireland, 47-48
Italy, 49-51
Luxembourg, 52-53
the Netherlands, 53-55
Portugal, 55-57
Spain, 57-59
United Kingdom, 60-62
Business plan, sharing the, 170-71
Business Week
  employment advertising in, 77
  International Hot Growth Company Survey, 67, 68
  on absorbing Eastern Europe economies into the EC, 25-26
  on Italy's position in the EC, 27

Candidates, locating job, 67-89
Career opportunities, defining, 171
Career-specific publications, 77
Cars, company, 133
Caterpillar Tractor Company, 37
Chase Manhattan Bank, 143
Chemical Engineering, 77
Chicago Tribune, 76, 184
Children
  declining birth rates, 18
  relocating, 189-91
  U.S. schools, 127
Citicorp, 19, 29-30
Cloning effect, 112
CNN, 191
Coca-Cola, 213
Colgate-Palmolive Company, 145
College campuses
  recruiting on, 81
  students as part-time employees, 157-58
Commonwealth of Indepdendent States, 12
Communications and Electrical Workers of Canada, 22

Communications Workers of America, 22
Community Charter of the Fundamental Social Rights of Workers, 123-24, 132, 162
Continental Bank, 69, 188
Corporate isolation, 176
Corporate tax structure
  Denmark, 39
  Ireland, 48
  Luxembourg, 52-53
  United Kingdom, 61
Council of Europe, 41
Crain's New York, 77
Cross-cultural training, 187-89
Currency, establishment of a single European, 26, 27
Customs and protocols
  Belgium, 38-39
  Denmark, 40-41
  France, 43
  Germany, 45
  Greece, 46-47
  Ireland, 48-49
  Italy, 51-52
  Luxembourg, 53
  the Netherlands, 55
  Portugal, 57
  Spain, 59-60
  United Kingdom, 62-63
Cyprus, 41
Czechoslovakia, 212

D'Arcy Masius Benton & Bowles (advertising agency), 29
De Telegraaf (Netherlands), 78
Deepeners, 17-18
Délégation l'Aménagement du Territoire et de l'Action Régionale (DATAR), 42, 43, 156
Delors, Jacques, 26, 123, 206-7
Denmark
  EC member state, 39-41, 206
  EFTA and EEC member state, 13

Index

parental leave programs, 165
percentage of women in the workforce, 163
use of part-time employees, 157
work permits, 132
Denver Post, 76
Detached-worker rule, 129
Digital Equipment Corporation, 47
Domestic hiring, basic steps for, 92
Dow Chemical, 49
DuPont (E.I. Du Pont De Nemours & Co.), 19

Eastern Bloc, the, 210–15
Economic integration, 12
Economic Promotion Zones, 59
Educational expenses, 127
El Pais (Spain), 78
Employee communications, forms of, 172–74
Employment contracts, 117–18, 119
Entering European arena, three ways of, 30–32
Europe, 143, 179, 213
Europe, hiring considerations for, 92–94
European Bank for Reconstruction and Development (EBRD), 212
European Coal and Steel Community (ECSC), 10, 11
European Community (EC), 2, 16–24, 25–34
 charter of workers' rights, 123–24, 132, 162
 Commission, 13–14, 15, 28, 207, 208
 Council of Ministers, 13, 14, 33, 155, 158
 Court of Auditors, 14–15, 52
 Economic and Social Committee, 13, 14
 healthcare professionals in the, 22
 member states, 35–63
 Ministry of Finance, 33
 name change to, 13
 rules of origin, 21

European contributions, reinforcement of, 175
European Council, 15, 123, 212
European Court of Justice, 13, 14, 28, 52, 164
European Economic Community (EEC), formation of, 12–13, 15
European Economic Space (EES), 206, 207
European Foundation for the Improvement of Living and Working Conditions, 15, 85, 155–56
European Free Trade Association (EFTA), 41, 114, 205
 formation of, 13, 18, 206–10
European Investment Bank (EIB), 15, 52, 212
European media, 78
European Parliament, 13, 14, 52
European Regional Development Fund, 50, 58
Exxon Company, 39, 49

Family fit, the, 179–93
Finland, EFTA member state, 18, 206, 209–10
Ford Motor Company, 19
Foreign hires, 119–20
Fortune, 77, 91
France
 coal and steel production problems, 10
 EC member state, 41–43
 S O S Racism, 19
 social security bilateral agreement, 128
 Treaty of Rome signatory, 12
 use of temporary workers, 156
 work permits, 131
French Institute/Alliance Francaise (FI/AF), 187
Fujitsu, 47

General Electric Company, 47
 joint venture, 31

237

General Motors, 143, 212–13
Germany
   1947 Moscow Conference, 9
   alien residence permits, 131
   coal and steel production problems, 10
   EC member state, 44–45
   German workers, 142–43
   parental leave programs, 165
   percentage of women in the workforce, 163
   reunification of East and West, 12, 27, 210
   social security bilateral agreement, 128
   use of temporary workers, 156
Glass-Steagall Act, 33
Global product managers, 20–21
Globalization of business, 22
Greece
   EC member state, 45–47
   EEC member state, 13
   parental leave programs, 165
Green card rules, 18, 131
Grey Advertising, 29, 67, 68
Gross domestic product (GDP), 16
   Belgium, 37
   Denmark, 39
   Germany, 27, 44
   Greece, 45
   Ireland, 48
   Luxembourg, 52
   Portugal, 56

Hardy, Maurice G., 60, 114
Harper's, 78
Harvard Business Review, 77
Health and medical insurance programs, 129–30
Hedlen Marshall v. Southampton Health Authority, 164
Hewlett-Packard Corporation, 19
Hiring process, 91–110
Hitachi Corporation, 39
Honeywell, Inc., 49

Housing differentials, 127
HR Magazine, 68, 111, 214
Human resource needs, determining, 69–70
Human resources managers, hiring, 144–45
Hungary, 212

Iceland, EFTA member state, 18, 206
Imperial Chemical Industries PLC, 143
Inc., 77
Industry Week, 77
In-house media, utilizing, 172–74
Intellectual publications, 78
Internal hire, the, 118–19
International Business Machines (IBM), 19, 39, 47, 49
International Federation of Chemical, Energy and General Workers' Unions (Brussels), 22
International joint ventures (IJVs), 31–32
International Orientation Resources (IOR), 188–89, 197
International personnel placement firms, 145, 180–81
Interviews, employment, 98–102, 117
Invest in Britain Bureau (IBB), 60, 62
Ireland
   EC member state, 47–49
   EEC member state, 13
   parental leave programs, 165
Italy
   coal and steel production problems, 10
   diversified business base, 27
   EC member state, 49–52
   social security bilateral agreement, 128
   Treaty of Rome signatory, 12

J. Walter Thompson (advertising agency), 29
Job descriptions, creation of, 70–72

Index

Job offer, making the, 111–22
Job-posting, 80

KPMG Peat Marwick survey, 32
Kraft, Inc., 37, 49
Kreicker, Noel, 188–89, 201

Language skills, 30, 74
Language training, 185–87
L'Express (France), 43, 78
Le Figaro (France), 43, 78
Le Monde (France), 43, 78
Liechtenstein, 41
   EFTA member state, 206
Local nationals
   hiring, 124, 144–46
   motivating, 175–76
Los Angeles Times, 76
Lundstrom, Leif, 211–12, 215
Luxembourg
   coal and steel production problems, 10
   EC member state, 52–53
   parental leave programs, 165
   Treaty of Rome signatory, 12
Luxembourg, Declaration of 1984, 206

McFadden Act, 33
Malta, 41
Management Accounting, 77
Mancuso, Angeli, 24
Maternity leave. *See* Parental leave programs
Matsushita, 39
Medical Concepts, Inc., 23–24, 68
Meier, Dr. Kurt, 207–8
Merger or acquisition of an existing operation, 30–31
Microsoft, Inc., 47
Milliken Textiles, 39
Mitsubishi Electric Corporation, 32
Mobil Oil Corporation, 37, 49
Money, 77
Monnet, Jean, 10
Monsanto Company, 37

1947 Moscow Conference, 9
Motivation, European staff, 169–77, 215–16
Motorola, Inc., 39, 184

N.V. Philips, 54
National Business Employment Weekly, 198–99
Netherlands' Foreign Information Service, 163–64
Netherlands Foreign Investment Agency, 131
Netherlands, the
   coal and steel production problems, 10
   EC member state, 53–55
   Treaty of Rome signatory, 12
   use of temporary workers, 156
Networking, job candidate, 82–84
New York Law Journal, 77
New York Times, 29, 67, 161
   employment advertising in the, 75–76
   on Eastern Bloc, 211
   on the Economic Community, 16
   on unified German market, 12
Newsweek, 20, 21
Nicholls, Donald G., 81–82, 141, 211
Nippon Electric Company, 47
Non-EC Europe, 205–16
North Atlantic Treaty Organization (NATO), 9
Norway
   EFTA member state, 13, 18, 206
   social security bilateral agreement, 128

Overseas hiring, basic steps for, 92

Pacific Rim nations, 11
Pall Corporation, 60, 81, 114, 141, 143, 147, 157, 211
Para-professionals, 152, 159
Parental leave programs, 165
Pepsico, 213

Periodicals, 77
Permanent part-time employees, 152, 157–58
Personal contact, maintaining, 174–75
Personnel Journal, 77
Pizza Hut, 213
Poland, 211, 212, 213
Portugal
  EC member state, 55–57, 206
  EFTA and EEC member state, 13
  social security bilateral agreement, 128
Pre-selecting and pre-screening job candidates, 79
Professional organizations, 191
Purchasing World, 77

Recruiting externally, 80–82
Recruiting internally, 79–80
Reference checking, 102–5, 117
Regional and local newspapers, 76–77
Relocation
  cost of, 126–27
  of a family to Europe, 179–93
Repatriation, employee, 115, 195–201
Resumes and *curriculum vitaes*, evaluating, 95–98
Robert Half International offices, 143, 181
Romania, 212

S O S Racism (organization), 19
Salaries and benefits, 116, 123–36
San Francisco Chronicle, 76
San Marino, 41
Schuman, Robert, 10
Scientific American, 78
Shell Oil Company, 53–54
Single European Act (SEA), 15–16
Single-market concept, 1, 15–16, 24
Smith, John F., Jr., 212–13
Smithsonian, 78
Snecma, 31–32
Social security benefits, 128–29
Socio-cultural fit, 182–85

Soviet Union, dissolution of the, 11–12, 211, 213–14
Spain
  EC member state, 57–60
  EEC member state, 13
  parental leave programs, 165
  percentage of women in the workforce, 163
  residence and work permits, 131
  social security bilateral agreement, 128
  work permits, 131
Start-up of a European operation, 32
Strasbourg, 41
Strategic staffing, 153
Sweden
  EFTA member state, 13, 18, 206
  social security bilateral agreement, 128
Switzerland
  EFTA member state, 13, 18, 206, 208–9
  social security bilateral agreement, 128

Taxes, 127–28
Temporary workers, 151–57
Territorial rule, 129
Thatcher, Margaret, 27
Third country nationals, 125–26, 146–47
  motivating, 175–76
3M Corporation, 49, 190
Time, 57
Translink's European Deal Review, 30
Treaty of Rome, 12–13, 15
Turkey, 41

Unification date, 1992, 1, 27
United Kingdom
  EC member state, 60–63, 206
  EFTA and EEC member state, 13
  Equal Pay Act of 1970, 164
  social security bilateral agreement, 128

Index

use of part-time employees, 157
use of temporary workers, 156
United Nations Educational, Scientific and Cultural Organization (UNESCO), 49
U.S. Chamber of Commerce International Division, 205, 213
U.S. management style, perceptions of, 142
U.S. nationals
  hiring, 147–49
  relocating, 124–25
U.S. schools, 127
  U.S. Department of State's Office of Overseas Schools, 189–90
United Technologies research centers, 21
University of Washington survey, 196–97, 198
University publications, 77
USA Today, 76, 142

Vacation policies, 133

Wage rates for local employees, lower, 130–31
Wall Street Journal, 51
  employment advertising in the, 76
  on failure rate of U.S. executives overseas, 169
  on hiring Euro-managers, 139
  on Italian government-owned holdings, 50
  on non-EC countries, 207
  on relocating working spouses, 180
  on women in the workforce, 164
Warsaw Pact, 9
Washington Flyer, 216
Washington Post, 22
  employment advertising in the, 76
West Germany, Treaty of Rome signatory, 12
Women
  declining birth rate, 18
  employment of, 18, 161–65
  as part-time employees, 157
Women's World Banking, 161
Work permits, 131–32
Workforce mix, achieving an effective, 139–50
Working spouse, relocating, 180–82

Yugoslavia, 212

NOTES

NOTES

NOTES